STOCK CAR RACING
CHRONICLE
THE 1990s

AL PEARCE, BEN BLAKE, AND NIGEL KINRADE

MBI Publishing Company

First published in 2001 by MBI Publishing Company, Galtier Plaza, Suite 200, 380 Jackson Street, St. Paul, MN 55101-3885, USA.

MBI Publishing Company books are also available at discounts in bulk quantity for industrial or sales-promotional use. For details write to Special Sales Manager at Motorbooks International Wholesalers & Distributors, Galtier Plaza, Suite 200, 380 Jackson Street, St. Paul, MN 55101-3885, USA.

Library of Congress Cataloging-in-Publication Data Available

ISBN: 0-7603-1019-X

Front cover *(clockwise from upper left):* NASCAR's Winston Cup champions of the 1990s: Dale Earnhardt, 35 wins and 4 titles in the decade; Dale Jarrett, 22 wins and 1 title; Jeff Gordon, 49 wins and 3 titles; Terry Labonte, 12 wins and 1 title; Alan Kulwicki, 4 wins and 1 title.

Frontispiece: Dale Earnhardt pushes his black number 3 Chevy Lumina down pit lane in 1995. He finished second to Jeff Gordon that year in the points standings.

Title page: NASCAR racing burst into the national spotlight in the 1990s.

Back cover:
Top: Jeff Gordon and Terry Labonte share a restful moment at Talladega in 1995.
Middle: NASCAR drivers became household names during the 1990s. Here autograph seekers ask Bobby Labonte to sign a few souvenirs.
Bottom: Two legends of racing battle it out at Lowe's Motor Speedway in 1992, Richard Petty's final year behind the wheel. Petty and Dale Earnhardt each one seven championships in their careers.

Edited by Paul Johnson
Designed by Dan Perry

Printed in China

CONTENTS

For Charlie Daniels of Rocky Mount, N.C., a friend, a mentor, and a guiding hand to so many of us during those years when we most needed one. The lessons you taught in the gym, on the field of play, and in the classroom are a part of who I am and what you helped me become. If I never thanked you publicly, I do now.

— Al Pearce

It can be argued with some degree of confidence that NASCAR and its premier Winston Cup Series came of age more in the decade of the 1990s than in the four previous decades *combined.* To review quickly:

Big-time stock car racing was born in the late 1940s, then wet-nursed through its fitful infancy in the 1950s. It moved from infancy into childhood—then found itself on the cusp of adolescence—during the uncertainty that marked the 1960s. Racing spread its wings and expanded its vision in the 1970s, a 10-year period when it first realized it was no longer a child clinging helplessly to its parents.

In the 1980s, NASCAR racing moved gingerly into young adulthood, unsure of precisely where it was going, but all the while being fairly confident it knew how to get there.

And so it did. So it did, indeed.

As the 1980s turned into the 1990s, one part of Winston Cup racing looked back on the path it had taken to that point. Another part looked forward to the likelihood of a prosperous decade and an ever-growing acceptance. Still another part of this man-child fought hard to maintain its roots and traditions, a battle it knew it would lose.

By the end of the 1990s, then, it was clear that Winston Cup racing had matured beyond anyone's wildest dreams. What had begun as a cast of rag tag characters racing souped-up street cars around rutted old tracks suddenly found itself the self-described "Sport of the 1990s."

Corporate America openly embraced NASCAR like a long-lost child with money in his pocket. Television, a half hearted suitor for years, eventually found that the bottom line looked better at 200 miles per hour. Likewise, opportunistic business-men noticed the same thing. And while racing would pose no threat to the lure of major-league and major–college team sports over most of America, neither would it sit quietly on the sidelines. Nor, as we have come to learn, should it have.

Ah, the 1990s.

It was a decade of notable comings and goings . . . some voluntary, others tragic. Former Winston Cup stars Richard Petty, Buddy Baker, Harry Gant, and Ernie Irvan retired after combining for 252 career victories. Alan Kulwicki and Davey Allison died in separate 1993 aviation accidents only months apart. Neil Bonnett died practicing for the 1994 Daytona 500, and pioneer racer Wendell Scott died of natural causes late in 1991. Long time tour regulars Jimmy Means, Lake Speed, Greg Sacks, Dick Trickle, Jimmy Hensley, and Phil Parsons began winding down in the 1990s. Sponsors came and sponsors went, but each contributed in its own way to moving the sport forward apace.

Truth-seekers wondered who would take the place of their long time favorites. After all, the Pettys, Allisons, Bonnetts, Kulwickis, and Bakers of this world were irreplaceable . . . or were they?

Jeff Gordon, a multi-time Winston Cup champion and poster boy for the "new-generation NASCAR driver" emerged as a superstar in the 1990s. The Burtons—Ward and younger brother Jeff—began their winning ways in the 1990s. Champions-in-waiting Dale Jarrett and Bobby Labonte didn't get their first career Cup victories until the 1990s. So, too, did Bobby Hamilton, Tony Stewart, John Andretti, Sterling Marlin, Jeremy Mayfield, Joe Nemechek, and Jimmy Spencer. Drivers who grew up dreaming about open-wheel racing—among them, Jeff Gordon, Robby Gordon, Wally Dallenbach, Stewart, and Andretti—found a comforting home in full-bodied stock cars on oval tracks.

The real estate that is NASCAR also changed dramatically during the 1990s. New superspeedways opened at Loudon, New Hamphire; Fort Worth, Texas; Fontana, California; Las Vegas, Nevada; and Homestead, Florida. After years of speculation and fervent hope, the Indianapolis Motor Speedway hosted its first Cup race in 1994. In addition to the new facilities, every "old" track on the circuit added seats and upgraded its amenities. By the end of the decade, the Cup tour was running 34 races at 21 tracks in 17 states. Every area of the country had at least one race except the Pacific Northwest, the Rocky Mountain states, and the Great Plains.

One of the most important reasons for stock car racing's maturation during the 1990s was television. Hard to believe, but the first live, start-to-finish, coverage of a major Winston Cup race wasn't until the 1979 Daytona 500. Even so, there was precious little live coverage by the mainstream, non cable net-works in the 1980s, a void aptly filled by ESPN. By the mid-1990s, though, virtually every network (cable and mainstream) was fighting for its slice of NASCAR's revenue-producing pie.

And, finally, not to be overlooked . . . the role of the Winston Cup automobile itself. Never in any decade have so many engineers—both classically trained and the shade tree variety—worked so tirelessly and spent so much money to improve the breed. Once little more than an afterthought, aerodynamics became a huge issue in the 1990s. Annual budgets grew as crew chiefs and car builders booked expensive wind tunnel time in hopes of reducing drag or adding downforce. Builders found ways to squeeze even more horsepower from their 358-ci, V-8, four-barrel, gasoline-powered engines. Tire specialists often found cherished hundredths of a second among their stack of Goodyear Eagles.

This book—written by motor sports journalists who attended virtually every race of the 1990s—celebrates the 10 years between Derrike Cope's miracle victory in the 1990 Daytona 500 and Dale Jarrett's championship season of 1999. It focuses on the top 30 drivers and cars as well as the honorable mentions in each year's final points standings; on the memorable and not-so-memorable championship duels; on the key moments and some that perhaps are already forgotten; and on the stars and also-rans who proudly showed their wares 309 times between February of 1990 and November of 1999.

Enjoy . . . and recall.

Chapter 1

1990

By the Narrowest of Margins

DALE EARNHARDT DENIES MARK MARTIN

Hardly anyone thought much about it at the time. It was, after all, only two races into the 29-race NASCAR season of 1990. Nobody was looking that far ahead, envisioning the day when a 46-point penalty imposed at Richmond in February would play a role in determining the Winston Cup championship at Atlanta in November.

Even now, driver Mark Martin and owner/engine-builder Jack Roush shake their heads sadly when the subject comes up. Except for an innocent mistake, they insist, they would have won the first Winston Cup of the 1990s.

Instead, Dale Earnhardt got the huge trophy and $1 million check from R.J. Reynolds Tobacco Co. After 29 races spread over 10 months at 16 tracks in 13 states, the difference was 26 points. Not surprisingly, there's a story behind that handful of points.

It begins at Richmond International Raceway on February 25, a week after Earnhardt had lost the

Dale Earnhardt

Dale Earnhardt won his fourth championship in 1990, becoming the first driver other than Richard Petty to win more than three. The key this season was having been through a title run before, and the grit and experience of Earnhardt and the Richard Childress team showed down the stretch. The battle this year was with newcomer Mark Martin, who led by close shaves through September and October. But Earnhardt won at Phoenix, taking a six-point lead, and the Martin team panicked at Atlanta, finally borrowing a car from Robert Yates. Earnhardt, sensing the weakness, grinned and finished third to Martin's sixth at Atlanta, winning the trophy by 26 points. *David Chobat*

Car No.: 3
Make & Model: Chevrolet Lumina
Team Owner: Richard Childress
Wins: 9
Top 10: 23

Dale Earnhardt finished in the top 10 in 23 of 29 races in 1990, including six checkered flags. He squeaked out a narrow 26-point edge over Mark Martin for the championship with a win and a third-place finish in the last two races.

Daytona 500 on the final lap. Martin, driving the Roush-owned, Steve Hmiel–prepared, Folgers-backed, No. 6 Ford Thunderbird, took the lead in the final laps and won the Pontiac Excitement 400 at Richmond International Raceway. His margin of victory over Earnhardt was 3 seconds, with pole-sitter Ricky Rudd, Bill Elliott, and Dick Trickle rounding out the top five in the annual spring race at the 3/4-mile track.

Martin and Roush went to Victory Lane, then made the usual rounds of print and TV interviews. Hmiel was with the winning car, helping as officials began their routine post-race inspection. All around them, crewmen from other teams were packing up and loading up, already planning for next weekend's 500-miler at Rockingham.

Soon after the last hauler pulled out, Hmiel, Roush, and Martin realized they had more to worry about than just getting ready for Rockingham. NASCAR inspectors

had taken exception to an aluminum spacer plate between the carburetor and intake manifold on the Roush-built engine. The plate was legal, but it was not attached according to the letter of the rule book. The victory would stand—after all, NASCAR is loath to overturn what its fans have paid to watch—but Roush Racing would be fined $40,000, and Martin would be penalized 46 Winston Cup points.

At the time, it seemed more a careless mistake than an attempt by Roush to cheat his way to an unfair advantage. The fine was steep, but the team's accountant had no trouble stroking the check. And what were 46 points in February, anyway? Twenty-seven races remained. More than 5,000 points were still out there for the taking. Within days, almost everyone had forgotten about the fine and penalty from Richmond.

Martin went on to win three poles and two more races in 1990. He added 13 more top fives and 7 finishes between sixth and 10th. He led the point standings with two races left, but stumbled just enough at Phoenix and Atlanta to lose the Winston Cup by 26 points.

"It's unfortunate what happened," Martin said late in the season when the Richmond penalty became an issue. "We didn't get any competitive advantage with the plate like it was. It was an honest mistake that cost us a championship." Roush didn't mince words. "They took the championship away from us," he said.

The 1990 title was Earnhardt's third in a five-year spell and fourth overall. It broke a tie with three-time champions Lee Petty (1954, 1958, 1959), David Pearson (1966, 1968, 1969), Cale Yarborough (1976, 1977, 1978), and Darrell Waltrip (1981, 1982, 1985). That seemed to mean as much to Earnhardt as anything else. "It's a real honor to win more championships than those guys," he said after the 1990 season. "They're all great racers, so I was really happy to be in their company. It's really great to move into second behind [seven-time champion] Richard Petty. As far as I'm concerned, it's a huge honor to be anywhere near him in anything."

Earnhardt won four poles. His nine victories were Atlanta, Darlington, and Talladega in the spring; then Michigan, Daytona Beach, and Talladega in the summer. His fall victories were at Darlington, Richmond, and Phoenix. He had nine other top fives, five other finishes between sixth and 10th, and completed 28 of the year's 29 races. At the time, his 26-point championship margin was the fifth-closest in series history.

The year before, several days after losing the Cup to Rusty Wallace by 12 points, Earnhardt went hunting in Alabama. He replayed the season time and time again, fretting over mistakes in some races and second-guessing decisions in others. He came back to Richard Childress

Racing more determined than ever to win another Winston Cup.

"The more I thought about 1989, the more it bothered me," Earnhardt said. "We gave the championship away with our performances in the fall at North Wilkesboro [from second to 10th after a last-lap incident] and Rockingham [20th to Wallace's second]. When I got back from hunting, I went to every member of the crew and we made each other a promise. If we had a problem at the track and could fix the car, we would. We'd get every bonus point for leading, no matter what it took. We'd lead the most laps we possibly could and not take any prisoners. It hurt to be so close in 1989 and then lose it. Nobody on the team wanted to go through that again."

Earnhardt's season was a model of consistency. After leading into Turn 3 on the last lap of the season-opening race in Daytona Beach, he finished a heartbreaking fifth in the No. 3 Goodwrench Chevrolet. He ran second the following weekend at Richmond and was 10th at Rockingham before winning back-to-back at Atlanta and Darlington. He stum-bled to 19th at Bristol, but rallied with three consecutive top 10s: third at North Wilkesboro, fifth at Martinsville and first in the May race at Talladega.

His worst slump of the season lasted only four races: 30th at Charlotte on Memorial Day weekend, 31st a week later at Dover, 34th at Sonoma, then 13th at Pocono the third Sunday in June. After 13 of 29 races, Earnhardt trailed Martin, Morgan Shepherd, Wallace, and Geoff Bodine in the standings. He moved to second behind Martin by winning on back-to-back weekends at Michigan and Daytona Beach. He was fourth at Pocono, first at Talladega, seventh at Watkins Glen, and eighth at Michigan and Bristol to close the summer portion of the season.

By Labor Day weekend, it was apparent that Martin and Earnhardt were the class of the field. They stood one-two in points, Martin leading by 61 with nine races remaining. Earnhardt immediately began his championship charge by winning at Darlington and Richmond. He was third at Dover, then second at Martinsville and North Wilkesboro the last weekend in September. After 25 of 29 races, Earnhardt trailed by 16 points.

Mark Martin's win at Michigan Speedway in August put him 48 points ahead of second-place Earnhardt. Martin held the top spot in the standings from June 3 to November 4, before finishing second to the Intimidator.

The deficit grew to 49 when Martin finished 14th and Earnhardt 25th at Charlotte. Neither fared very well two weeks later: Earnhardt was 10th and Martin 11th at Rockingham. With only Phoenix and Atlanta left, Martin's lead was down to 45 points. Suddenly, that 46-point penalty he suffered back in the spring at Richmond loomed large, indeed.

Darrell Waltrip (left) and Alan Kulwicki (right) both finished in the top 20 in 1990. Kulwicki had his best season in 5 years as owner-driver of the number 7 Ford, while Waltrip struggled to his lowest finish (20th) in 18 years.

The season turned at Phoenix. Earnhardt qualified third, led the final 262 laps, won the race, and earned the maximum 185 points. Martin started eighth, didn't lead any laps, finished 10th, and earned only 134 points. Instead of taking a 40-point lead into the Atlanta finale the third Sunday in November, Martin went into it trailing by six.

With everything on the line, Martin, Hmiel, and Roush tuned and tweaked six Ford Thunderbirds in a three-day test prior to Atlanta. Unhappy with all six, they borrowed a Davey Allison car from fellow Ford owner Robert Yates. In hindsight, they may have been better off with the devil they knew rather than the one they didn't.

Given an opening, Earnhardt wasn't about to blow it. He qualified sixth, led three times for 42 laps, and finished third behind Shepherd and Bodine. Alas, Martin started 11th, didn't lead, finished a lap-down sixth, and lost the championship by 26 points. That, after having been No. 1 in points following 16 of the year's 29 races.

The spring victory at Richmond was one of Martin's three. He also won the second summer race at Michigan, and North Wilkesboro in the fall. He was second in five races, third on four occasions, fourth in two races, and fifth in two. What's more, he finished between sixth and 10th on seven occasions, had only one DNF, and won three poles. His fans were understandably bitter about the costly penalty, but Earnhardt's fans quickly pointed out that he'd won three times as many races. Besides, they added smugly, Roush should have known better than to use an unapproved part.

Third-ranked Bodine won three poles and three races for Junior Johnson, and loitered among the top five almost all season. Even so, he wasn't a serious contender to finish first or second in points. He won at Martinsville in the spring, at Pocono in the second summer race, then back at Martinsville in the fall. He was top five in eight other races and between sixth and 10th on eight occasions in the No. 11 Budweiser Ford.

Elliott was fourth-ranked in what for him was a poor season for owner Harry Melling: two poles and the fall victory at Dover. He had 11 other top fives and four other finishes between sixth and 11th, but wasn't the consistent force he'd been for so many years. Nobody knew it until late in the year, but 1990 marked the beginning of the end of his long and often-glorious relationship with Melling and the No. 9 Coors Ford.

The only victory for fifth-ranked Shepherd and owner Bud Moore was the season finale at Atlanta. The No. 15 Motorcraft Ford team had six other top fives and nine more finishes between sixth and 10th.

Sixth-ranked Wallace won at Charlotte in May and Sonoma in June, but seven DNFs in the No. 27 Miller Pontiac doomed his shot at winning another Cup for owner Raymond Beadle. Rudd won the summer race at Watkins Glen in the No. 5 Levi Garrett Chevrolet for Rick Hendrick. Owner-driver Kulwicki won the fall race at Rockingham in the No. 7 Zerex Ford. Relative newcomer Irvan got his breakthrough victory in the No. 4 Kodak Chevrolet for Morgan-McClure at Bristol in the summer. Tenth-ranked Ken Schrader won three poles and had 15 top 10s, but didn't win a race for Hendrick in the No. 25 Kodiak Chevrolet.

The other seven victories were divided among five drivers: Cope won the season-opener at Daytona Beach and the summer race at Dover. Allison won the spring race at Bristol and the fall race in Charlotte. Harry Gant won the first summer race at Pocono, Kyle Petty won the spring race at Rockingham, and Brett Bodine got his breakthrough victory in the spring race at North Wilkesboro.

Two tragedies struck the tour. Mike Rich, the right-rear tire-changer for Elliott, died from injuries suffered when Rudd's car slid into Elliott's during a late-race pit stop in the finale at Atlanta. (Several weeks later, at the Winston Cup awards banquet in New York, rules were announced restricting when and how fast drivers could pit.)

In the other incident, 22-year-old Rob Moroso died in a two-car accident on a blacktop near Charlotte. It was Sunday night, September 30, several hours after he'd finished 21st in the Holly Farms 400 at North Wilkesboro. Moroso failed to negotiate a right-hand turn and slid into an oncoming car shortly after leaving a popular restaurant-bar. His girlfriend was injured, but the driver of the other car—Tammy Williams, a 27-year-old nursing assistant and mother of two—died at the scene. An autopsy showed Moroso's blood-alcohol content at .22, more than twice the North Carolina standard for being legally drunk.

With almost no fanfare—his driving record turned out to be nothing short of abysmal—Moroso was posthumously named the series' Rookie of the Year. So young . . . so talented . . . so promising.

And, ultimately and tragically, so undisciplined.

Dale Earnhardt's Fateful Daytona 500

It remains the most famous deflating tire in NASCAR Winston Cup history. Hands down, no question about it, no contest. If you don't believe it, ask anybody who was there that Sunday afternoon in February of 1990.

After coming so close so many times, Dale Earnhardt was about to finally win the Daytona 500. He took the white flag comfortably ahead of Derrike Cope, Terry Labonte, Bill Elliott, and Ricky Rudd. He easily stayed ahead through Turns 1 and 2, then down the backstretch at Daytona International Speedway.

The (then) three-time NASCAR champion seemed home free until his No. 3 Chevrolet Lumina began slowing in Turn 3. Instead of its usual low line, it shot up the track, toward the wall. Cope and Labonte immediately cut left and passed on the inside. Seconds later in Turn 4, Elliott and Rudd did the same as Earnhardt's car slowed even more.

And just like that—in the blink of an eye—he had lost the one race he desperately yearned to win. The culprit this time was a deflating right-rear tire, cut when it clipped a shard of metal in the final laps. After leading eight times for 150 of 200 laps and holding a 38-second lead at one point, it was the most heartbreaking of Earnhardt's first 12 Daytona 500 losses.

At the time, he had nine victories at Daytona International Speedway: three in the Busch Series, three in the Gatorade 125-mile qualifiers, and three in the Busch Clash. He'd finished lead-lap in five of his first 11 Daytona 500s and been in position to win several. But all he had to show were five top fives and two other top 10s.

He took his latest loss better than many NASCAR-watchers would have imagined. "I was just riding along, waiting for the finish," he said moments after climbing from his car. "I felt the tire going down, but I had to ride it out. Derrike won the race, but we beat everybody all day. They didn't outrun us, they just lucked into it. When it shredded, it was all I could to keep it off the wall.

"The thing is, you can't do anything about it. You can't kick the car and cry and pout and lay down and squall and ball. You've just got to take it and walk on. But I'll tell you, this is the biggest letdown I've ever had in racing."

2nd

Car No.: 6
Make & Model:
 Ford Thunderbird
Team Owner: Jack Roush
Wins: 3
Top 10: 23

Mark Martin

Of all the disappointing seconds and thirds Mark Martin endured during the decade, the 1990 season had to be the most heartbreaking—and a testimonial to the fact that every point counts. On a frigid afternoon at Richmond in February (seen here), Martin won the Pontiac 400, but afterward, NASCAR found that his team had used an illegally thick carburetor-spacer plate. Martin kept the trophy, but the team was fined $40,000 and, more important, 46 points, judge Dick Beaty ruling that amount to be the difference between first and 10th place. After a desperately close stretch run for the championship with Dale Earnhardt, Martin fell short by 26 points. *David Chobat*

3rd

Geoff Bodine

One of the oddest owner-driver combinations in NASCAR history was formed in 1990, with New Yorker Geoff Bodine joining quintessential Carolina moonshiner Junior Johnson. Johnson was the ultimate insider among NASCAR's old guard, with Bodine, at least through the 1980s, the pioneer outsider. Bodine joked that he and Johnson had chickens in common, Bodine growing up on a chicken farm near Elmira, New York, and Johnson being one of Holly Farms' top producers. The alliance paid off, with Bodine winning three races (both Martinsvilles and Pocono, shown here) and hanging tough in the points race through August. *David Chobat*

Car No.: 11
Make & Model:
 Ford Thunderbird
Team Owner: Junior Johnson
Wins: 3
Top 10: 19

4th

Bill Elliott

A strong finish propelled Bill Elliott to fourth in points, two spots better than in 1989, and he counted that an achievement after being out of the top 10 at mid season. From the July Pocono on, Elliott finished out of the top five in only five of the 14 events, and he peaked at Dover in September, winning from the pole. Elliott surpassed $1 million for the fifth time, so considering the slow start the year was a success. At Martinsville (shown here), NASCAR's shortest track and not (up until then) one of Bill's best, he showed gains, starting 13th and finishing 10th in April, then starting 10th and finishing eighth in September. *David Chobat*

Car No.: 9
Make & Model: Ford Thunderbird
Team Owner: Harry Melling
Wins: 1
Top 10: 16

5th

Morgan Shepherd

Morgan Shepherd's first season with legendary car owner Bud Moore was a puzzle. The cars just would not qualify, with Shepherd making top five only twice (second at Michigan, third at Atlanta). However, through the first half, Morgan was able to push those same cars to an amazing 11 top 10s in a row, from Daytona through Dover. From there, however, Shepherd made just five top 10s over the final 18 runs. Nevertheless, he wrapped up the season with a victory at Atlanta, his best track, after finishing second at Charlotte and third at Phoenix in the homestretch, offering encouragement for 1991. *David Chobat*

Car No.: 15
Make & Model: Ford Thunderbird
Team Owner: Bud Moore
Wins: 1
Top 10: 16

6th

Car No.: 27
Make & Model:
Pontiac Grand Prix
Team Owner:
Raymond Beadle
Wins: 2
Top 10: 16

Rusty Wallace

Rusty Wallace set out to defend his 1989 Winston Cup championship amid a deteriorating team situation. By mid year, Wallace had sued long time team owner Raymond Beadle for money owed from the championship season, and it became clear that the No. 27 team had miraculously rag-tagged to the title. The hard core—Wallace, Barry Dodson, Harold Elliott, Jimmy Makar, and Buddy Barnes—held together through 1990 scoring victories at Charlotte and Sonoma and poles at the last two races of the season, at Phoenix and Atlanta. By the end of the year, however, shadow-backer Roger Penske, a board member at Miller Brewing, had asserted control. *David Chobat*

7th

Car No.: 5
Make & Model:
Chevrolet Lumina
Team Owner: Rick Hendrick
Wins: 1
Top 10: 15

Ricky Rudd

After two years with Kenny Bernstein, Ricky Rudd was the choice to replace founding partner Geoff Bodine at Hendrick Motorsports. Bodine and crew chief Harry Hyde had gotten Hendrick off the ground in No. 5 in 1984, and although Hendrick since had added two or three new teams, the owner's affection for No. 5 was deep-seated. Gritty Rudd, a racer's racer, kept the Levi Garrett car in the spotlight off the starting line with a pole at Richmond in February. Ricky also confirmed his road-course expertise with a pole at Sonoma in May (finishing third) and a victory at Watkins Glen in August. *David Chobat*

8th

Alan Kulwicki

The multiple abilities of Alan Kulwicki—as racer, team owner, businessman, and competitor—became evident in 1990. Kulwicki, once considered a brush-off oddball from Wisconsin, began to open eyes. Alan got off to a halting start. Always a good qualifier, he started third at Richmond, Rockingham, and Charlotte. The pace increased the second time through the tracks, with Kulwicki winning the pole at Michigan in August and finishing top 10 in the final six races, including Rockingham (shown here), where he won for the first time in 1990 and the second time in his career, leading the last 55 laps. *David Chobat*

Car No.: 7
Make & Model: Ford Thunderbird
Team Owner: Alan Kulwicki
Wins: 1
Top 10: 13

Ernie Irvan

Talented Ernie Irvan got his big career break in 1990. Irvan, from California farm country, had driven scrub cars for three years and had taken up with veteran Junie Donlavey at the start of the season. Donlavey had no solid sponsorship, however, and after three races, Irvan was called to replace Phil Parsons in Morgan-McClure's upscale No. 4 Kodak car. Ernie made the move pay by winning the pole at Bristol (Morgan-McClure's home track) in April and the night race at the brutal half-mile in August, his first victory in Winston Cup. Despite a tendency to try too hard at times, Irvan had arrived. *David Chobat*

9th

Car No.: 4
Make & Model: Oldsmobile Cutlass
Team Owner: Larry McClure
Wins: 1
Top 10: 13

10th

Car No.: 25
Make & Model: Chevrolet Lumina
Team Owner: Rick Hendrick
Wins: 0
Top 10: 14

Ken Schrader

As usual, Ken Schrader was in the spotlight at the start, winning the Daytona 500 pole at 196.515 miles per hour—his third Daytona 500 pole in a row—and out-gassing the field in the Busch Clash warm up. In the race, however, Kenny's engine quit after 58 laps, and he played a supporting role the rest of the season. Always fast on Fridays, Schrader also won poles at Charlotte and Rockingham (shown here), and he managed two second-place runs, at Dover and Phoenix. Schrader qualified sixth or better 14 times in 1990, but eight DNFs crippled the effort, and he ended the season winless. *David Chobat*

11th

Kyle Petty

Fifty miles south of his home in Randolph County, North Carolina, North Carolina Motor Speedway became Kyle Petty's personal playground in the early 1990s, under the leadership of crew chief Gary Nelson, who would become NASCAR's tech chief in 1993. From 1990 through 1992, Petty won five poles and three races at the aging, 1.017-mile oval, and in March 1990, he was unbeatable. Kyle started from the pole, led 433 of the 492 laps, and won by an astonishing 26 seconds, with only one other driver, Geoff Bodine, on the lead lap. Elsewhere, Kyle was a little better than average, with a best of fourth at Charlotte in October. *David Chobat*

Car No.: 42
Make & Model: Pontiac Grand Prix
Team Owner: Felix Sabates
Wins: 1
Top 10: 4

12th

Brett Bodine

After two graduate-school years in Bud Moore's Ford, Brett Bodine hired on as driver of Kenny Bernstein's No. 26 in 1990, one of only three full-time Buicks on the tour. In an otherwise ordinary year, Bodine pulled a rabbit out of the hat at .625-mile North Wilkesboro in April, scoring his one and only career victory—with an asterisk. During caution on Lap 321, a pace-car snafu left Bodine in a lap by himself, and although NASCAR tried to rectify the problem, Bodine won easily. Bodine earned the victory, however, leading 146 of the 400 laps. He also had two thirds and two fourths. *David Chobat*

Car No.: 26
Make & Model: Buick Regal
Team Owner: Kenny Bernstein
Wins: 1
Top 10: 9

13th

Davey Allison

In his fourth full season, Davey Allison, son of legendary Bobby Allison, had become NASCAR's most beloved and respected young star. With Davey as center of gravity, Robert Yates acquired Harry Ranier's operation in 1987, building it to powerhouse stature in five years. Yates could produce horsepower, and Davey could drive it, but the difficulty was in keeping it in a straight line. Guidance would come a year later, when crew chief Larry McReynolds came aboard. In 1990, on cubic inches and guts alone, Allison and Yates won at Bristol (shown here) and Charlotte. At Bristol, Davey beat Mark Martin by no more than a bumper. *David Chobat*

Car No.: 28
Make & Model: Ford Thunderbird
Team Owner: Robert Yates
Wins: 2
Top 10: 10

Sterling Marlin

Sterling Marlin made a game try in four years with Billy Hagan's team, even sporting a brand of women's underwear as a sponsor in the late 1980s. In 1990, the veteran flatfoot was still looking for his first Winston Cup victory, although he had shown his potential in winning The Winston at Charlotte the previous two seasons; most believed he was due. Sterling was mid pack most of the season despite new sponsorship from Sunoco. His best results were a third at Talladega in August, fourth at Rockingham in March, and fifths at Dover, summer Daytona, and August Bristol. *David Chobat*

14th

Car No.: 94
Make & Model: Oldsmobile Cutlass
Team Owner: Bill Hagan
Wins: 0
Top 10: 10

15th

Car No.: 1
Make & Model: Oldsmobile Cutlass
Team Owner: Richard Jackson
Wins: 0
Top 10: 9

Terry Labonte

Turned loose by Junior Johnson after 1989, Terry Labonte teamed with Richard Jackson in 1990 and endured his first winless season since 1982. Jackson, brother of Harry Gant car owner Leo Jackson, had decent cars and decent sponsorship from Skoal (which also backed Leo's team), and Terry's results were, well, *decent.* He ran second in the Daytona 500—his best of the season—and added fourths at summer Daytona and in the two Bristol races. Second place at Daytona paid Labonte $117,800, his biggest single-day paycheck to date. However, he finished down on the money list, making just $450,230 all year. *David Chobat*

16th

Michael Waltrip

Michael Waltrip, Darrell's little brother, had been the cornerstone of Chuck Rider's newly formed team in 1988, and the team made gradual gains in 1990. Waltrip and crew competed under a peculiar, dual-branded sponsor situation, which gave the cars the look of a rolling argument. Nevertheless, the Bill Ingle–led group produced five top-five finishes and an outside-front starting spot at Richmond in September. Overall, Mikey turned in 10 top 10s, 16th in points, and $400,000 in winnings, pushing him past the million-dollar threshold. All of those were career bests for the 27-year-old. Waltrip's high point was Charlotte in October, where he rallied from 36th at the start to finish third. *David Chobat*

Car No.: 30
Make & Model: Pontiac Grand Prix
Team Owner: Chuck Rider
Wins: 0
Top 10: 10

17th

Car No.: 33
Make & Model: Oldsmobile Cutlass
Team Owner: Leo Jackson
Wins: 1
Top 10: 9

Harry Gant

Harry Gant, who retired unhurt in 1994, was one of the extraordinary characters of the decade. He was serious as a racer, but he never let racing take over his life, and was always more comfortable building a house or shingling a roof. He skipped the Bristol race in April due to the death of his father, then won at Pocono in June, becoming, at 51, the oldest driver to win in Winston Cup. Overall, the season was spotty and not one of Gant's best. Gant drove one of five full-time Oldsmobiles in the circuit in 1990, and his relationship with sponsor Skoal was one of the longest lived in the business. *David Chobat*

18th

Derrike Cope

Derrike Cope will remain one of NASCAR's all-time favorite footnotes, and his victory in the Daytona 500 in 1990 goes down as one of racing history's all-time great upsets, with sure-fire winner Dale Earnhardt suffering a flat tire on the last lap. What people forget is that Cope's No. 10 car was competitive (running second behind Earnhardt) and that veteran Buddy Parrott was making the calls from the pits for Bob Whitcomb's Purolator team. More unlikely was that Cope dominated at Dover in June, then never won again. At all other stops, Derrike was no better than average, with a dreadful count of 10 DNFs. *David Chobat*

Car No.: 10
Make & Model: Chevrolet Lumina
Team Owner: Bob Whitcomb
Wins: 2
Top 10: 6

Bobby Hillin Jr.

Bobby Hillin, a wealthy young Texan, spent 10 years trying, unsuccessfully, to show that his lone victory at Talladega in 1986 was not a fluke. The 1990 season was basically his last chance after seven years with the Stavola Brothers' team, armed with sponsorship from Mars candy. Hillin probably had the best of the Buicks, but that was not good enough. Hillin began his wanderings in the wilderness the next year, and the Stavolas, paving contractors from New Jersey, had a new driver. Hillin started brightly enough, finishing sixth at Daytona, but had only three other top 10s, including fifth (from 31st) at Sonoma. *David Chobat*

19th

Car No.: 8
Make & Model: Buick Regal
Team Owner: Stavola Brothers
Wins: 0
Top 10: 4

20th

Darrell Waltrip

The 1990 season was pivotal for Darrell Waltrip, three-time Winston Cup champion. He crashed badly in practice for the summer race at Daytona, breaking his thigh and missing six races after surgery. Many believed Darrell never was quite the same afterward, although he won five more races on his own in 1991 and 1992, padding his career victory total to 84. Toward the end of 1990, Waltrip decided to set out on his own, with the blessing of owner Rick Hendrick, who helped set up the champ as owner-driver, with sponsorship from Sears/Western Auto. In 1990, Waltrip failed to win for the first time since 1974. *David Chobat*

Car No.: 17
Make & Model: Chevrolet Lumina
Team Owner: Rick Hendrick
Wins: 0
Top 10: 12

21st

Dave Marcis

Dave Marcis, from the old school, came late to the notion that a team needed a sponsor to be competitive. Marcis, who had driven for the likes of Nord Krauskopf, Roger Penske, and Rod Osterlund in the post Detroit 1970s, maintained his independent nature, and that cost him. Big Apple Market, shown on the side of his Chevrolet here at Daytona in 1990, was the business of a Pennsylvania friend of Dave's, but hardly in the league with Texaco and Tide. Marcis, who finished second in points (to Richard Petty) in 1975, made all the races in 1990 and ran steady, but without a single top 10. *David Chobat*

Car No.: 71
Make & Model: Chevrolet Lumina
Team Owner: Helen and Dave Marcis
Wins: 0
Top 10: 0

22nd

Car No.: 66
Make & Model: Pontiac Grand Prix
Team Owner: Stavola Brothers Racing
Wins: 0
Top 10: 4

Dick Trickle

Dick Trickle, undisputed king of Midwest short tracks, had been Rookie of the Year in 1989 with the Stavola Brothers, at age 48, replacing injured Bobby Allison. In 1990, he turned up with Cale Yarborough, who had switched from Oldsmobile to Pontiac, sporting new sponsor colors and a new car number to match. The highlight was a pole at Dover in June, but there were few others before or after, the combination producing an amazing 13 DNFs, including five engine failures. The season concluded on a low note, with Trickle finishing 30th or worse in the final four races. *David Chobat*

23rd

Rick Wilson

The Rahmoc team, led by former driver Butch Mock, took a chance in 1990 on stocky Rick Wilson, on the rebound from Morgan-McClure. For whatever reasons, just about anything that could go wrong did. Wilson made all 29 races (this in the days when NASCAR occasionally had trouble summoning a full field) but failed to finish 15 times, which has to be close to some kind of record. The team's season earnings fell by half, from $544,255 in 1989, with Morgan Shepherd, to $242,067. Wilson made just three top 10s, at Bristol, Sonoma (seen here), and Michigan. *David Chobat*

Car No.: 75
Make & Model: Oldsmobile Cutlass
Team Owner: Butch Mock
Wins: 0
Top 10:

Jimmy Spencer

The second coming of Rod Osterlund went pale through 1990, with sponsor Heinz increasingly dissatisfied. That was unfortunate for driver Jimmy Spencer, former Modified champion from Pennsylvania coal country, who had boot strapped into Winston Cup with Buddy Baker in 1989. Osterlund, a California land developer, had launched the career of Dale Earnhardt in 1979 and 1980, producing Rookie of the Year in 1979 and a Winston Cup in 1980, the only time that has been done in consecutive years. Spencer was not as fortunate, and after a wreck at Charlotte in October, he and the team split. After the season, Osterlund and Heinz were gone as well. *David Chobat*

24th

Car No.: 57
Make & Model: Ford Thunderbird
Team Owner: Rod Osterlund
Wins: 0
Top 10: 2

25th

Dale Jarrett

Dale Jarrett was flat on his back after his dismissal by Cale Yarborough after 1989, and was all but resigned to a career in the Busch Series. When the Wood Brothers' regular driver Neil Bonnett was badly hurt in a wreck at Darlington in April, Jarrett got the call, and when Bonnett's injuries turned out to be disabling, Jarrett kept the ride, boosting him up the ladder of success which culminated in his 1999 championship. The Wood boys had fallen a long way from their peak in the 1970s, and Jarrett helped stabilize the ancient organization, constructing four top 10s in the last seven races. *David Chobat*

Car No.: 21
Make & Model: Ford Thunderbird
Team Owner: Wood Brothers
Wins: 0
Top 10: 7

26th

Richard Petty

The end was near for Richard Petty, NASCAR's greatest champion, but it took him two more years to figure a way out. Petty's last decent season had been 1987, his last winning one 1983, and at 53 the repeated beatings of a 30-year career had taken a toll. The legendary King did not break the top 15 until Michigan in June, and he qualified only once in the top 10 all year, that being seventh at Daytona in July. Petty made all the races in 1990 after missing four in 1989; the Petty exemption (champion's provisional) was in force in 1990, although he had to use it only twice. *David Chobat*

Car No.: 43
Make & Model: Pontiac Grand Prix
Team Owner: Richard Petty
Wins: 0
Top 10: 1

27th

Butch Miller

Owner Travis Carter struggled to his feet in 1990 with a coalition of sponsors and with driver Butch Miller, American Speed Association standout from Michigan. Winn-Dixie, a supermarket chain (shown here), later achieved success as backer of Mark Martin's splendid Busch Series effort. Miller was steady, running consistently in the low 20s and teens, which probably was about all the cars could do. Nevertheless, Miller was out toward the end of the season, with Rick Mast taking over for the final five races. This turned out to be Miller's one full-time try in the big leagues; he was no more than a fringe player afterward. *David Chobat*

Car No.: 98
Make & Model: Chevrolet Lumina
Team Owner: Travis Carter
Wins: 0
Top 10: 1

Hut Stricklin

Waymond (yes, Waymond) Stricklin, better known as Hut, has spent most of his career looking for a proper home. The former Alabama and Tennessee short-tracker got what looked like a big break with Rod Osterlund and Heinz in 1989, but Stricklin was dismissed after the season and started 1990 without a full-time job. However, when Mike Alexander was unable to come back from off-season injuries, Stricklin got a call from owner Bobby Allison, jumped in the car at Talladega, and performed well, finishing ninth. He added a sixth place at Michigan a month later and was solid through the fall. *David Chobat*

28th

Car No.: 12
Make & Model: Buick Regal
Team Owner: Bobby Allison
Wins: 0
Top 10: 2

Jimmy Means

Jimmy Means made an acceptable living in racing through the 1970s and 1980s, bringing dependable, presentable cars to the tracks—finishing 15th and lower and earning $5,000 a week. By 1990, $5,000 a week hardly covered the bills, and Means proudly showed small sponsorship from Alka-Seltzer, which helped cover expenses. Means stuck it out through 1990 and 1991, but the death of old pal J.D. McDuffie at Watkins Glen in 1991 (with Means first to the accident scene) gave him second thoughts, and he reorganized his priorities shortly afterward. Means' take in 1990 was $135,165. *David Chobat*

29th

Car No.: 52
Make & Model: Pontiac Grand Prix
Team Owner: Jimmy Means
Wins: 0
Top 10: 0

Rob Moroso

Robbie Moroso was the bright young star of 1990. His father, Dick Moroso, well-known racing equipment producer, set up his son's rookie run this season, around a concerted effort by Oldsmobile, Crown gasoline, and Fas Mart, a growing chain of convenience stores. Young Moroso did well enough to earn Rookie of the Year honors. However, he died in a highway accident (which also killed a woman in another car) near Charlotte in October. Dead at 25, he became NASCAR's only posthumous Rookie of the Year. Dick Moroso's team struggled on for a few years, but nothing was the same, and Dick died before the end of the decade. *David Chobat*

30th

Car No.: 20
Make & Model: Oldsmobile Cutlass
Team Owner: Dick Moroso
Wins: 0
Top 10: 1

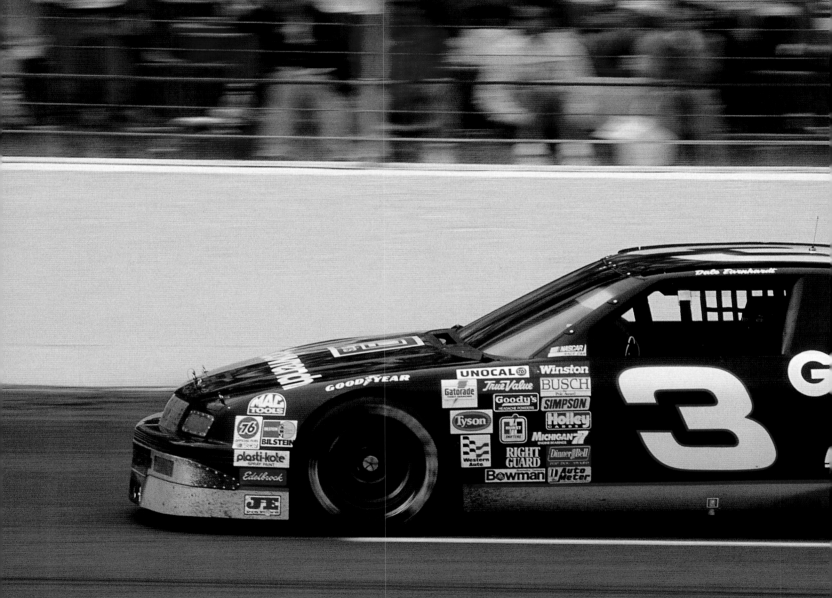

Chapter 2

1991

A Two-Horse Season

DALE EARNHARDT WINS SECOND CONSECUTIVE CHAMPIONSHIP

It was over by the first weekend of May. Nobody knew it at the time, of course, so they raced on and on and on. They raced on, in fact, until the third weekend of November. And when the 328th lap of the 29th and last race of the 1991 NASCAR Winston Cup season was completed, the same drivers who'd been one-two in points the first weekend in May were still one-two.

Their names were Dale Earnhardt and Ricky Rudd.

In one of the oddest seasons in recent memory, Earnhardt and Rudd were ranked one-two virtually all year. Ernie Irvan and Sterling Marlin were one-two after the season-opening race in February, then Earnhardt and Rudd were one-two after the next three races. It was Rudd-Earnhardt for a week in April, Rudd-Irvan the next week, then Rudd-Earnhardt for the last two weeks in April. It didn't change—Earnhardt first and Rudd second—from Talladega the first weekend in May through the season-ending race at Atlanta the third weekend in November.

Dale Earnhardt

Secure again at the top of the championship ladder, Earnhardt and crew pitched into 1991 with gusto, starting at Daytona. The 500, however, became yet another in a long string of Earnhardt disappointments in NASCAR's biggest race. He had taken the lead before caution on Lap 190, yielded it to Ernie Irvan on the restart, then wrecked with Davey Allison while running for the second two laps from the finish. He followed up with his first of four 1991 victories the next week at Rockingham. At Charlotte in May (seen here), Earnhardt was a contender all day, finishing third behind Davey Allison and Ken Schrader.

Car No.: 3
Make & Model: Chevrolet Lumina
Team Owner: Richard Childress
Wins: 4
Top 10: 24

And how's this for another statistical oddity: other than Irvan and Marlin (each for one week), Earnhardt and Rudd were the only drivers to rank second in points. In a series that prides itself on parity, it remains hard to believe that only four drivers would be first or second in points after 29 races.

Earnhardt won his second consecutive Cup and fifth overall with what some would consider a mediocre season.

Dale Earnhardt waves to his fans during the 1991 championship run. This was Earnhardt's fifth championship. The "Intimidator" racked up four victories and 24 top-10 finishes for the year.

He won only four times: Richmond, Martinsville, and Talladega in the spring; then North Wilkesboro in the fall. That was fewer than half the nine races he won en route to the 1990 title. But Earnhardt, crew chief Kirk Shelmerdine, and team owner Richard Childress piled on the consistency. They had three runner-up finishes and were third in four races. They added one fourth-place finish and two fifths, and finished between sixth and 10th an amazing 10 times. They had only two DNFs: at Darlington in the spring and at Charlotte in the fall.

In light of his fierce battles with Rusty Wallace in 1989 and Mark Martin in 1990, Earnhardt admitted 1991 felt somewhat odd. "We took the lead after first Talladega and never gave it up," he said at the time. "But every weekend I felt I was defending the team [to the media] for not dominating races. We've built such a tradition at Richard Childress Racing and with GM Goodwrench that everybody expects us to be at the front and in victory lane every weekend. That would be the perfect scenario and a perfect season, but the competition is so fierce that total domination is virtually impossible for anyone."

Maybe so, but Earnhardt made a run at it. He opened by finishing fifth in the season-opening Daytona 500 in Daytona Beach. He won the following weekend at Richmond, was eighth a week later at Rockingham, then third at Atlanta. His only bad finishes throughout the spring portion of the schedule were at Darlington (an engine-related 29th) and Bristol (a wreck-related 20th). Bristol was his last poor finish until the end of June.

He had nine consecutive top-10 finishes between late-April and mid-July: second at North Wilkesboro, first at Martinsville, third at Talladega, third at Charlotte, second at Dover, seventh at Sonoma, second at Pocono, fourth at Michigan, and seventh in the July race at Daytona Beach. The streak ended with a 22nd in the rain-shortened July race at Pocono.

To the surprise of hardly anyone, he bounced back by starting fourth, leading the most laps, and winning the late-July race at Talladega. But he stumbled again the next two weekends: 15th at Watkins Glen and 24th at Michigan. He regained his form by finishing seventh at Bristol late in August, then eighth at Darlington, 11th at Richmond, 15th at Dover, third at Martinsville, and first at North Wilkesboro, all in September.

Except for an engine-related DNF 25th at Charlotte in October, Earnhardt finished strong: seventh at Rockingham, ninth at Phoenix, and fifth in the season-finale at Atlanta the third weekend in November. The title was securely his by then, leaving his team free to take chances without worrying about the points consequences.

"You can't win races on your past history and you certainly can't win championships that way," Earnhardt said. "It takes work, painstaking, blood-and-guts work that people outside the racing world never see. Nobody worked harder that year than we did. We didn't just show up for 1991 resting on our 1990 laurels. Two days after we finished that season with the Winston Cup, everybody was back in the shop working on the '91 Daytona 500 car. That's the kind of dedication it takes."

Rudd pulled to within 36 points with six races remaining, the closest they'd been since May. But Earnhardt beat his only challenger in the last six races and won it all by 195 points. Rudd's only victory for crew chief Waddell Wilson and team owner Rick Hendrick was in the spring at Darlington. But he had eight other top fives (three of them second places), eight other finishes between sixth and 10th, and only one DNF, a wreck-related 32nd at Charlotte in the fall.

And while fans might not recall much else about Rudd's 1991 season, they recall his most controversial finish. It was in June at Sonoma, where Davey Allison and Rudd were one-two in the final laps of the Banquet Frozen Foods 300 at Sears Point Raceway. Rudd, running hard in second, nudged Allison aside as they came through the hairpin turn to begin the next-to-last lap on the 2.5-mile road course. Allison spun out, but quickly recovered and set off in hot pursuit of the new leader.

Given time to think about it—a lap around the track took about 105 seconds at the time—officials agreed to black-flag Rudd's No. 5 Tide Chevrolet and show Allison the white "one-lap-to-go" flag. Despite getting back to the start-finish line 5 seconds ahead of Allison, Rudd was penalized 6 seconds for rough driving and scored second. It later was determined that officials would have penalized Rudd 1 second more than any apparent margin of victory. Even today, the official margin of victory remains 1 second.

Rudd's understandable reaction was to compare NASCAR racing to professional wrestling. He accused

officials of wanting a popular, second-generation Ford Thunderbird driver to win during what was turning into a season dominated by General Motors products. Hendrick briefly talked of appealing before realizing the folly of publicly second-guessing the decisions of NASCAR officials.

When all was said and done though, Rudd had the last laugh. He beat Allison by six finish positions in the season-ender at Atlanta four months later to move from third to second in the final points. Allison's controversial victory at Sonoma was one of five (plus the non-points Winston all-star race) in the No. 28 Texaco Havoline Ford of owner Robert Yates. They also won at Charlotte in the spring, Michigan in the summer, then back-to-back at Rockingham and Phoenix in the fall. Allison had seven

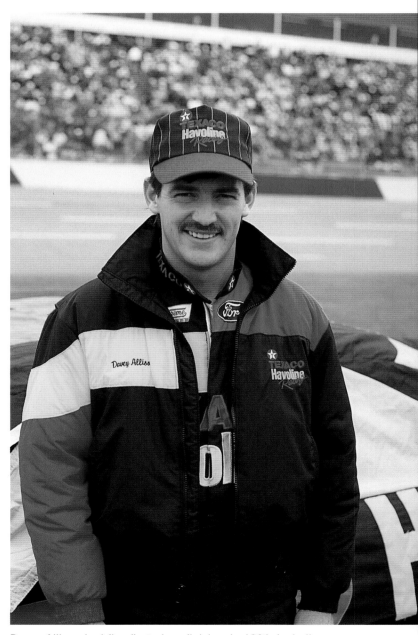

Davey Allison had five first-place finishes in 1991, including a controversial win at Sears Point in June. He ended the season third-best overall, four points behind Ricky Rudd in second place.

other top fives (including four runner-up finishes) and four other finishes between sixth and 10th. But four DNFs (three more than Rudd) cost him in the final standings.

Fourth-ranked Harry Gant provided one of the year's most heartwarming stories. At 51, an age when most drivers have retired or are leaning that way, the popular No. 33 Skoal Oldsmobile driver won five times: in the spring at Talladega, then on four consecutive weekends in September. Suddenly, "Handsome Harry" had another nickname: "Mr. September."

He started his record-tying streak for owner Leo Jackson by beating Ernie Irvan by 11 seconds at Darlington on Labor Day weekend. He beat Allison by less than a second a week later at Richmond and beat Geoff Bodine by more than a lap at Dover. He made it 4-for-4 by beating Brett Bodine by 1 second at Martinsville the following weekend. Gant was a handful of laps from sweeping all five September races when brake problems slowed him in the final laps at North Wilkesboro. Even so, his second-place finish behind Earnhardt that Sunday

Returning to the dual role of owner-driver for the first time since 1975, Darrell Waltrip climbed to an eighth-place finish in 1991. He earned a trophy—and a nice big check—for his victory at North Wilkesboro in April, the first of two wins on the year.

afternoon capped the most successful month any NASCAR driver had ever enjoyed.

Irvan's season was a roller coaster with the No. 4 Kodak Chevrolet team of Morgan-McClure. It began with an upset victory in February's season-opening Daytona 500, only the second checkered flag of his Cup career. Irvan also won the bittersweet summer road race at Watkins Glen, had nine other top fives, and eight other top 10s. But his team's inconsistency—he dropped out of six races, five of them because of accidents—relegated them to fifth in points.

As for sixth through 10th in the final standings:

Mark Martin won the season finale at Atlanta and had 16 other top 10s for owner Jack Roush. Marlin was 0-for-29 (but had 16 top 10s) in his first season with legendary owner Junior Johnson. Rookie owner-driver Darrell Waltrip won at North Wilkesboro in the spring and Pocono in the summer, and had 15 other top 10s. Ken Schrader won at Atlanta in the spring and Dover in the summer, and finished 16 other races in the top 10 for Hendrick. And Wallace won at the spring race at Bristol and the summer race at Pocono and was top 10 in 12 other starts for new owner Roger Penske.

Five drivers outside the top 10 also won races: Kyle Petty dominated the spring race at Rockingham. Bill Elliott won the summer race at Daytona Beach. Dale Jarrett got his breakthrough Cup victory at Michigan in the summer by beating Allison by a matter of inches. Alan Kulwicki won the summer night race at Bristol, and Geoff Bodine won the fall race at Charlotte.

Bobby Hamilton, a veteran of Tennessee's short tracks and a Busch Series regular, was the Rookie of the Year. He had four top 10s in 28 starts (including a best of sixth in the fall race at Rockingham) for team owner George Bradshaw. Among the tour's other rookies: Ted Musgrave, Wally Dallenbach Jr., and Stanley Smith.

And in a return to form—after all, he'd been No. 1 for five consecutive years before Waltrip beat him in 1989 and 1990—Elliott was named NASCAR's Most Popular Driver. (At the time, most NASCAR-watchers judged popularity on souvenir sales, where Earnhardt was the uncontested leader. Maybe so, but Elliott's well-organized fan club was almost impossible to beat.)

The season was marred by tragedy. Veteran owner-driver J.D. McDuffie died in a horrific crash with Jimmy Means in the early laps of the summer road race at Watkins Glen. The night before, at nearby Owego Speedway, the ever-popular McDuffie had basked in the glory of winning an exhibition dirt-track race. Truly, it is a harsh business, indeed.

Joe Gibbs Begins His NASCAR Adventure

By the early 1990s NASCAR was attracting athletes from other major-league sports. Chief among them was NBA star Brad Daugherty, part-owner of Busch Series and Craftsman Truck teams, and a friend of the Pettys.

Up in Washington, Joe Gibbs was scratching his racing itch. A North Carolina native and long time race fan, he wanted a sports business to share with college-age sons, J.D. and Coy. Thus was born Joe Gibbs Racing, a refreshing diversion from the pressure of coaching the Washington Redskins.

Even as J.D. played football at William and Mary and Coy at Stanford, their father juggled two jobs: preparing the Redskins for 1991 while building a NASCAR team for 1992. "Some people in Washington didn't like the idea of me racing," Gibbs said. "I saw a sign at an exhibition game saying, 'Cars or Quarterbacks.' I never let racing interfere with coaching."

He began with a sponsorship pitch to Norm Miller, president of Interstate Batteries. Next, he called Jimmy Johnson (not the ex-Dallas coach) and ordered cars and engines from Hendrick Motorsports. He hired Dale Jarrett as his driver and Jarrett's brother-in-law, Jimmy Makar, to be crew chief. By the fall of 1991, Joe Gibbs Racing was fully operational at a small shop in Charlotte.

"But I didn't have any idea what I was getting into," Gibbs said years later. "The first time I went to a party with the other team owners I realized how deep I was in over my head. Those guys had yachts, private jets, lots of money . . . and I didn't have anything. We left a party one night and I told my wife, 'How in the world did we get into this?'"

Jarrett, Makar, and Gibbs stayed together for three eventful years. They had two top fives and eight top 10s in 1992, then won the 1993 Daytona 500 and the 1994 Charlotte fall race. By Charlotte, everyone knew Jarrett was leaving to drive the No. 28 Ford owned by Robert Yates, and Bobby Labonte was coming in after a mediocre rookie season with Bill Davis.

In the long run, everything worked out. Jarrett and Yates won the 1999 Winston Cup and Labonte and Gibbs won it in 2000. Gibbs (140-65 in 12 seasons) retired from the NFL early in 1993, five weeks after winning his third Super Bowl in four tries. "Go back?" he said after the 1993 season. "No, I love it right here."

2nd

Car No.: 5
Make & Model:
 Ford Thunderbird
Team Owner:
 Rick Hendrick
Wins: 1
Top 10: 17

Ricky Rudd

In 1991, Ricky Rudd's second season with Rick Hendrick, he made his first real charge at a championship, finishing second to Dale Earnhardt, although both faltered down the stretch. Rudd was part of one of the strangest scripts in NASCAR history at Sonoma (shown here) in June, where for one of the very few times in series history, NASCAR penalized a driver out of a win. Rudd bumped past Davey Allison in the downhill hairpin with a lap to go and took the checkered flag, but NASCAR ruled Rudd had been too rough and gave the win to Allison, Rudd finishing second. *David Chobat*

Davey Allison

Davey Allison definitely broke out of his father's shadow in 1991, winning five races (beginning at Charlotte in May) and three poles and emerging as a championship contender. The difference in 1991 was the arrival of crew chief Larry McReynolds, who brought organization and discipline to the raw horsepower out of the Robert Yates shop and to the raw talent of the 30-year-old driver. Yates stayed a few horsepower ahead in the engine game throughout the 1990s, especially on the 1.5-mile tracks such as Charlotte, where Davey won The Winston and $325,000 in May. He won back-to-back at Rockingham and Phoenix in the fall, but could not get a clear shot at champ Dale Earnhardt. *David Chobat*

3rd

Car No.: 28
Make & Model: Ford Thunderbird
Team Owner: Robert Yates
Wins: 5
Top 10: 16

4th

Harry Gant

Good old Harry Gant had his best season in 1991, thanks largely to a phenomenal four-race winning streak in the fall, which tied the "modern-era" record. Gant reeled off consecutive victories at Darlington, Richmond, Dover, and Martinsville, not only tying the record but becoming the oldest driver (at 51) to win in Winston Cup. Gant, who began racing for money in 1964, emerged as a Cup rookie in 1979, and became a modest star via the participation in the team of movie producer Hal Needham (*Smokey and the Bandit*) in 1982. Harry enjoyed the ride, made money, and won races. *David Chobat*

Car No.: 33
Make & Model: Oldsmobile Cutlass
Team Owner: Leo Jackson
Wins: 5
Top 10: 17

Ernie Irvan

In his second season driving the Morgan-McClure Kodak Chevrolet, Ernie Irvan established himself as a front runner. He climbed four championship positions from ninth in the 1991 point standings to fifth in the final 1992 points tally. The hard-driving Californian claimed one pole, two race wins, and 20 top 10 finishes. Starting from the second row, Irvan proved he knew how to road race as well as oval race. He took control of the lead and went on to win the Budweiser at the Glen event. Irvan beat talented road racer Ricky Rudd by seven seconds. But Irvan will be forever etched in people's minds for his performance in the Daytona 500. In the waning stages of the race, Irvan was leading when Dale Earnhardt and Davey Allison came together sending each other out of the race. Irvan was in the right place at the right time and took the checkered flag under full course caution conditions. *David Chobat*

5th

Car No.: 4
Make & Model: Chevrolet Lumina
Team Owner: Larry McClure
Wins: 2
Top 10: 19

6th

Mark Martin

Mark Martin had caught the tail of the championship comet in 1990, finishing a desperate second to Dale Earnhardt. From then to the end of the decade, Martin never finished lower than sixth in points, a phenomenal run of consistency despite 10 years of ebb and flow within the Jack Roush–owned No. 6 team. Martin continued to dominate on pole days, winning five staves to bring his career total to 14. His one victory of the season came in the November run at Atlanta, where Davey Allison's battery went dead at halfway, allowing Martin to take control. He beat Ernie Irvan by 10 seconds. *David Chobat*

Car No.: 6
Make & Model: Ford Thunderbird
Team Owner: Jack Roush
Wins: 1
Top 10: 17

7th

Car No.: 22
Make & Model:
Ford Thunderbird
Team Owner:
Junior Johnson
Wins: 0
Top 10: 15

Sterling Marlin

Junior Johnson had a new sponsor, Maxwell House, and thus a new, second car, the No. 22, in 1991, and veteran plugger Sterling Marlin was the surprise choice to fill the seat. Always at his fearless best on the big tracks, Marlin made his debut with a second place (behind Ernie Irvan) at the Daytona 500. Otherwise, however, results were disappointing, at least relative to the reputation of the Johnson organization, which had won six championships between 1976 and 1985. Sterling also picked off poles for the summer races at Daytona and Talladega, and he finished second at Bristol in August, but he won no races.

Darrell Waltrip

The trend at the turn of the decade was toward owner-drivers, and Darrell Waltrip was one of the first to grasp the concept. Having driven four seasons for mega-owner Rick Hendrick, Waltrip, with a boost-up from Hendrick, launched his own team in 1991 with Western Auto sponsorship, and he got the hang of it pretty quickly, winning twice and finishing second twice. One of the victories came at North Wilkesboro in April (seen here), where he evaded 17 cautions to win by nearly a second over closing Dale Earnhardt, with Jimmy Spencer third. Waltrip also scored at Pocono in June. *David Chobat*

8th

Car No.: 17
Make & Model: Chevrolet Lumina
Team Owner: Darrell Waltrip
Wins: 2
Top 10: 17

9th

Car No.: 25
Make & Model: Chevrolet Lumina
Team Owner: Rick Hendrick
Wins: 2
Top 10: 18

Ken Schrader

Ken Schrader had begun to pay off on the promise he had shown as a rookie with Junie Donlavey in 1987, winning twice in 1991 and improving to ninth in points. Car owner Rick Hendrick had adjusted his roster after 1990, spinning off Darrell Waltrip's No. 17 and contracting to Schrader's No. 25 and the No. 5 of Ricky Rudd. Schrader won his second race of the season in June at Dover (seen here), leading the last 78 laps and finishing more than a second ahead of Dale Earnhardt. Strangely, this was Schrader's last win of the 1990s, leaving him with a 269-race losing streak by decade's end. *David Chobat*

Rusty Wallace

With a new owner (Roger Penske) and a new number (No. 2), Rusty Wallace set sail toward one of the most successful decades in NASCAR history, piling up 33 victories. Wallace actually took a tumble with the owner change, falling from sixth in points in 1990 to 10th in 1991, but he won twice (Bristol, Pocono), and with Penske's resources came confidence and a future. At Sears Point in June (seen here), Wallace dominated, leading 45 of the 74 laps on the road course. He finished third, after misfortune on a pit stop on Lap 60 left the final struggle to Ricky Rudd and Davey Allison. *David Chobat*

10th

Car No.: 2
Make & Model: Pontiac Grand Prix
Team Owner: Roger Penske
Wins: 2
Top 10: 14

Bill Elliott

Through his career, Bill Elliott has shown an uncanny ability to focus on his racing, no matter what else was going on in his life. By 1991, Elliott, sponsor Coors, and long time patron and owner Harry Melling were looking in different directions, but Elliott still found the fortitude to win the summer race at Daytona and finish 11th in points. Bill and the family team had been the most spectacular in NASCAR through the 1980s, but after a 15-year run, Elliott saw the handwriting and cast in with Junior Johnson for 1992. Elliott also rang up two second places and two poles in 1991. *David Chobat*

11th

Car No.: 9
Make & Model: Ford Thunderbird
Team Owner: Harry Melling
Wins: 1
Top 10: 12

12th

Car No.: 15
Make & Model:
Ford Thunderbird
Team Owner: Bud Moore
Wins: 0
Top 10: 14

Morgan Shepherd

At age 49, Morgan Shepherd, one of NASCAR's elder statesmen, posted a string of 12 top-10 finishes for the Bud Moore team, but the 1991 campaign wasn't nearly as successful as the 1990 season that garnered them fifth position in the final standings. The 1980 NASCAR National Sportsman champion's top finishes were two thirds at the Tyson Holly Farms 400 and the Peak Antifreeze 500. In addition, he posted two sixth-place and three eighth-place finishes. *David Chobat*

13th

Car No.: 7
Make & Model: Ford Thunderbird
Team Owner: Alan Kulwicki
Wins: 1
Top 10: 11

Alan Kulwicki

The 1991 season began in the shadow of the Gulf War, and several teams lacked major sponsorship. R.J. Reynolds impresario T. Wayne Robertson created a patriotic motif at Daytona, backing five teams, which then would be painted in the colors of the Armed Services; Kulwicki drew Army. The turning point came at Atlanta in March, where Kulwicki, backed provisionally by the Hooters restaurant chain, finished eighth, thus earning him patronage for the rest of the season, and beyond. Kulwicki, ultimate long-shot, went on to win at Bristol in August and finish 13th in points.

14th

Geoff Bodine

Geoff Bodine's second and final year with owner Junior Johnson continued the soap opera of Bodine's quirky career. At Charlotte in May, Bodine was injured in practice, and Johnson chose Sportsman veteran Tommy Ellis to stand in. Ellis finished 14th in The Winston, but the car afterward was found to have an over-sized engine, and Johnson and crew chief Tim Brewer were suspended for four weeks. Thus, when Bodine returned at Dover, he was driving a No. 97 car nominally owned by Junior's wife, Flossie. Seen enough? Stay tuned. Bodine also won at Charlotte, NASCAR's soap capital, in the fall and took poles at Darlington and Phoenix. *David Chobat*

Car No.: 11
Make & Model: Ford Thunderbird
Team Owner: Junior Johnson
Wins: 1
Top 10: 12

Michael Waltrip

Michael Waltrip and the Bahari team continued to plug in 1991, and the yellow Pennzoil car had become one of the familiar icons on the tour. Certainly, however, Waltrip and crew chief Bill Ingle hoped for better results. Waltrip was at least as good as he was in 1990, scratching out a third-place finish at tough Darlington in April and recording nine other top 10s. The race at the Watkins Glen road course (shown here) in August was not one of the team's best, with Waltrip finishing 21st, two laps behind winner Ernie Irvan. Waltrip improved to 15th in points, best yet in four years with Bahari. *David Chobat*

15th

Car No.: 30
Make & Model: Pontiac Grand Prix
Team Owner: Chuck Rider
Wins: 0
Top 10: 12

Hut Stricklin

The team formed around legendary Bobby Allison in 1990 was Allison's in name only, and it struggled to get to its feet. Allison's partners had promising sponsorship from Raybestos brakes. Hut Stricklin, Alabama neighbor of Allison, had given the team a good try at the end of 1990 and continued into 1991. Hut's best performance was at Michigan in June, where he contended all day, led 27 laps, and finished second to Allison's son Davey. Stricklin also posted two fourth places and four other top 10s, making 1991 one of the Allison team's better seasons. Stricklin had married Bobby's niece, Pam. *David Chobat*

16th

Car No.: 12
Make & Model: Buick Regal
Team Owner: Bobby Allison
Wins: 0
Top 10: 7

17th

Car No.: 21
Make & Model:
Ford Thunderbird
Team Owner:
Wood Brothers
Wins: 1
Top 10: 8

Dale Jarrett

The 1991 season was a turning point for Dale Jarrett, who had labored for 15 years on short tracks, in Sportsman cars, and with inferior Winston Cup teams. In his second year with the fabled Wood Brothers, Jarrett finally won his first Winston Cup race, beating Davey Allison to the line by inches at Michigan in a thriller. That one brilliant moment may have helped Jarrett move to the next peg; by the end of the season, he had agreed to suit up for coach Joe Gibbs' new NASCAR team in 1992—history in the making. Elsewhere, Jarrett and the Woods were middling, with nine DNFs hurting the effort. *David Chobat*

Terry Labonte

For a spell around the turn of the decade, 1984 champion Terry Labonte pulled in two directions—toward forming a team of his own and toward finding a steady ride. The dynamic landed him in the middle, back with old partner Billy Hagan in 1991, who was rejuvenated with sponsorship from Sunoco. Racing always was a game to Hagan, and the 1991 season reflected growing pains. Labonte finished 18th in points with nine top 10s, including a best of fifth at Darlington in September. Labonte also performed well at Charlotte (shown here) with 10th in May and sixth in October.

18th

Car No.: 94
Make & Model: Oldsmobile Cutlass
Team Owner: Bill Hagan
Wins: 0
Top 10: 7

Car No.: 26
Make & Model: Buick Regal
Team Owner: Kenny Bernstein
Wins: 0
Top 10: 6

Brett Bodine

Buick was near the end of its Winston Cup trail in 1991, with General Motors looking to consolidate its efforts behind Chevrolet. Kenny Bernstein's King Racing was one of the last of the Buick loyalists, and engine reliability proved to be a costly issue, with driver Brett Bodine failing to finish 12 of the 29 events. Competent Bodine ran well enough in the other 17, marking down a fourth at Martinsville in the spring and a second at Bristol in the fall. He also won the pole at North Wilkesboro in the spring (shown here) and started outside-front twice. *David Chobat*

Joe Ruttman

West Coast warrior Joe Ruttman, by now 45, had one of his few full-season runs in Winston Cup in 1991, becoming the fourth driver in four years for the nerve-wracked Rahmoc organization. Ruttman, brother of 1952 Indianapolis 500 winner Troy Ruttman, never had a minute's care on the big tracks, and his best moment of 1991 was his third place in the Daytona 500, where in three-and-a-half hours he earned $111,450. That was a third of his total take for the season; Ruttman stayed largely out of trouble, with only two DNFs, but finished lower than 10th, running at the finish, an amazing 23 times. *David Chobat*

Car No.: 75
Make & Model: Oldsmobile Cutlass
Team Owner: Bob Rahilly & Butch Mock
Wins: 0
Top 10: 4

Rick Mast

Rick Mast found job security at last in 1991, landing steady work with Richard Jackson's U.S. Tobacco–sponsored No. 1 car, a job he held for six largely fruitless years. Despite the best efforts of driver and owner, the No. 1 Skoal car was middle-of-the-pack most of the time, although the new marriage got off to a strong start with fourth place in the Daytona 500. The 500 had been Mast's showcase in 1989, when, driving a white, unsponsored car fielded by Travis Carter, he had led the big race toward the end before losing the draft and finishing sixth. *David Chobat*

Car No.: 1
Make & Model: Oldsmobile Cutlass
Team Owner: Richard Jackson
Wins: 0
Top 10: 3

22nd

Car No.: 68
Make & Model:
 Oldsmobile Cutlass
Team Owner:
 George Bradshaw
Wins: 0
Top 10: 4

Bobby Hamilton

Opportunist Bobby Hamilton got his first meaningful break in 1991, when George Bradshaw's Tri-Star crew, having given Hamilton a brief tryout late in 1990, agreed to a full-year effort. With engines from crafty Mark Smith, results likely were better than expected, with Hamilton, so far seen as little more than a short-tracker and movie stuntman, carving out four top 10s and 22nd in points. Other than the team's garish car, little stood out that season, although many recognized Hamilton's determination and car savvy. He finished 27th and 29th in the two races at Charlotte (seen here).

23rd

Car No.: 55
Make & Model: Pontiac Grand Prix
Team Owner: Ray DeWitt and
 D.K. Ulrich
Wins: 0
Top 10: 0

Ted Musgrave

Few knew much about this Ted Musgrave fellow when owners Ray DeWitt and D.K. Ulrich gave him a full-year shot in 1991. DeWitt was familiar with Musgrave from his work in the Midwestern ASA circuit, which had fed to NASCAR stars such as Rusty Wallace, Mark Martin, and Dick Trickle; for a time, ASA was NASCAR's primary nursery. In 1991, Musgrave began to show those who really were watching that he was a shrewd, heady race car driver. He did not bring home a single top 10, but only four times all season did he fail to bring the car back in one piece.

24th

Richard Petty

Richard Petty continued to enjoy mass adoration from the fans even though his skills were deteriorating and the results were few and far between. From 1989 to 1991, he finished no higher than 22nd in the final points. But Petty could always be counted on to share a smile, a warm comment, and soldier on despite the adversity. King Richard's best showing came at the upstate New York road course of Watkins Glen where he captured 9th place. He was only the second Pontiac in the top 10 in a race won by Robert Yates driver Ernie Irvan. *David Chobat*

Car No.: 43
Make & Model: Pontiac Grand Prix
Team Owner: Richard Petty
Wins: 0
Top 10: 1

Jimmy Spencer

Jimmy Spencer, from the untamed coal country of north-central Pennsylvania, had at least a two-year degree in big-time racing, having been champion (and terror) of NASCAR's Modified division in 1986 and 1987, then schooling with Buddy Baker (1989) and Rod Osterlund (1990). In 1991, restless Spencer joined with one of NASCAR's most calming mentors, Travis Carter, thus beginning a long friendship. Carter had dipped in and out of car management-ownership for 20 years. Spencer rewarded Travis, and the fans, with a stout third place at North Wilkesboro in April.

25th

Car No.: 98
Make & Model: Chevrolet Lumina
Team Owner: Travis Carter
Wins: 0
Top 10: 6

26th

Rick Wilson

Rick Wilson had helped Morgan-McClure get off the ground from 1986 through 1990. After an unsteady year with Rahmoc in 1990, Wilson was hired by Bill and Mickey Stavola for work in their Mars-sponsored cars in 1991. The 38-year-old Floridian managed a full season with the New Jersey contractors, pulling in $241,375 in purse. The next year, Wilson and the Stavolas came to dispute during and after the Daytona 500, and when Dick Trickle became available, Wilson was put aside. He reemerged as a historical footnote in 1993, as the man who replaced the retired Richard Petty in Petty's famous No. 43

Car No.: 8
Make & Model: Buick Regal
Team Owner: Stavola Brothers
Wins: 0
Top 10: 0

27th

Car No.: 19
Make & Model:
Ford Thunderbird
Team Owner:
Chuck Little
Wins: 0
Top 10: 1

Chad Little

The Spokane, Washington native Chad Little drove part-time in Winston Cup competition from 1986 to 1991 with mixed success. After winning the 1987 Winston West championship, Little moved to Charlotte, North Carolina, to pursue a Winston Cup career. For 1991, Little ran 27 races and wound up 28th in points. He had one top-10 finish that came at the Mello Yellow 500 won by Geoff Bodine in a Ford. After his Winston Cup rides failed to produce the necessary results, Little competed in the Busch Grand National series taking six wins and 11 top-10 finishes en route to runner-up position in the 1995 championship point standings. *David Chobat*

Derrike Cope

Whatever magic had produced a Daytona 500 victory for Cope and owner Bob Whitcomb in 1990 had fled elsewhere by 1991, with Cope drifting from 18th to 28th in final points. Either cause or symptom of the team's decline was the departure of crew chief Buddy Parrott mid year. Cope occasionally made himself troublesome, such as at Darlington in September, where he finished fourth, but he managed only one other top 10. Among the best of the rest was Cope's 12th-place finish at Charlotte in May (pictured here); he finished two laps down and received a check for $19,700.

28th

Car No.: 10
Make & Model: Chevrolet Lumina
Team Owner: Bob Whitcomb
Wins: 0
Top 10: 2

Dave Marcis

For many, Dave Marcis is one of NASCAR's unsung heroes. The independent race-team owner and driver has five Winston Cup career victories to his credit and was runner-up to Richard Petty in the 1975 points standings. In the early 1990s, the tide had turned to the large multi-car race teams, but Marcis continued the fight. Big Apple markets continued to sponsor the extremely modest race team. Considering the caliber of his equipment, Marcis put in a creditable performance for the year. He qualified for 27 events and scored a 10th-place finish at the Peak Antifreeze 500 and a 12th at the Hardees 500. *David Chobat*

Car No.: 71
Make & Model: Chevrolet Lumina
Team Owner: Helen and Dave Marcis
Wins: 0
Top 10: 1

Car No.: 20
Make & Model:
  Oldsmobile Cutlass
Team Owner:
Wins: 0
Top 10: 1

Bobby Hillin Jr.

In 1982, Bobby Hillin Jr. entered Winston Cup in 1982 at the tender age of 17 and failed to score a top-10 finish in his first three years of competition, but the rookie showed some promise. By 1985, his career took an upswing with five top-10 finishes. But Hillin astonished the NASCAR community by capturing the 1986 Talladega 500 and becoming the youngest driver to win a superspeedway race. For Hillin, the 1991 season was a struggle with only one top-10 finish to show for 22 starts. *David Chobat*

Kyle Petty

A catastrophe at Talladega in April both ruined Kyle Petty's season and focused his mind on the business of racing. A multi-car disaster on the backstretch, with Petty going airborne, left him with a fractured thigh, a long recovery, and a lot of time to think; he was not able to return until the Southern 500 at Darlington in September. Petty had won with his usual ease at Rockingham in March, leading all but 112 of the 492 laps. Bobby Hillin Jr. subbed for Kyle at Charlotte in May, with Kyle returning for a 15th-place run (shown here) in the fall. *David Chobat*

Car No.: 42
Make & Model: Pontiac Grand Prix
Team Owner: Felix Sabates
Wins: 1
Top 10: 2

Chapter 3

1992

Against All Odds

UNDERDOG ALAN KULWICKI PREVAILS

Hardly anyone associated with NASCAR racing bothered to look up and take note when Alan Kulwicki quietly arrived from Greenfield, Wisconsin, to run five Winston Cup races late in 1985. And truth be told, why should they have? After all, Kulwicki was just another Midwestern short-track star looking to conquer big-time stock car racing. Some who'd come before him had made it; many had not.

Good luck, kid, but don't quit your day job. You may have graduated from college and won a bunch of American Speed Association races, but Daytona Beach in February ain't Salem on a Sunday afternoon. Matter of fact, Darlington on Labor Day weekend ain't Elko at any time of the year. If you can't run with the big dogs . . .

Turns out the NASCAR family should have paid closer attention. In 1987, less than two seasons after coming to North Carolina with all his belongings in a battered pickup, Kulwicki won his first Cup pole. A year later, in his 85th career start, he won his first Cup race.

Alan Kulwicki

Alan Kulwicki, in the No. 7 Hooters Ford, tows Dale Jarrett's No. 18 Chevrolet off the fourth turn in Charlotte's Mello Yello 500. By the time of this race in October, long-shot Kulwicki had closed from 278 points behind to make a close, three-way points race which culminated in his impossible-dream championship. Kulwicki won the pole at Charlotte and led 64 laps before Mark Martin ran him down at the end. Kulwicki nevertheless finished second and closed to 47 points behind leader Bill Elliott. The climax was to come three races later at Atlanta, where Kulwicki, with Ford's permission, dubbed his Thunderbird the "Underbird."

Car No.: 7
Make & Model: Ford Thunderbird
Team Owner: Alan Kulwicki
Wins: 2
Top 10: 17

And in 1992, by the slimmest margin in series history, the owner-driver of the No. 7 Hooters Ford "Underbird" won the championship and reigned ever-so-briefly as king of NASCAR.

If the rest of the racing fraternity found it hard to believe, imagine how Kulwicki felt. "The reality of winning the championship didn't set in until December, at the awards banquet in New York," he said early in 1993. "I was sleeping in the master bedroom of the Presidential Suite of the Waldorf-Astoria. It had been the resting place for every U.S. president since 1931 as well as kings and queens from around the world.

"John F. Kennedy's rocking chair was in the living room and General MacArthur's desk was in the second of the four bedrooms. When I woke up that morning, the reality of the championship hit me like a ton of bricks. The first thing I asked myself was, 'How did I get here?'"

How, indeed?

In many ways, 1992 was among the most eventful Winston Cup seasons of the 1990s. Richard Petty closed out his brilliant 34-year career with a "Fan Appreciation Tour" that generated worldwide attention and enormous income from endorsements and souvenirs. A young Busch Series driver named Jeff Gordon caught the eye of Rick Hendrick and began his meteoric climb up the stock-car ladder to fame and fortune. Davey Allison solidified his place as a superstar and Ernie Irvan began showing the promise so many had predicted for so long. Bill Elliott continued to weave his magic with a Ford, this time with new owner Junior Johnson.

Then, there was the matter of the closest finish in series history. The season began with 500 miles at Daytona Beach in February and ended with 500 miles at Atlanta in November. It included 29 races at 16 tracks in 13 states from Florida to New York, from Delaware to California, and from Arizona to Michigan. There were 19 superspeedway races, 8 short-track races, and 2 on road circuits.

Six drivers arrived at the season-ending race in Atlanta still thinking championship. Surprisingly, two-time defending champion Dale Earnhardt was not among them. After winning the 1980, 1986, 1987, 1990, and 1991 Cups, his Richard Childress–owned, Kirk

Bill Elliott and Davey Allison each had more victories and led more laps than Alan Kulwicki in 1992, but they finished second and third, respectively, behind Kulwicki. Elliott and Allison are shown here at Daytona before the July 4th Pepsi 400.

Driving Rick Hendrick's Chevrolet, Ricky Rudd finished seventh-place in the 1992 championship.

Shelmerdine–led, No. 3 Goodwrench Chevrolet team struggled. For only the second time since 1979, the Intimidator finished outside the top 10 in points.

Kulwicki's improbable run began with a fourth at Daytona Beach in February. He was 31st the next weekend at Rockingham, then second by a matter of feet a week later in Richmond. He was seventh at Atlanta, 18th (an engine-related DNF) at Darlington, then first at Bristol. After six of 29 races he was fifth in points behind Allison, Elliott, Harry Gant, and Terry Labonte.

He was seventh in the spring race at North Wilkesboro, 16th a week later at Martinsville, sixth in the May race at Talladega, then seventh in the Memorial Day weekend race at Charlotte. He finished 12th at Dover late in May and 14th at Sears Point the first weekend in June. With almost half the season behind him, Kulwicki was fifth in points—but only 83 behind Allison.

His up-and-down struggles continued throughout the summer portion of the schedule: first at Pocono, third a week later in Michigan, 30th at Daytona Beach, third at Pocono, and 25th at Talladega. He was seventh at Watkins Glen, 14th at Michigan, and fifth at Bristol. The good news was that Kulwicki reached the two-thirds mark of the season behind only Elliott and Allison in points. The bad news was that he was 133 behind Elliott and 24 behind Allison, and showing no real sign of enough staying power to hang with the larger, better-funded teams of Junior Johnson and Robert Yates.

In fact, Kulwicki's ride got much, much worse before it got much, much better. Witness:

He was eighth in the rain-shortened Labor Day weekend race at Darlington. Elliott was third and Allison fifth, leaving Kulwicki 161 points behind Elliott and 42 behind Allison with eight races remaining.

None of the top three ran well at Richmond the following weekend: Elliott was 14th, Kulwicki 15th, and Allison 19th. Elliott's lead grew to 134 points over Allison and 164 over Kulwicki.

Some NASCAR-watchers wrote off Kulwicki following the fall race at Dover. Elliott was second and Allison fourth, but Kulwicki was 34th, victim of an early-race accident. With six chances remaining, Elliott's lead was 154 over Allison, 239 over Gant, and a near insurmountable (everyone thought) 278 over fourth-place Kulwicki.

But Kulwicki quickly showed his resolve. He was a lead-lap fifth in the next race at Martinsville, well ahead of Allison (16th), Gant (19th), and Elliott (30th). After 24 of 29 races, Kulwicki was back to third in points, but 191 behind Elliott and 79 behind Allison.

He made up even ground at North Wilkesboro the following weekend. Allison finished 11th and Kulwicki

12th (each was three laps behind in the caution-free race), and Elliott was 26th, plagued by engine problems. The standings after 25 of 29 races showed Elliott 67 points ahead of second-ranked Allison and 144 ahead of third-ranked Kulwicki.

The key race for Kulwicki—other than the finale, that is—was at Charlotte on the second Sunday in October. He finished second to Martin and was 17 positions better than Allison and 28 positions better than Elliott. The threesome headed into the last three races almost deadlocked: Elliott by 39 points over Allison and only 47 points ahead of Kulwicki. (Fourth-ranked Martin was 91 behind Elliott, but hardly anyone at that point considered him a serious championship threat.)

Elliott opened the gap a little at Rockingham on the last Sunday in October. He finished fourth to Allison's 10th and Kulwicki's 12th. That built Elliott's lead to 70 points over Allison, 85 over Kulwicki, 94 over Kyle Petty, and 113 over Gant. (Martin was 30th at The Rock and fell to sixth, 178 points behind Elliott.)

The championship chase took a dramatic turn at Phoenix the first Sunday in November. Elliott qualified

Despite not winning any poles during the season, Harry Gant finished fourth overall. He struggled to 23rd place at the Pepsi 400, but still attracted the attention of autograph seekers.

only 18th, didn't run especially well, and was an engine-related DNF 31st. Allison won the race and took the points lead by 30 over Kulwicki, the new second-ranked driver. Elliott dropped to third, 40 behind Allison, followed by Gant, 97 behind. Petty was fifth, 98 behind, and sixth-ranked Martin was 113 behind, the longest of long shots.

The entire 1992 season—29 races covering more than 10,000 miles—came down to 500 miles at Atlanta Motor Speedway the third Sunday in November. The weekend oozed with anticipation, given that never had six drivers been chasing the Cup this late in any season. As if that weren't enough, the Hooters 500 was Gordon's first race and Richard Petty's last.

Barely 16 months earlier—in June of 1991 at his shop in Level Cross, North Carolina—the seven-time champion and 200-race winner announced his retirement plans. He was 54 at the time, as popular as ever, and an American original. But he hadn't won in more than seven years, and indeed had grown increasingly and embarrassingly mediocre in his No. 43 STP Pontiac. The 1992 finale at Atlanta would mark his 1,177th and final NASCAR race. It's a record every bit as safe for all time as his 200 career victories and 27 victories (including 10 in a row) in 1967.

Interest in seeing The King's last ride was so great that track owner Bruton Smith scrounged up 18,000 extra bleacher seats—and promptly sold them out. Petty and his family spent most of the week at media functions and accepting farewell gifts. He qualified 39th on Friday, was treated to a lavish farewell banquet that night, then recognized at a concert by the musical group Alabama on Saturday night in the Georgia Dome in downtown Atlanta. Little wonder he was happy to see Sunday finally come and go.

Allison needed to finish the season-ending race fifth or better to win the Cup. He started 17th, led several laps, and seemed poised to close the deal when he and Ernie Irvan crashed on the front stretch at lap 253. With Allison on the sidelines and Gant, Petty, and Martin well off the pace, the 1992 Winston Cup suddenly seemed headed to Elliott or Kulwicki.

They stayed one-two most of the second half of the 328-lap race, swapping the lead several times. It quickly became evident that Elliott would win the Cup if he led the most laps and finished at least two places ahead of Kulwicki. If Elliott led the most laps and finished one spot ahead of Kulwicki, he'd make up 10 points and forge a tie. Since he had more victories (4-2), the championship tiebreaker would favor him. But if Kulwicki led the most laps and finished within one spot of Elliott, he'd be the champion outright.

Which is precisely what happened.

Elliott won the race and led 102 laps. Kulwicki finished second and led 103 laps. That one-lap difference—worth five bonus points—kept Elliott and Kulwicki from tying for the title. Elliott might have led the most laps and won the title if he hadn't pitted under green at Lap 209. If he could have stayed out until at least 210, he would have led one more lap than Kulwicki and won the Cup.

Petty, in the meantime, wasn't faring very well. He started 39th and was involved in a fiery, early-race incident that damaged and burned his Pontiac. In the final laps, though, he got back in the car and was running at the finish of his last race. "I wanted to go out in a blaze of glory," he quipped. "I just forgot to bring along the 'glory' part. There was plenty of blaze, I can tell you that."

Gordon's debut with crew chief Ray Evernham went almost unnoticed. He started 21st, crashed out after 164 laps, and finished 31st. The team's only real bright spot was being the second-round, fastest qualifier in the Hendrick Motorsports No. 24 Chevrolet. It would be one of the last times the No. 24 team did anything almost unnoticed.

Elliott's bittersweet victory at Atlanta was his fifth of the season for Johnson in the No. 11 Budweiser Ford. He won consecutive races at Rockingham, Richmond, Atlanta, and Darlington in the spring, then the finale in Atlanta. He had nine other top fives and three finishes between sixth and 10th. He led or was near the top in most statistical categories, but it wasn't enough for the Cup.

Third-ranked Allison also won five races: Daytona Beach, North Wilkesboro, and Talladega in the spring, then Michigan in the summer and Phoenix in the fall. He had 10 more top fives and two more top 10s in the No. 28 Texaco Ford of owner Robert Yates. His best drive might have been to simply start the summer race at Talladega. After all, he'd spent four days in a hospital for treatment of head, arm, and wrist injuries suffered the previous weekend at Pocono.

Harry Gant and owner Leo Jackson finished fourth for the second consecutive season. Gant won the spring race at Dover and the second Michigan summer race. He had eight more top fives and five finishes between sixth and 10th in the No. 33 Skoal Bandit Oldsmobile.

Kyle Petty took Sabco Racing to fifth in the final standings, winning at Watkins Glen in the summer and Rockingham in the fall. He and the No. 42 Mello Yello Pontiac added seven other top fives and eight more finishes between sixth and 10th.

The back-five in the standings were Mark Martin, Ricky Rudd, Terry Labonte, Darrell Waltrip, and Sterling Marlin. Three of them won races.

Martin and team owner Jack Roush won at

Martinsville in the spring and Charlotte in the fall. Rudd won the fall race at Dover for owner Rick Hendrick. Labonte was 0-for-29 for owner Billy Hagan. Waltrip won the summer Pocono and Bristol races, and the rain-shortened Labor Day weekend race at Darlington in his own car. And Marlin was 0-for-29 as Elliott's teammate for Johnson.

Irvan won summer races at Sears Point, Daytona Beach, and Talladega, but finished 11th in points. Twelfth-ranked Earnhardt's only victory was the summer race at Charlotte. Rusty Wallace won the fall race at Richmond and finished a surprising (and bitterly disappointing) 13th in points.

Jimmy Hensley, who joined the tour at Martinsville in April, was named the top rookie in a relatively weak class. The long time Late Model and Busch Series star was so nervous during his acceptance speech at the Waldorf in New York that he left his $50,000 check on the podium.

And in case you're wondering . . . no, Kulwicki didn't forget his $1 million check. It's called attention to detail, and it's why he was the champion.

One year after being named the Busch Series Rookie of the Year, Jeff Gordon was driving a Bill Davis Ford in 1992. He finished fifth in the Busch Series that year.

Jeff Gordon's Meteoric Climb to the Top

It's now clear that Jeff Gordon was destined to be a superstar. His impressive open-wheel resume led to a 1990 tryout at Buck Baker's driving school, where he earned a ride for that fall's Busch Series 200 at Rockingham. First, the good news: Gordon stunned everyone by qualifying second. Now, the bad news: He lasted only 33 laps before crashing out to 39th.

But the die was cast, and NASCAR would be the beneficiary of his sudden fondness for stock cars.

Gordon was the 1991 Busch Series Rookie of the Year in Fords owned by Bill Davis. They won 11 poles and three races in 1992, and finished fifth in points. For part of 1992, it seemed that Davis, Gordon, and Fords would climb the NASCAR ladder together to the Cup.

But everything changed on Saturday, March 14, at Atlanta Motor Speedway. That's when Cup owner Rick Hendrick noticed Gordon's immense potential.

Hendrick and Charlotte Motor Speedway promoter Humpy Wheeler were walking through the grandstands during the Busch Series 300. Before boarding a VIP elevator, Wheeler stopped Hendrick and motioned toward Gordon. "He said if we stood there long enough, the kid in the 1 car would crash," Hendrick recalled years later. "I mean, there was smoke coming off the tires and the car was hanging out. I thought Humpy was right, that he was going to crash."

Not only did Gordon not crash, he won ahead of Cup stars Harry Gant, Hut Stricklin, Davey Allison, and Morgan Shepherd. Several days later, after asking around, Hendrick learned that Gordon was obligated to Davis and Ford, and likely wouldn't be available. "I didn't think much about it other than realizing he was a great talent," Hendrick said. "At the time, I didn't expect he'd ever drive for me."

In truth—as Hendrick later discovered—Gordon wasn't committed to anyone or any brand. What's more, he and a Hendrick Motorsports employee were roommates. It wasn't long before Hendrick and Chevrolet offered to fast-track Gordon directly to Winston Cup in 1993. Davis and Ford were stunned at the news, but were powerless since there was no contract.

Gordon's Cup debut at Atlanta in November of 1992 was forgettable. He led second-round qualifying in a Hendrick-owned No. 24 Chevrolet, but crashed out midway through Richard Petty's 1,177th and final race. Out with the old and in with the new, just like nature has always intended.

2ⁿᵈ

Car No.: 11
Make & Model:
Ford Thunderbird
Team Owner:
Junior Johnson
Wins: 5
Top 10: 17

Bill Elliott

Bill Elliott, rejuvenated in his first year driving Junior Johnson's No. 11 Budweiser Fords, won five races (including four in a row in the spring) and took the points lead at Pocono in July. Elliott was one of five drivers within 113 points of the lead with two races to go—the most exciting points race of the decade. He yielded the lead, however, when his engine blew at Phoenix, bringing the season to a one-round-takes-all finish at Atlanta. In Atlanta's Hooters 500, Elliott ran neck-to-neck with Alan Kulwicki through the second half, snatching the lead, and the race victory, with a fuel-only stop 18 laps from the finish. Kulwicki finished second and won the 1992 title by 10 points.

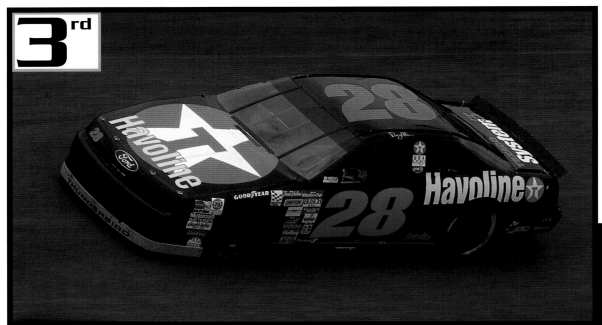

3ʳᵈ

Car No.: 28
Make & Model:
Ford Thunderbird
Team Owner: Robert Yates
Wins: 5
Top 10: 17

Davey Allison

Davey Allison's 1992 season summarized the triumph and tragedy that marked the Allison clan's journey in racing. At the Daytona 500 (shown here), Allison won, completing the promise shown in 1988, when he finished second to father Bobby. Then, at Pocono in July, Allison crashed terribly; many initially feared him dead, but he came out with no worse than a broken wrist. He came to Atlanta in November leading in points and needing to finish only sixth to win the Winston Cup, but a crash with Ernie Irvan and Rusty Wallace left him 27th and cost him the championship, by 63 points.

4th

Car No.: 33
Make & Model:
 Oldsmobile Cutlass
Team Owner:
 Leo Jackson
Wins: 2
Top 10: 15

Harry Gant

Harry Gant seemed to save his best for the end. In 1991, at 51, he had tied the Winston Cup record for consecutive victories with four (and nearly five) in the fall. In 1992, at 52, he produced two victories, three second places, and fourth in points. Harry's vitality was amazing. While younger men needed ice and oxygen after a hot afternoon at, say, Richmond, Gant could be seen, already dressed, sprinting across the garage to a waiting get-away car. Gant's run at Rockingham in February was typical. In the four-hour race, Gant hung in for third place, behind Bill Elliott and Davey Allison.

5th

Car No.: 42
Make & Model:
 Pontiac Grand Prix
Team Owner:
 Felix Sabates
Wins: 2
Top 10: 17

Kyle Petty

Kyle Petty was riding high in 1992, putting together the best season of his career. He improved from 31st to fifth in points, notched two victories (Rockingham, of course, and Watkins Glen), and recorded his first million-dollar season. Robin Pemberton was the crew chief this year, replacing Gary Nelson. Petty, driving for long time patron Felix Sabates, was competitive at most stops, scoring 17 top 10s. The night race at Bristol in August was one of his better efforts. Starting 26th and thus pitting on the backstretch, Kyle nevertheless survived to finish fourth, the last man on the lead lap.

6th

Car No.: 6
Make & Model: Ford Thunderbird
Team Owner: Jack Roush
Wins: 2
Top 10: 17

Mark Martin

Perennial championship contender Mark Martin sported new sponsorship and colors in 1992, with Valvoline replacing Folgers coffee, thus creating an identity that lasted for a decade. Martin won two races in 1992, at Martinsville and Charlotte, and was in a six-way dogfight for the championship until a wreck at Rockingham in October eliminated him from contention. Equally costly was the August night race at Bristol (shown here). Martin started fourth and led twice early, then was caught in a multi-car accident which left him 25th in the final order. The Bud 500 was the first race on Bristol's new concrete surface.

7th

Car No.: 5
Make & Model:
Chevrolet Lumina
Team Owner:
Rick Hendrick
Wins: 1
Top 10: 18

Ricky Rudd

Ricky Rudd has been a model of consistency throughout his career. During the 1980s, he finished in the top 10 of the final points standings 8 out of 10 times; and he has won at least one race per year since 1983. For 1992, Rudd captured one pole, 18 top-10 finishes, and took a fantastic win at the Peak Anti-Freeze 500 held at New Hampshire International Raceway. In 1991, Rudd drove for Hendrick Motorsports and had been as close as 36 points to the eventual points champion Earnhardt in the points chase. In the end, Rudd wound up second in points. Despite a solid season, Rudd slid from second to seventh in the 1992 point standings. Thus, his performance was somewhat of a disappointment. But Rudd did claim a championship. Racing against Indy car and stock car drivers, he won the 1992 International Race of Champions (IROC) championship. *David Chobat*

8th

Terry Labonte

Terry Labonte, 1984 champion with Billy Hagan, returned to Hagan in 1991, in Sunoco colors, after three years with Junior Johnson and one with Richard Jackson. In 1992, the team changed from Oldsmobiles to Chevrolets, and Labonte gained from 18th to eighth in the points picture. North Wilkesboro, a now-defunct .625-mile track in the North Carolina hills, rewarded Labonte with a ninth-place, lead-lap finish in the spring and eighth place, two laps down, in October. Labonte would spend one more year with Hagan and sponsor Kellogg's, then move on with Kellogg's to Hendrick Motorsports' No. 5 Chevrolets in 1994, resulting in another Winston Cup title in 1996.

Car No.: 94
Make & Model:
 Chevrolet Lumina
Team Owner: Bill Hagan
Wins: 0
Top 10: 16

Car No.: 17
Make & Model: Chevrolet Lumina
Team Owner: Darrell Waltrip
Wins: 3
Top 10: 13

9th

Darrell Waltrip

Darrell Waltrip, 45, seemingly had taken control of his destiny in 1991, leaving owner Rick Hendrick to become owner and driver of his No. 17 Western Auto Chevrolets. In 1992, legendary Waltrip won three races, including Bristol's Bud 500. Bristol, of course, always had been Waltrip's best track; he won 12 races at the freakish Tennessee half-mile, more than anyone. He made victory look easy in the August night race, leading the last 133 laps and beating Dale Earnhardt to the finish line by an untouchable 9.28 seconds. Waltrip also won the next weekend, in a thunderstorm at Darlington. So, oddly, the last two of Waltrip's 84 career trophies came back-to-back.

10th

Sterling Marlin

The 1992 season began brightly for Sterling Marlin, as he won the pole for the Daytona 500. It turned dark 92 laps into the big race, when he, teammate Bill Elliott, and Ernie Irvan tangled on the backstretch. Although Sterling was not strictly to blame, that may have been the beginning of the end of his two-year tenure with Junior Johnson, who let him go at the end of the year. Marlin recorded five poles (second to Alan Kulwicki's six) and three second-places, but no victories. At Rockingham in the fall (shown here), Marlin started 19th and battled to fifth place at the finish.

Car No.: 22
Make & Model: Ford Thunderbird
Team Owner: Junior Johnson
Wins: 0
Top 10: 13

Car No.: 68
Make & Model: Ford Thunderbird
Team Owner: Morgan McClure
Wins: 3
Top 10: 11

Ernie Irvan

By the end of 1992, Ernie Irvan (No. 4 Kodak Chevrolet) was an established star, having won the 1991 Daytona 500 and the Pepsi 400 in 1992, finishing 11th in points. Bobby Hamilton (No. 68 Country Time Ford) was still struggling along in the middle, driving for the ever-hopeful Tri-Star team of George Bradshaw and Mark Smith. Here, Hamilton moves over to allow Irvan's faster car room on the outside at Atlanta. Irvan later was involved in the controversial wreck which took Davey Allison out of the championship chase.

Car No.: 3
Make & Model:
   Chevrolet Lumina
Team Owner:
   Richard Childress
Wins: 1
Top 10: 15

Dale Earnhardt

Dale Earnhardt fumed through 1992, finishing 12th in points, the only time in the decade he failed to make the top 10. He said later that, in 1992, he and the Richard Childress team were called to pay for the investment in success that brought them championships in 1990 and 1991. Earnhardt won only once in 1992, at the May spectacular at Charlotte, with a streak of bad luck and a decade-high four DNFs holding him under $1 million in race earnings for the first (and only) time since 1985. Earnhardt led early in the season-ender at Atlanta, one of his better tracks—and there are many—but he was caught in a wreck and limped home 26th. *David Chobat*

13th

Rusty Wallace

By late 1992, Rusty Wallace was on the verge. He had won a championship in 1989 with the chaotic Raymond Beadle team, and by 1992, his second season with Roger Penske, he had begun to put the parts in place. Rusty won just one race in 1992, at Richmond in September, but he added two second-places, a third, a fourth, and seven other top 10s, all that equaling 13th in points. Better yet, he and the team cut their DNFs in half, with only five in 1992 compared with 10 in 1991. Wallace had begun to show that the Pontiac Grand Prix was a workable racecar, despite the general trend toward Ford. At Bristol, easily his best track, Wallace ran ninth (April) and 10th (August).

Car No.: 2
Make & Model: Pontiac Grand Prix
Team Owner: Roger Penske
Wins: 1
Top 10: 12

Morgan Shepherd

Morgan Shepherd migrated from one veteran team to another for 1992, leaving Bud Moore's No. 15 to begin a fruitful association with the Wood Brothers. Right away, Shepherd and the Woods surprised many by finishing second at the Daytona 500, two lengths behind winner Davey Allison. Shepherd also racked up second place at Watkins Glen, in the rain-shortened race won by Kyle Petty. Atlanta always was Shepherd's personal briar patch, with three of his four career victories coming at the 1.5-mile oval. In 1992, he ran 10th (March) and 11th (November). The overall tally gave Shepherd 14th in points.

14th

Car No.: 21
Make & Model: Ford Thunderbird
Team Owner: Wood Brothers
Wins: 0
Top 10: 11

15th

Brett Bodine

Brett Bodine, middle of three racing Bodine brothers, was in the middle of a five-year tenure with owner Kenny Bernstein, the drag-racing star. In the wake of new engine rules for 1992, Bernstein had converted from Buicks to Fords, with Brett racking up 13 top 10s and a best finish of third (at Martinsville in September). The final counting in November showed him 15th in points, his second best through the 1990s. Bodine showed commendably at concrete Bristol, finishing 11th, six laps down, in the Food City 500 in April and ninth, one lap down, in the night race in August. Through the 1990s, Brett was always at his best on the short tracks.

Car No.: 26
Make & Model: Ford Thunderbird
Team Owner: Kenny Bernstein
Wins: 0
Top 10: 13

16th

Car No.: 15
Make & Model: Ford Thunderbird
Team Owner: Bud Moore
Wins: 2
Top 10: 11

Geoff Bodine

Battler Geoff Bodine had taken up with patriarch Bud Moore in 1992 after six years with Rick Hendrick and two with Junior Johnson. The Bodine-Moore partnership was curiously inconsistent, with two victories and seven top fives, but also seven DNFs and 16th place in points. Moore, a Ford loyalist since the late 1960s, had acquired Ford Motorcraft sponsorship in the middle 1980s and maintained it through 1995. Geoff's two victories for Moore in 1992 came at Martinsville and North Wilkesboro. At Bristol's Bud 500 in August (shown here), Bodine started 11th and finished 11th, three laps behind winner Darrell Waltrip.

17th

Car No.: 25
Make & Model:
Chevrolet Lumina
Team Owner:
Rick Hendrick
Wins: 0
Top 10: 14

Ken Schrader

The 1992 season was not a bad one for Ken Schrader, but it had to be disappointing for him to fire blanks after winning twice in 1991. The Hendrick Motorsports No. 25 team endured some internal turmoil and reorganization in 1992, with long time Hendrick insider Ken Howes replacing Richard Broome as crew chief in the spring. Schrader's best finishes were two third-places, both at Bristol, one with Broome and one with Howes. Always fearless on the big tracks, Schrader also put up a good result, sixth, in the Pepsi 400 at Daytona in July (shown here).

18th

Car No.: 55
Make & Model: Ford Thunderbird
Team Owner: Ray DeWitt and D.K. Ulrich
Wins: 0
Top 10: 7

Ted Musgrave

Ted Musgrave was on his way up in 1992, his second full season. He had begun to show he could make the most out of less, including the No. 55 DeWitt-Ulrich Fords. The team, co-owned by Ray DeWitt and former Winston Cup independent D.K. Ulrich, had fair support from Indiana-based Jasper Engines but was not in the sponsorship league with the big boys. Still, Musgrave managed an impressive fifth place at Pocono and six other top 10s, leaving him 18th in the final standings. At Atlanta's Hooters 500, Musgrave politely moves over for one of the championships contenders, Davey Allison, driving Robert Yates' No. 28.

Dale Jarrett

A champion was hatched in 1992, when Dale Jarrett got his first legitimate shot at front-running. After a journeyman career in sportsman cars and with fair-to-middling teams, Jarrett was hired by Super Bowl–winning coach Joe Gibbs, who had turned his interest to NASCAR racing. In the long run, both Jarrett and Gibbs prospered, with Jarrett winning the Winston Cup in 1999 and Gibbs (with Bobby Labonte) in 2000. In 1992, the effort was barely underway, although Jarrett scored a second place (Bristol in the spring) and a third place (Daytona in the summer). Results for the Interstate Batteries Chevrolets were not consistent enough, however, to give Jarrett more than a 19th-place ending.

19th

Car No.: 18
Make & Model: Chevrolet Lumina
Team Owner: Joe Gibbs
Wins: 0
Top 10: 8

20th

Dick Trickle

Dick Trickle won Rookie of the Year with the Stavola Brothers team in 1989—at age 47, in his first full season in Winston Cup. The Wisconsin latecomer migrated to Cale Yarborough's team in 1990, then returned to the Stavolas in 1992, replacing Rick Wilson and supporting the team's sponsorship from Mars candy. As it turned out, this was one of many stops on the road for Trickle, whose 1,000 (give or take) short-track victories in the Midwest had made him a figure of respect. Bill and Mickey Stavola had joined the general rush to Ford in 1992, changing over from their long time Buick allegiance. Trickle finished 20th in points.

Car No.: 8
Make & Model: Ford Thunderbird
Team Owner: Stavola Brothers
Wins: 0
Top 10: 9

Car No.: 10
Make & Model: Chevrolet Lumina
Team Owner: Bob Whitcomb
Wins: 0
Top 10: 3

Derrike Cope

Driver Derrike Cope and owner Bob Whitcomb had discovered magic at Daytona in 1990, when Cope followed sure-winner Dale Earnhardt's flat tire to a singular victory in the Daytona 500. The operation had not kept pace since, with the team seemingly unable to find its way. This was Cope's last year with Whitcomb, who closed down not long afterward; he took up the next year with Cale Yarborough. Cope had one of his better runs of the season at Darlington in September, running 12th in the Purolator Chevrolet—for which he earned $10,690, a sign of those times.

Car No.: 1
Make & Model:
Oldsmobile Cutlass
Team Owner:
Richard Jackson
Wins: 0
Top 10: 1

Rick Mast

Probably no one had more 11th-or-worse finishes through the 1990s than did Rick Mast, a good-natured Virginian who probably deserved better. From 1990 through 1999, Mast finished out of the top 10 198 times in 294 starts, with an additional 61 DNFs. Rick's six-year acquaintance with owner Richard Jackson and U.S. Tobacco impresario Johnny Hayes brought long-term benefits, however, so Rick was secure. Mast made only one top-10 finish in 1992, his second season with Jackson, but he finished the season on a high note by winning the pole at Atlanta, the first pole dash of his career.

23rd

Michael Waltrip

The 1992 season was Michael Waltrip's fifth with car owner and friend Chuck Rider, with steady backing from Pennzoil and Pontiac. By 1992, the yellow No. 30 Pennzoil car had become one of the most-recognized on the circuit, despite the fact that the team had not won. Crew chief Mike Beam had not helped the results, neither had Bill Ingle. The one constant during those years was Waltrip, who gave his best at every stop, especially on the big tracks. Waltrip made his best result in the second race of the season, at Rockingham, where he finished fourth, a lap down, in what was then a grueling, four-hour, 492-lap race.

Car No.: 30
Make & Model: Pontiac Grand Prix
Team Owner: Chuck Rider
Wins: 0
Top 10: 2

Wally Dallenbach Jr.

Road-racer Wally Dallenbach had been a Ford protégé and a one-time championship driver for Jack Roush in Trans-Am. When Roush set up a second team (companion to his pioneer No. 6 with Mark Martin), Dallenbach was the natural choice. The No. 16 Fords bore sponsorship from Keystone beer—a Coors product—and Dallenbach, who'd had an 11-race tryout with Junie Donlavey in 1991, completed the switch from sports cars to NASCAR in 1992. The team had teething pains in 1992, with only one top five (a fifth at the Watkins Glen road course, a Dallenbach specialty). The car is shown here entering the pits at Darlington.

24th

Car No.: 16
Make & Model: Ford Thunderbird
Team Owner: Jack Roush
Wins: 0
Top 10: 1

25th

Bobby Hamilton

By 1992, Tennessee short-tracker Bobby Hamilton had gotten both feet in the door and was working his second full season with mid pack car owner George Bradshaw. The vividly painted, lemon-and-pink Country Time cars were an eyesore, but Hamilton continued to show his savvy, seldom wrecking and usually bringing the car home better than where it started. The team showed flashes down the stretch, with Hamilton starting 23rd and finishing 10th at Dover in September and starting 21st and finishing eighth at Phoenix in November, his best of the season. Hamilton ended up 23rd in points and with $367,065 in the bank.

Car No.: 68
Make & Model: Chevrolet Lumina
Team Owner: George Bradshaw
Wins: 0
Top 10: 2

Car No.: 43
Make & Model:
  Pontiac Grand Prix
Team Owner:
  Richard Petty
Wins: 0
Top 10: 0

Richard Petty

What can be said about Richard Petty that has not already be said? Aside from his amiable manner and gracious relationship with his fans, he is simply the greatest stock car driver of all time. His amazing career spanned three decades and countless NASCAR changes. He started 1,184 events, captured 126 poles, won a record number 200 races—a record that most likely will never be broken—and won the Winston Cup championship seven times (1964, 1967, 1971, 1972, 1974, 1975, and 1979). This year was the swan song for the great master. Many wanted to see Richard finish out his career with a podium or top-10 finish. Alas, it was not to be. In the 26 races "The King" qualified for, he did not crack the top 10. In the last race of the season at Atlanta, he was caught up in a wreck that knocked him out of the race. After the race, he made one last lap in a fenderless car to say goodbye to his fiercely loyal fans. Later that year, he was awarded the Medal of Freedom, the highest civilian award for an American. *David Chobat*

Car No.: 12
Make & Model:
  Chevrolet Lumina
Team Owner: Bobby Allison
Wins: 0
Top 10: 4

Hut Stricklin

Hut Stricklin, a native Alabaman, continued to race for the Bobby Allison team in 1992. After battling with leaders during the June race at Michigan in 1991, Stricklin showed the ability was there if the equipment was up to the task. But this underfunded team in its third year with Stricklin struggled to find success. For 28 races entered in 1992, Stricklin made his way into the top 10 only four times. His best performance was a seventh at the Budweiser 500.

28th

Jimmy Hensley

Virginian Jimmy Hensley began his racing career in old Modified coupes in the late 1960s and had long been a workhorse in NASCAR's Sportsman (later Grand National) divisions. His one big chance came in 1992, when Cale Yarborough shed season-starter Chad Little after the April Bristol race and put Hensley in the car. Hensley, as always, ran steadily, bringing in four top 10s in 22 races and, improbably at age 47, won Rookie of the Year, despite not running the full schedule. Only Dick Trickle, who won rookie honors in 1989 at 48, beat Hensley for high age as top freshman. Hensley finished seventh at Bristol (shown here), his best run of the year.

Car No.: 66
Make & Model: Ford Thunderbird
Team Owner: Cale Yarborough
Wins: 0
Top 10: 4

Dave Marcis

It seems odd to see Dave Marcis in any colors other than his familiar blue No. 71. Marcis takes the word "independent" to the third or fourth power, and only in brief spells during his 35-year career has he stepped aside to drive for someone else. One of those spells came in 1992, when Marcis accepted an offer to drive Larry Hedrick's No. 41 Chevrolet, with Kellogg's breaking in as sponsor. Marcis never really *said* he'd break from his own team (in fact, he put Jim Sauter in No. 71), and Hedrick never really committed to Marcis either. Let the record show that from the August Bristol race on (shown here), Marcis drove seven races for Larry Hedrick, then went back to his own business.

29th

Car No.: 41
Make & Model: Chevrolet Lumina
Team Owner: Larry Hedrick
Wins: 0
Top 10: 0

30th

Greg Sacks

Former Modified driver Greg Sacks appeared finally to have found a home in Winston Cup when Larry Hedrick hired him as starter in 1992. Sacks' one great claim to fame had been his implausible victory at the Daytona Firecracker in 1985, driving an unsponsored one-off from Bill Gardner, coached by Gary Nelson. He had bounced around a good bit since, with not a single full-season run in 10 years. He ran 20 races for Hedrick in 1992 before he and Hedrick agreed to disagree and Dave Marcis took over the No. 41 Chevrolets. Sacks, who did not break the top 10 with Hedrick, ran 28th in the spring race at Darlington, with engine failure.

Car No.: 41
Make & Model: Chevrolet Lumina
Team Owner: Larry Hedrick
Wins: 0
Top 10: 0

Chapter 4

1993

So Close

DALE EARNHARDT'S CONSISTENCY CINCHES CHAMPIONSHIP

When he's deep into his retirement years, maybe while flying one of his jets to an old-timer's autograph session, Rusty Wallace will think back to the 1993 NASCAR Winston Cup season as the one that got away. He won one more pole and four more races than Dale Earnhardt. He had more top fives and an equal number of top 10s, and led more races and more laps.

But when all the ciphering was done, Wallace was still 80 points behind. Instead of having another huge trophy to bookend his 1989 Winston Cup, he was a disappointed and frustrated runner-up. "We did all we could, so I can't fault anybody on this team," he said after getting his 10th victory in the season finale at Atlanta in November. "This is a season I'll savor, but I never thought we'd win 10 races and not the championship."

Earnhardt collared his sixth NASCAR title (his third

Dale Earnhardt

After a puzzling hiatus in 1992, Dale Earnhardt rallied strong in 1993 under new crew chief Andy Petree and returned to the top of the pile, winning championship No. 6. Earnhardt took the lead for good with his first-ever road-course victory at Sears Point in May, built a huge margin during the summer, and coasted home with an 80-point cushion. The year brought six victories, 17 top fives, and $3.3 million, a record at the time. On the horizon, though, was rookie Jeff Gordon, shown here chasing Earnhardt in the soon-to-be-famous Rainbow car. Gordon, who finished second twice, began to emerge as the champ's primary rival in the public eye.

Car No.: 3
Make & Model: Chevrolet Lumina
Team Owner: Richard Childress
Wins: 6
Top 10: 21

of the 1990s) on the strength of two poles, six victories, 11 other top fives, and four finishes between sixth and 10th. Despite a new crew chief (Andy Petree replaced Kirk Shelmerdine) and winning four fewer races than Wallace, he led the standings from Round 10 at Sonoma in May through the Atlanta finale in mid-November.

He went into Atlanta leading Wallace by 126 points, setting up this comfortable scenario: even if Wallace led the most laps and won the race, Earnhardt needed to finish only 34th or better for the title. "I'm willing to give Rusty the battle," he said in the days before the race, "as long as I win the war. The championship is the thing. It's what we've been racing for since February."

It can be argued that both men got what they wanted that Sunday afternoon at Atlanta Motor Speedway. Wallace qualified 20th, led nine times for 189 of the 328 laps, and won ahead of Ricky Rudd, Darrell Waltrip, Bill Elliott, and Dick Trickle. Earnhardt qualified 19th, led once for only two laps, and finished 10th. He lost 46 points to Wallace, hardly worth mentioning in light of his $1.25 million champion's payoff.

Earnhardt's sixth championship came a year after he'd won just one race and finished 12th in points. "What's so special about this one is how the team rebounded after that poor year," he said. "The crewmen never got down on

Though Rusty Wallace won more races, Dale Earnhardt was on top again in 1993, holding an 80-point lead when the season ended in Atlanta. It was championship number six for "The Intimidator."

themselves or questioned their abilities [after their poor 1992 season]. They knew they were a championship team and this proves they were right. Kirk was the only crew chief most of the guys had ever known, but they accepted Andy right away. As much as anything else, that helped us win this one."

Earnhardt began the season by leading the most laps and finishing second to Dale Jarrett in February's season-opening Daytona 500. He was second to Wallace two weeks later at Rockingham, fourth at Richmond, 11th at Atlanta, won the pole and the late-March race at Darlington, then ran second to Wallace at Bristol. After six of 30 races, the champion-to-be had one victory, three seconds, a 10th and an 11th, and a 47-point lead over Wallace.

But he lost the lead during his only "slump" of the season: a 16th at North Wilkesboro and an engine-related DNF 22nd at Martinsville in races Wallace won. Earnhardt quickly set things straight with a third at Talladega early in May and a sixth two weeks later at Sonoma. In the span of five races—from Bristol the first Sunday in April through Sonoma the third Sunday in May—Earnhardt had gone from 47 points ahead to 101 behind and back to 20 ahead. The lead change at Sonoma (Wallace was a transmission-related DNF 38th) was the fifth and final one of 1993.

Despite being No. 1, Earnhardt ran like he was trying to get there. He won on back-to-back weekends at Charlotte and Dover, was 11th at Pocono and 14th at Michigan, then won the early-July race at Daytona Beach. He was an uncharacteristic 26th in the inaugural race at New Hampshire, then won late-July races at Pocono (where Wallace was second) and Talladega (where Ernie Irvan was second). After 18 of 30 races, Earnhardt had built his lead over Jarrett to 234 points.

He stumbled a few times down the stretch, but not enough to matter. He was 18th at Watkins Glen, ninth at Michigan, and third at Bristol, all in August. He opened the fall stretch finishing fourth at Darlington on Labor Day weekend, third at Richmond, then 27th at Dover (crash damage) and 29th at Martinsville (axle-related DNF). His 305-point lead that had looked virtually insurmountable in August was down to 72 with four races remaining. "I saw a mischievous glint in Dale's eye that let me know he enjoyed the pressure of the chase," said Kevin Triplett, one of Earnhardt's publicists at the time. "It was like he was glad things were going to be close. It was like he wanted people to know he would be racing hard right to the end."

But Earnhardt promptly put an end to the suspense. He led some laps and finished third at Charlotte in October, gaining 10 points on fourth-place Wallace. He was second at Rockingham, but still lost 10 points because

Wallace won the race and led the most laps. But any fear of a total collapse ended on Halloween at Phoenix, where Earnhardt was fourth to Wallace's 19th. That crucial swing gave Earnhardt 54 more points, and he went to Atlanta leading by 126.

(The Cup chase tells only part of Earnhardt's season. He, Petree, and team owner Richard Childress also won the Busch Clash and their 125-mile qualifier at Daytona Beach in February. In May, they won The Winston all-star race at Charlotte for the third time. "All in all," Earnhardt said in November, "it was an unbelievable year. I just can't get over the things that have happened to me.")

Wallace's three poles for owner Roger Penske and crew chief Buddy Parrott came in the spring at Atlanta and at Bristol, and in the fall at Dover. Their victories were in the spring at Rockingham, then three straight: Bristol, North Wilkesboro, and Martinsville. The No. 2 Miller Pontiac won only once during the summer—at Loudon in July—but closed with fall victories at Richmond, Dover, North Wilkesboro, Rockingham, and Atlanta.

"You don't win championships with five bad runs like we had," Wallace said in his post-Atlanta press conference. "Give me back those races and I've got 14 or 15 wins and the championship. We crashed [32nd] at Daytona Beach, had transmission troubles at Sears Point [38th], suspension problems at Charlotte [29th], crashed at Dover [21st], and blew up [39th] at Pocono. We came back to make it close, but we'd put ourselves into too much of a hole. We did everything we could do at the end, and I'm proud of the team for that."

Despite five poles and five victories, Mark Martin, crew chief Steve Hmiel, and owner Jack Roush never were serious title contenders in their No. 6 Valvoline Ford. Martin was third in the final accounting, 296 behind Wallace and 376 behind Earnhardt. He won the spring and fall poles at Rockingham, and in the summer at Loudon, Watkins Glen, and Bristol.

Four of his five victories came on consecutive weekends in August and early September: Watkins Glen, Michigan, Bristol, and Darlington. He also won the fall race at Phoenix, a bittersweet victory since he was eliminated from the championship hunt that weekend.

Fourth-ranked Jarrett won the Daytona 500 for second-year owner Joe Gibbs and crew chief Jimmy Makar. It was his only victory of the season (the second of his career) in his No. 18 Interstate Chevrolet Lumina. He had 12 other top

Robert Yates (left) and crew inspect the RYR No. 28 Ford. Ernie Irvan took over as the car's driver following Davey Allison's tragic death in a helicopter crash at Talladega in July.

fives and five other finishes between sixth and 10th, but fell from second in points to fourth in the year's final 10 races.

Kyle Petty was fifth in points for owner Felix Sabates, crew chief Robin Pemberton, and the No. 42 Mello Yello Pontiac team. They won the Daytona 500 pole and the summer 500-miler at Pocono, had eight other top fives, and six other finishes between sixth and 10th.

Sixth-ranked Irvan won the spring race at Talladega for the No. 4 Kodak-backed Chevrolet team of Morgan-McClure Racing. He switched rides in September and promptly won at Martinsville and Charlotte for new owner Robert Yates and crew chief Larry McReynolds. Irvan also had nine more top fives and two more finishes between sixth and 10th. His downfall was six DNFs in his first 16 starts with Morgan-McClure.

Seventh-ranked Morgan Shepherd won the spring race at Atlanta, eighth-ranked Bill Elliott (the tour's Most Popular Driver) was 0-for-30, ninth-ranked Ken Schrader won a Cup-high six poles but no races, and 10th-ranked Ricky Rudd won the first of two summer races in Michigan. Davey Allison won the spring race at Richmond, and Geoff Bodine won at Sonoma in May.

One of the 1993 season's most interesting stories focused on a handful of promising newcomers. After three relatively weak years—Rob Moroso in 1990, Jimmy Hensley in 1991, and Bobby Hamilton in 1992—the 1993 rookie class featured Busch Series graduates Jeff Gordon, Bobby Labonte, and Kenny Wallace. It didn't take long for Gordon to become the class of the class. He won a Daytona 125-miler, was fifth in the Daytona 500, and had two more top 10s in the next three races. He ended 1993 with a pole, seven top fives, four other top 10s, and won Rookie of the Year in something of a runaway.

For the second year in a row, Kyle Petty finished fifth in Winston Cup points in 1993. He won the pole at the Daytona 500 and had 15 top-10 finishes.

Dale Jarrett's only checkered flag for Joe Gibbs Racing in 1993 came in the Daytona 500, but his 13 top-five finishes were good enough to place him fourth on the season.

After scheduling 29 races for the previous seven years, NASCAR finally added a 30th in 1993. It went to Bob Bahre, a crusty, no-nonsense New England banker who converted Bryar Motorsports Park near Loudon, New Hampshire, into a picturesque 1.017-mile superspeedway. NASCAR was so enamored of Bahre and the marketing potential of New England that it gave New Hampshire International Speedway CNHIS lower-division races in 1990, 1991, and 1992. When New Hampshire International Speedway got its first Cup race in July of 1993, a record New England sports crowd of more than 70,000 saw Martin win the pole and Wallace win the race.

Tragically, 1993 was marred by two off-the-track deaths. In a span of barely three months, defending Winston Cup champion Alan Kulwicki and young superstar Davey Allison died in aviation crashes.

Kulwicki and three other men perished when their private plane plunged 3,000 feet on final approach to Tri-Cities Airport near Bristol. It happened in light fog and rain at 9:38 on Thursday night, April 1. On board the twin-engine, turbo prop Merlin Fairchild were the 38-year-old Kulwicki, 26-year-old Mark Brooks, 44-year-old Dan Duncan, and 48-year-old Charles Campbell, the pilot. The tragedy stunned the racing community. Despite being a loner driven by perfection, Kulwicki was highly respected as an owner and driver. He had overcome enormous odds en route to winning the 1992 championship, a crown he got to enjoy for barely four months.

In some ways, Allison's death hit even harder. He was, after all, a much-beloved racing insider, the eldest son of long time fan favorite Bobby Allison. Just 32 and already a 19-time winner, he was considered a cinch to win scores of races and multiple titles. He died less than 24 hours after his helicopter crashed on the infield at Talladega Superspeedway on Monday, July 12.

Allison and long time friend Red Farmer were arriving at Talladega to watch David Bonnett, son of Neil Bonnett, test his Busch Series car. His death was the latest tragedy to strike the Allisons. In June of 1988, on the first lap of the Miller High Life 500 at Pocono, Bobby suffered life-threatening and career-ending injuries in a multi-car crash. Four years later, younger son Clifford died during practice for a Busch Series race in Michigan. Then, less than a year later, Davey at Talladega.

"Things will never be the same out here," Earnhardt said after winning at Pocono six days after Allison's death. "I don't think anybody will ever look at the 7 and 28 cars again and not think of Alan and Davey."

NASCAR's New England Playground— New Hampshire International Speedway

By the early 1990s, NASCAR had spread its wings into virtually every area of America. Granted, 10 of the 16 Winston Cup tracks were in the Southeast, jammed into Virginia, the Carolinas, Tennessee, Alabama, Georgia, and Florida. But there also were major speedways doing well in Delaware, Pennsylvania, Michigan, New York, California, and Arizona.

Bob Bahre, a veteran short-track owner-operator from Maine, watched the expansion with envy. Why, he wondered, can't New England have a Cup track? The area loves racing, witness the large crowds for Sportsman and Modified races, and for the Cup visit to Watkins Glen. Bahre's own third-mile Oxford Plains Speedway was legendary for behaving like a superspeedway.

And New England was home to its fair share of stars. Daytona 500 winner Pete Hamilton was one. Multiple Sportsman champion Rene Charland was another, plus Modified stars Ernie Gahan, Bugs Stevens, Fred DeSarro, Mike Stefanik, the Fuller brothers, and Reggie Ruggiero. Even Rob Moroso and the Bouchard and Bodine brothers carried New England bloodlines.

Using 18 million of his own dollars, Bahre began planning a superspeedway. It didn't happen in Maine, so he drove into neighboring New Hampshire in 1988 and bought the once-glorious Bryar Motorsports Park near Loudon. In less than two years, he and his son, Gary, turned the aging road course into a 1-mile, low-banked, paved speedway with wonderful amenities.

"Why shouldn't he build a track if he wants one?" Gary said of his much-beloved father. "It's his money; he can do anything with it he wants because he's earned it. He's always wanted a big track and now he's going to have one."

NASCAR was impressed with New Hampshire International Speedway, but not enough to dispatch its top series without first testing the waters. Bahre got two Busch Series races each in 1990, 1991, and 1992 before landing a Cup race in 1993. He got a second one in 1997 by shifting a date from North Wilkesboro Speedway. (Bruton Smith took the other North Wilkesboro Speedway date to his new track in Texas.)

One story speaks volumes about how Bahre does business. A fire marshal reportedly told the zoning board that the ladder on his best truck wouldn't reach the press and VIP level, or the top row of the grandstands. Unflinchingly, Bahre opened his briefcase and stroked a six-figure check for a new, state-of-the-art truck.

The zoning was approved and New Hamphire International Speedway was on its way.

2nd

Car No.: 2
Make & Model:
  Pontiac Grand Prix
Team Owner:
  Roger Penske
Wins: 10
Top 10: 21

Rusty Wallace

Rusty Wallace enjoyed high highs and endured low lows in 1993. With veteran crew chief Buddy Parrott aboard, Wallace won a career-high 10 races, including a near-sweep of the short tracks—he won six of the eight under-a-mile events and finished second in the other two. However, at Talladega in May, Wallace flipped violently down the front stretch after an ill-advised restart with two laps to go and was lucky to come away with no worse than a mouthful of dirt and a broken wrist. He wouldn't admit it, but that probably cost him the championship; he finished second to Earnhardt by 80 points. Wallace here leads Kyle Petty at Martinsville, where he was first (spring) and second (fall).

3rd

Car No.: 6
Make & Model:
  Ford Thunderbird
Team Owner:
  Jack Roush
Wins: 5
Top 10: 19

Mark Martin

Mark Martin got off to a slow start, with engine failures at Atlanta, Charlotte, and Pocono dimming the picture. Then, suddenly in late summer, no one could touch him, with Martin ripping off a record-tying four wins in a row, at Watkins Glen, Michigan, Bristol, and Darlington—an amazing run on four different kinds of tracks. He finished with five victories and was third in points.

4th

Dale Jarrett

Dale Jarrett broke through in 1993, holding off Dale Earnhardt to win the Daytona 500, with his father Ned making an emotional call from the broadcast booth. That was Jarrett's second career victory and the first for the fledgling Joe Gibbs Racing team, and suddenly, after 10 years as Ned's son, people began taking Jarrett seriously. Jarrett hung in the points race into the spring before wrecks at Atlanta and Bristol and a blown engine at North Wilkesboro dropped him off the pace. Nevertheless, he posted his best-ever points finish, ninth, and his first million-dollar season. Jarrett finished third in the spring race at Martinsville, one of only four drivers on the lead lap.

Car No.: 18
Make & Model: Chevrolet Lumina
Team Owner: Joe Gibbs
Wins: 1
Top 10: 18

Kyle Petty

Kyle Petty was close, but not quite there, in 1993. When opportunity knocked in the way of late-day rain at Watkins Glen, he stayed out front under the caution to claim his only victory of the season, somewhat sheepishly. Petty and Team Sabco, owned by colorful Felix Sabates, put together a solid season, adding a second, two thirds, and 11 other top 10s—good enough for fifth in points the second year in a row. Petty acquired a teammate this season, with Kenny Wallace joining Team Sabco in the No. 40 car, Sabco following the trend toward multi-car operations. Here, Petty leads Davey Allison at Martinsville, where he finished fifth.

5th

Car No.: 42
Make & Model:
  Pontiac Grand Prix
Team Owner:
  Felix Sabates
Wins: 1
Top 10: 15

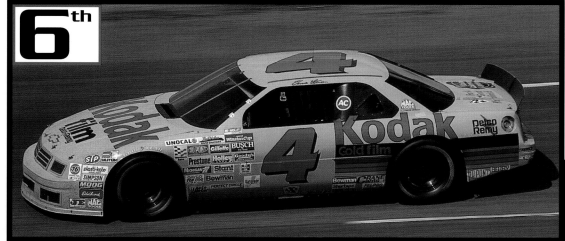

6th

Car No.: 4
Make & Model: Chevrolet Lumina
Team Owner: Larry McClure
Wins: 3
Top 10: 14

Ernie Irvan

A trying year for many was perhaps most trying for Ernie Irvan, who began his third season as driver of Morgan-McClure's Kodak Chevrolets. The McClure cars, as always, were exceptional at the restrictor-plate tracks, and Ernie came through the last-lap chaos at Talladega in May to bring the team a victory. Everything changed in July, when Davey Allison, driver of Robert Yates' powerful Texaco No. 28, died in a helicopter crash. By fall, Texaco bought out Irvan's contract and put him in No. 28, starting at Darlington. Irvan went on to win at Martinsville, becoming one of very few drivers to win for two teams in one year. He finished sixth in points.

7th

Morgan Shepherd

Veteran Morgan Shepherd enjoyed the most-stable four years of his career with the Wood Brothers from 1992 to 1995, and in 1993 he rewarded the legendary team with its first win in two years (and unfortunately, its last of the decade). At Atlanta in March, Shepherd and the Woods found superior gas mileage and took the lead for good when Jeff Gordon, apparently on his way to his first Winston Cup victory, suffered a blown tire with 12 laps to go. All in all, it was a good season for Shepherd, who at 52 still had the stamina of a younger man. His seventh-place finish in points was the Wood Brothers' best since 1987, when Kyle Petty drove.

Car No.: 21
Make & Model: Ford Thunderbird
Team Owner: Wood Brothers
Wins: 1
Top 10: 15

Bill Elliott

Although it wasn't obvious at the time, the clock had begun to run down in the house of Junior Johnson. Driver Bill Elliott, partnered this year with Hut Stricklin, endured his first non-winning season since 1984. In fact, neither of Johnson's teams won that year, giving the veteran owner his first blank since 1988. Elliott, 1988 Winston Cup champion, did produce six top fives, including a second place at Richmond in September, and he rode to eighth in points, which was fair enough, all things considered. Bill and the Budweiser No. 11 are shown here in the Goodwrench 500 at Rockingham, where he finished 11th, a lap down.

8th

Car No.: 11
Make & Model: Ford Thunderbird
Team Owner: Junior Johnson
Wins: 0
Top 10: 15

9th

Car No.: 25
Make & Model: Chevrolet Lumina
Team Owner: Rick Hendrick
Wins: 0
Top 10: 15

Ken Schrader

Although Ken Schrader and Hendrick Motorsports' No. 25 took something of a back seat to newly arrived teammate Jeff Gordon in 1993, they still fashioned one of Schrader's better seasons in the decade—ninth in points. Schrader had one of the fastest cars in the pack, at least on Fridays, winning six poles to lead all contenders. His best results on Sundays were two second places (at Pocono and Dover) and seven other top fives. The Martinsville race in April (shown here) was not one of Schrader's best. Although he had run top 10 most of the day, his transmission dropped out 11 laps from the finish, leaving him 18th in the final order.

10th

Ricky Rudd

Ricky Rudd was in the last of his four years with Hendrick Motorsports and his second with crew chief Gary DeHart, finishing 10th in points. Rudd also managed to keep alive his record streak of consecutive seasons with at least one race won. In 1993, he landed his trophy at Michigan in June, stretching his fuel mileage nine laps longer than prior leader Mark Martin (who had to pit on Lap 192) and cruising home 1.74 seconds ahead of new teammate Jeff Gordon. Rudd also scored second place (behind Rusty Wallace) at Atlanta in the fall and third at Sears Point in June.

Car No.: 5
Make & Model: Chevrolet Lumina
Team Owner: Ricky Rudd
Wins: 1
Top 10: 15

Car No.: 33
Make & Model: Chevrolet Lumina
Team Owner: Leo Jackson
Wins: 0
Top 10: 12

11th

Harry Gant

Harry Gant, said to be ageless, turned 53 before the 1993 season but showed few signs of wear. He won the pole for the season-ending race at Atlanta and surged to third place at Pocono in June, his best result of the season. The final count gave Harry 11th place in points, a dip from the previous two seasons, in which he finished fourth. At the end of the season, without much fanfare, Gant announced that 1994 would be his last year behind the wheel. Gant, accustomed to hard work as a carpenter and roofer, was in splendid physical shape, able to endure heat and physical strain better than anyone. He is shown here at Daytona in July, where he finished 21st.

12th

Jimmy Spencer

Spencer, finally set with a full-time ride, performed well for Bobby Allison in 1993, making the No. 12 Meineke Ford look better than it was. Spencer's 12th-place in points was his career best, and he could see only up as the season went on. Reputed to be a rough-neck, Spencer had only four DNFs in 1993. He missed victory by a car-length in May at Talladega, and he added third places at Watkins Glen and Martinsville down the stretch. All that attracted the eye of owner Junior Johnson, who was looking to replace Hut Stricklin in his No. 22 car, and late in the year, Spencer got the call. At Charlotte in the fall, Spencer carried the No. 12 car to a sixth-place finish.

Car No.: 12
Make & Model: Ford Thunderbird
Team Owner: Bobby Allison
Wins: 0
Top 10: 10

Car No.: 17
Make & Model:
Chevrolet Lumina
Team Owner:
Darrell Waltrip
Wins: 0
Top 10: 10

Darrell Waltrip

Darrell Waltrip's tenure as owner-driver had begun brightly enough, with winning seasons in 1991 and 1992. Hard reality caught up to Waltrip in 1993, although he was slow to see it. Waltrip suffered only his second non-winning season since 1974, a span which included three Winston Cup championships and 84 victories. From 1993 on, however, Waltrip never won again. He was 13th in points in 1993, with two third-places and 10 top 10s, enough to keep the 46-year-old encouraged. The thirds came at Dover in September and Atlanta in November, leaving Waltrip hopeful for 1994. He is shown here passing Sterling Marlin at Darlington in April.

Car No.: 24
Make & Model:
Chevrolet Lumina
Team Owner:
Rick Hendrick
Wins: 0
Top 10: 11

Jeff Gordon

A star was born in 1993 with the arrival of Indiana's Jeff Gordon from United States Auto Club sprints, via NASCAR Grand National. He was graduated to Winston Cup in 1993 with Hendrick Motorsports' new No. 24 team amid great expectations, but he needed a year of schooling before he was ready for victory lane. Gordon showed he was for real off the bat, starting third and finishing fifth in the Daytona 500, then running sixth at Richmond two weeks later. Next time out, he nearly won the Motorcraft 500 at Atlanta, but a blown tire near the end cost him. He went on to score second places at Charlotte and Michigan, finished 14th in points, and won Rookie of the Year. This was the beginning...

15th

Sterling Marlin

After two years in what should have been a dream ride with Junior Johnson, Sterling Marlin found himself looking for a job, and he took an interim turn with the Stavola Brothers' No. 8 in 1993. Sterling did not have a bad year. He finished 15th in points and picked off a best of second place, to Dale Earnhardt, in Daytona's summer Pepsi 400. The cars, however, were not what he needed. Marlin had only three DNFs but nevertheless finished out of the top 10 19 times in 30 tries. The TransSouth 500 at Darlington, shown here, was typical. Sterling started 18th and finished 21st, running at the finish but 21 laps down.

Car No.: 8
Make & Model: Ford Thunderbird
Team Owner: Stavola Brothers
Wins: 0
Top 10: 8

Geoff Bodine

Geoff Bodine had begun his second season with the declining Bud Moore team when the earth shook in April, upon the death of defending NASCAR champion Alan Kulwicki in a plane crash. Kulwicki had owned his championship team, and his estate, headed by his father, Gerald, had no interest in running it. In a transaction brokered by Felix Sabates, Bodine acquired the remains of the Kulwicki operation and arranged to leave Moore late in the year to take the wheel of No. 7. Bodine had notched a victory with Moore, at the Sears Point road course in May, but the lure of ownership was strong. Despite the divided season, Bodine finished 16th in points.

16th

Car No.: 15
Make & Model: Ford Thunderbird
Team Owner: Bud Moore
Wins: 1
Top 10: 9

17th

Car No.: 30
Make & Model: Pontiac Grand Prix
Team Owner: Chuck Rider
Wins: 0
Top 10: 5

Michael Waltrip

Michael Waltrip's relationship with owner Chuck Rider paralleled that of old pal Kyle Petty's with owner Felix Sabates—as much friendship as business. Waltrip and Rider, a suave auto-parts retailer, held together for eight years, always with the promise that business would improve, and always as friends. Michael truly appreciated the opportunity Rider had given him in 1988, and results *did* pick up a bit in 1993, with five top 10s and only four DNFs. This also was the year Waltrip, poignantly, waited until he won a race (the Busch race at Bristol in April) to propose marriage to now-wife Buffy from victory square. Buffy grandly accepted.

18th

Car No.: 14
Make & Model:
 Chevrolet Lumina
Team Owner:
 Bill Hagan
Wins: 0
Top 10: 10

Terry Labonte

Terry Labonte's patience with the struggling Billy Hagan team reached its limit by mid-1993, and he and sponsor Kellogg's neatly tied up a deal for both to migrate to Hendrick Motorsports in 1994, replacing Ricky Rudd and Tide. Meanwhile, Labonte and the Hagan group labored to 18th in points, with Terry suffering six DNFs and not a single top-five run. Labonte's best was sixth place at his home away from home, North Wilkesboro, in April. By late in the year, it was known Labonte would leave, and at Charlotte's Mello Yello 500 in October, he scratched to 16th place, three laps down, a pretty typical Sunday for Labonte in 1993.

19th

Car No.: 22
Make & Model:
 Ford Thunderbird
Team Owner: Bill Davis
Wins: 0
Top 10: 6

Bobby Labonte

The 1993 rookie crop was advertised as the best in years, and Bobby Labonte, Terry's younger brother, was one of three reasons why. Labonte, 1991 Grand National champion, had been drafted by Bill Davis after the sudden departure of Jeff Gordon—Davis had planned to move to Winston Cup with Gordon in 1993 but instead took on Labonte. In a strange, back door deal with Junior Johnson, Davis also acquired a car number (22), a sponsor (Maxwell House), and a crew chief (Tim Brewer). Labonte was overshadowed by super-rookie Jeff Gordon and finished 19th in points, but he demonstrated he was cool under fire and able to make the most of equipment.

20th

Brett Bodine

Brett Bodine had yet another average season with Kenny Bernstein and sponsor Quaker State, finishing 20th in points with a best finish of second (to Mark Martin) in the Southern 500 at Darlington in September. When the team was good it was decent; Bodine won poles at North Wilkesboro and Michigan. When it was bad it was horrid, with six DNFs and seven finishes in the 30s. The rest of the time, Bodine and crew were almost exactly in the middle, with the Daytona 500 (shown here) as an example. Bodine started 20th and finished 17th, the next-to-last man on the lead lap. All three Bodine brothers raced in Winston Cup this season.

Car No.: 26
Make & Model: Ford Thunderbird
Team Owner: Kenny Bernstein
Wins: 0
Top 10: 9

Rick Mast

Rick Mast continued his relationship with owner Richard Jackson and sponsor Skoal, which was comfortable but unproductive. Over the winter, Jackson had converted from the unsupported Oldsmobile brand to Ford, but the change did not show on the meter, with Mast picking up one position in points, from 22nd in 1992 to 21st in 1993, with a fifth place at Bristol in August his best result. One highlight came in The Winston Select all-star race at Charlotte in May (shown here). Mast drafted in by finishing fifth in the Winston Open qualifying race and made the feature field at the tail end. He finished 11th, pocketing $30,200 for his night's work.

21st

Car No.: 1
Make & Model: Ford Thunderbird
Team Owner: Richard Jackson
Wins: 0
Top 10: 5

22nd

Car No.: 16
Make & Model: Ford Thunderbird
Team Owner: Jack Roush
Wins: 0
Top 10: 4

Wally Dallenbach Jr.

Expert road-racer Wally Dallenbach was chafing in the Jack Roush stable through most of 1993. His No. 16 Keystone beer team was companion to Roush's No. 6 with Mark Martin, and Dallenbach had begun to grumble that the 16 amounted to a test car, for the benefit of Martin and crew. Dallenbach's best finish came, of course, at Watkins Glen in August. Martin won, giving Roush a one-two sweep. Oddly, Wally was furious after the race, complaining again that he'd been given off-brand treatment and equipment. Dallenbach finished the year 22nd in points, and his discontent pointed him out the door, and toward an uncertain future.

23rd

Car No.: 40
Make & Model:
 Pontiac Grand Prix
Team Owner: Felix Sabates
Wins: 0
Top 10: 3

Kenny Wallace

Third of the 1993 rookie triumvirate, after Jeff Gordon and Bobby Labonte, came Kenny Wallace, Rusty's cheerful, chatty little brother. Owner Felix Sabates, perceiving the benefits of a two-car team, sold Kenny to sponsor Dirt Devil and launched the No. 40 team as mate to Kyle Petty's primary No. 42. Kenny did not do badly, finishing 23rd in points, but the team never really got its feet on the ground, with Wallace scoring only three top 10s. The experiment ended after one year, with Bobby Hamilton getting the 40 car and Wallace returning to Busch with old pal Fil Martocci. Wallace would be back, but it would take a couple of years.

24th

Car No.: 27
Make & Model:
 Ford Thunderbird
Team Owner:
 Junior Johnson
Wins: 0
Top 10: 2

Hut Stricklin

The strange career of Hut Stricklin took another switchback in 1993. After a scattershot 1992 with four different car owners, Stricklin suddenly found himself teamed with Bill Elliott in Junior Johnson's still-prestigious stable—in an operation with a whole new look. Gone were driver Sterling Marlin, sponsor Maxwell House, even the No. 22. The cars now bore No. 27 and boasted sponsorship from McDonald's, one of the world's top-10 advertisers. Results somehow failed to materialize, with Stricklin showing only two top 10s and 24th in points. At the end of the year, Johnson dished off Stricklin and most of the team to Travis Carter, under the Camel banner.

Car No.: 55
Make & Model: Ford Thunderbird
Team Owner:
  Ray DeWitt and D.K. Ulrich
Wins: 0
Top 10: 5

Ted Musgrave

Ted Musgrave continued to surprise in 1993, consistently performing better than expected in the Ray DeWitt/D.K. Ulrich No. 55, with cobbled sponsorship from Jasper Engines and US Air. With freebooters DeWitt and Ulrich, few knew exactly what the decals on the car represented, or meant. Regardless, Ted consistently drove hard, presenting fifth-place finishes at Pocono and Michigan, his two best tracks, and earning 25th place in points. Musgrave also notched three other top 10s, including a 10th-place run in the Pepsi 400 at Daytona in July, shown here. Musgrave, meanwhile, had caught the eye of Mark Martin, who suggested him to owner Jack Roush for 1994.

Car No.: 66
Make & Model: Ford Thunderbird
Team Owner: Bob Whitcomb
Wins: 0
Top 10: 1

Derrike Cope

After the departure of nice-guy car owner Bob Whitcomb in 1992, Cope landed with the questionable Cale Yarborough team in 1993. Driving legend Yarborough had a knack of pulling sponsors out of a hat, and for 1993 he dressed his Fords in the colors of Bojangle's, a fried-chicken chain, which replaced departed Phillips 66. Strangely, Yarborough kept No. 66 on the car through the Daytona 500, then switched to No. 98 the next time out at Rockingham, the number the team held through the rest of the decade. Cope labored through the season with just one top 10, eight DNFs, and a 26th-place finish in Winston Cup points.

Car No.: 90
Make & Model: Ford Thunderbird
Team Owner: Junie Donlavey
Wins: 0
Top 10: 0

Bobby Hillin Jr.

Car owner Junie Donlavey, who had been around since the dawn of time (fielding his first Winston Cup entry in 1950), finally acquired a real sponsor in 1993, Heilig-Meyers, an expanding furniture retail chain. Bobby Hillin, who had knocked around a good bit since his days with the Stavola Brothers in the 1980s, was the in choice as driver. New sponsor and new driver did not immediately produce more than the usual results for the Donlavey team, with Hillin failing to register a top 10 and finishing 27th in points. Hillin did not help his case with early-season (and televised) on-track run-ins with Kyle Petty (Daytona) and Dale Jarrett (Bristol), and he was out early the next year.

28th

Car No.: 43
Make & Model: Pontiac Grand Prix
Team Owner: Richard Petty
Wins: 0
Top 10: 1

Rick Wilson

The hiring of veteran cast off Rick Wilson to replace legend Richard Petty in the STP No. 43 came as a surprise to many. Wilson thus took on the most thankless job in NASCAR history—following The King. The 43 team had lost direction over the years as Petty's career wound down, and Wilson, never a winner in Winston Cup, stepped into a no-win situation. Hardly a superstar, Wilson managed a best of eighth at, of all places, Sears Point in May, and did not come close elsewhere. Wilson was out at the end of the season, having finished 28th in the standings, and Petty Enterprises, once the royalty of racing, stumbled a while longer before finding winning form again.

29th

Car No.: 41
Make & Model: Chevrolet Lumina
Team Owner: Larry Hedrick
Wins: 0
Top 10: 2

Phil Parsons

Phil Parsons, younger brother of NASCAR champ (now television commentator) Benny Parsons, had made his splash in 1988, winning Talladega in Leo Jackson's car. His career fell apart when he was let go, for undisclosed reasons, by Morgan-McClure early in the 1990 season. His last full-season chance came in 1993, when he drove for Larry Hedrick, still struggling to find his feet in Winston Cup. Hedrick, who ran a major used-car auction in Statesville, North Carolina, paid out-of-pocket to keep the team going. Parsons could do no better than 29th in points and was on his own after the season. Since then, he has made a pretty good living in the Busch Series.

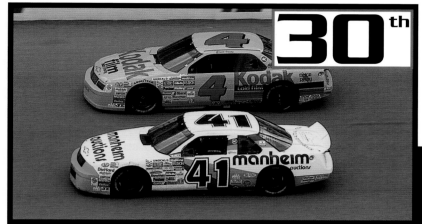

Car No.: 41
Make & Model: Chevrolet Lumina
Team Owner: Larry Hedrick
Wins: 0
Top 10:

Dick Trickle

Dick Trickle's rookie-of-the-year award in 1989 masked the fact that, by 1993, he was past 50 and set in his ways. As a result, he bounced around a good bit through the 1990s. After initial success as Bobby Allison's replacement with the Stavolas, he gave a try with Rahmoc, which itself was on the ropes by mid-1993, following the break-up of partners Butch Mock and Bob Rahilly. The season marked a steady downslide, and Trickle spent the last third of 1993 driving for Larry Hedrick's newly founded No. 41 team. The split season produced no wins and only one top 10.

Car No.: 28
Make & Model: Ford Thunderbird
Team Owner: Robert Yates
Wins: 1
Top 10: 8

Davey Allison

The tale is almost too sad to tell. Davey Allison, driver of Robert Yates' supreme No. 28, died in July 1993 when the helicopter he was flying crashed at the Talladega speedway, one day after the race at New Hampshire. Davey's death at 32 followed debilitating injuries to his father, racing legend Bobby Allison, and his brother, Clifford, in a crash at Michigan in 1992. Davey, contender to the end for the 1992 championship, won the last of his 19 Winston Cup races at Richmond in March. He had been as high as second in points in early June and finished third at New Hampshire. Yates, who mourned deeply, held the team together with Robby Gordon and Lake Speed before hiring Ernie Irvan.

Alan Kulwicki

There is no measure of tragedy. Let it be said only that NASCAR lost two of its very best in 1993 in self-made champion Alan Kulwicki and bright star Davey Allison. On an icy April Fool's night in Tennessee, Kulwicki's plane went down in the hills near Bristol, the night before qualifying for the Food City 500. Kulwicki thus never got to defend his magical 1992 championship, or really enjoy his triumph; he was gone at 38. Kulwicki had started with fourth at Rockingham, third at Richmond, and sixth at Darlington, his last race. Control of his team eventually passed to Geoff Bodine, but Kulwicki's legacy lived as drivers continued to perform his "Polish victory lap" in respectful tribute.

Car No.: 7
Make & Model: Ford Thunderbird
Team Owner: Alan Kulwicki
Wins: 0
Top 10: 3

Chapter 5

1994

An Iron Hand and a Lead Foot

DALE EARNHARDT GRABS CHAMPIONSHIP NO. 7

Tony George and Bill France got together in Indianapolis in the spring of 1993 for a joint announcement that reverberated to the very core of American motorsports. For the first time in its long and glorious history, NASCAR was being invited to take its enormously popular Winston Cup show to the legendary Indianapolis Motor Speedway. To some, it was akin to the Beatles playing not Shea Stadium, but Carnegie Hall.

Long time NASCAR-watchers couldn't recall anything even remotely as crucial to stock car racing's reputation. After decades of being the best show in town, the "taxicab tour" was getting to strut its stuff on the world's biggest and most famous stage. "I imagine that somewhere, my father and Tony's grandfather are smiling," France, the NASCAR president, said years later. "I think

Dale Earnhardt

Only four times in 1994, on the way to his record-tying seventh Winston Cup championship, did Dale Earnhardt finish out of the top 25. The June race at Dover brought one of those few stumbles. Earnhardt was caught early in a wreck and limped home 28th, 75 laps behind winner Rusty Wallace. He rallied the next week at Pocono, however, launching a streak of three seconds and a third-place finish, which cemented his points lead. He also avenged the June fumble at Dover upon return in September, racing from the 37th starting spot to second at the finish, Wallace winning again.

Car No.: 3
Make & Model: Chevrolet Lumina
Team Owner: Richard Childress
Wins: 4
Top 10: 25

they'd approve and be proud of what we've done. This is one of those relationships that's good for both parties."

Keenly aware of Indy's storied tradition, George worked hard to make sure its first NASCAR race had its own distinctive personality. Instead of 500 miles on a Sunday afternoon with a title sponsor, he and France settled on a 400-mile, unsponsored race on a Saturday afternoon in summer. Thus was born the first Brickyard 400, the most eagerly anticipated race in American motor sports history.

Never has any new event at any venue—including the 2000 U.S. Grand Prix at Indy—generated such national interest. All 350,000-plus tickets were sold within days of becoming available in August of 1993. Motels, hotels, campsites, and rooms in private homes were booked a year out. Rental cars and restaurant reservations were in short supply. More media credentials and sponsor passes were requested for the 400 than for any race in NASCAR history. And a NASCAR-record 85 drivers entered, including Indy 500 veterans A. J. Foyt, Danny Sullivan, Geoff Brabham, and John Andretti.

With all eyes on Indy, the good ol' boys didn't disappoint. Rick Mast won the pole at 172.414 miles per hour,

then charmed the unsuspecting "outside" media with his oft-told tale of selling a cow to finance his first racecar. Hometown hero Jeff Gordon thrilled the record crowd by winning after a late-race flat tire relegated leader and apparent winner Ernie Irvan to a lap-down 17th. And how did Gordon celebrate his $613,000 victory? He and wife Brooke hunkered down in a nearby motel for a night of TV and take out pizza.

It's still difficult to decide which was the biggest story of the 1994 Winston Cup season. Was it NASCAR running Indy for the first time or Dale Earnhardt winning his record-tying seventh championship? Some series-watchers leaned toward the former, saying getting to Indy showed just how far NASCAR had come in a relatively short span. Others felt the Intimidator's seventh title was at least as important since it pulled him even with seven-time champion Richard Petty. (Their closest pursuer at the time was three-time champ Darrell Waltrip, and nobody believed for a second he would ever come close to catching up.) Indy for four magical days in August or Earnhardt over the course of 31 races? Hey, nothing says it can't be a tie.

Once again—for the fourth time in five years—the series champion wasn't the tour's leading winner. In 1991,

In 1994, Dale Earnhardt joined "King" Richard Petty as the only racers to win seven Winston Cup championships. Earnhardt already had a comfortable points lead when this photo was taken at the season finale in Atlanta.

Harry Gant and Davey Allison won more (5-4) than Earnhardt. In 1992, Allison and Bill Elliott won more (5-3) than Alan Kulwicki. In 1993, Rusty Wallace won more (10-6) than Earnhardt. And in 1994, despite winning twice as many (8-4) as Earnhardt, Wallace ended the season ranked third behind Earnhardt and two-race winner Mark Martin.

Earnhardt, crew chief Andy Petree, and owner Richard Childress won two poles in 1994—Daytona Beach and Talladega in the summer. They won at Darlington, Bristol, and Talladega in the spring, then Rockingham in the fall. That's not a great season until you consider these numbers: seven second-place finishes, six thirds, a fourth, two fifths, and five more times finishing between sixth and 10th. Earnhardt and the No. 3 Goodwrench Chevrolet Lumina team took the points lead for good by finishing fifth in Round 19, the Brickyard 400. He padded his lead from 27 points that afternoon to 444 at season's end.

"To be honest about it, I didn't make many mistakes this year," Earnhardt said with unusual candor. "I made

Ken Schrader didn't win any poles in 1994, and the Bud 500, where this photo was taken, was one of only nine top-five finishes. Schrader still finished a career-best fourth place in the championship.

one when I wrecked at Michigan in August, but there weren't many more. We approached every race with the idea of getting as many points as we could, wherever we had to finish to get them. But I'll tell you again, I never expected to win the championship by this kind of margin. It might have been different if Ernie had been out there all season. That was a tough team, one that would have given me all I wanted."

The champ-to-be began his season with back-to-back seventh-place finishes in the spring races at Daytona Beach and Rockingham. He was fourth at Richmond early in March, then a mediocre 12th at Atlanta before winning back-to-back at Darlington and Bristol. He reached the quarter point of the season with a fifth at North Wilkesboro and 11th at Martinsville. After eight starts, he was second in points, 25 behind fellow two-race winner Irvan.

Earnhardt won the spring race at Talladega, was third at Sonoma three weeks later, then finished ninth in the night race at Charlotte over Memorial Day weekend. He stumbled home to a wreck-related 28th at Dover the following weekend, but recovered with back-to-back runner-up finishes to Wallace in the June races at Pocono and Michigan. He marked the mid point of the season with a third in the July race at Daytona Beach. Despite three victories and 12 top 10s, he remained 88 points behind Irvan.

A week later, he closed the gap by running second to Ricky Rudd (28 finish positions ahead of Irvan) at Loudon. Earnhardt was seventh at Pocono before suffering the first of three DNFs, an engine-related 34th at Talladega. He took the points lead with a fifth at Indy in August, was third a week later at Watkins Glen, and a wreck-related 37th DNF at Michigan. He was third in Bristol's grueling late-summer Saturday night race and second to Elliott in the Labor Day weekend race at Darlington.

Earnhardt won only once in the fall. That eight-race stretch included a third at Richmond and seconds to Wallace in back-to-back races at Dover and Martinsville. He was seventh at North Wilkesboro, third a week later near Charlotte, then clinched the title by winning two weeks later at Rockingham. He was an engine-related DNF 40th in the next-to-last race at Phoenix, then capped his championship season by finishing second to Martin in the season finale at Atlanta the second weekend in November.

Martin's second in points was his fourth top five and sixth top 10 in seven years with owner Jack Roush. He won one pole (Watkins Glen) and two races (Watkins Glen and the Atlanta finale). He and crew chief Steve Hmiel had four second-place finishes, two thirds, four fourths, and three fifths. They also had five finishes between sixth and 10th in their No. 6 Valvoline Ford.

Wallace's bittersweet season for owner Roger Penske and crew chief Buddy Parrott included poles at

Martinsville in the spring and Pocono in June. He won in the spring at Rockingham and Martinsville; in the summer at Dover, Pocono, and Michigan; then in the fall at Bristol, Dover, and Martinsville. But the No. 2 Miller Ford team's downfall was inconsistency. Wallace had only nine other top fives and only three other top 10s, and dropped out of five races.

Ken Schrader had something of an odd season in the No. 25 Kodiak Chevrolet for owner Rick Hendrick and crew chief Ken Howes. He didn't win a pole (he'd won seven in 1993) and his losing streak reached three-plus seasons. Schrader finished top five only nine times and was between sixth and 10th nine other times. But he managed to finish fourth in the final standings, his best showing in 10 full years on the tour.

After driving for Hendrick from 1990 to 1993, Rudd broke away to become owner-driver of the No. 10 Tide

The Diehard 500 saw Morgan Shepherd take a disappointing 15th place, but the 52-year-old finished sixth overall for the Wood Brothers in 1994.

Ford. His first season with crew chief Bill Ingle was marvelous: the fall pole at Rockingham, a summer victory at Loudon, five other top fives, and nine other finishes between sixth and 10th. Rudd's fifth in points was his best showing since being a distant second to Earnhardt in 1991.

Morgan Shepherd finished sixth in points for the Wood Brothers. Hendrick Motorsports teammates Terry Labonte and Jeff Gordon were seventh and eighth, owner-driver Darrell Waltrip was ninth, and Elliott with owner Junior Johnson was 10th. Labonte won at North Wilkesboro in the spring and Richmond and Phoenix in the fall. Gordon got his career breakthrough victory at Charlotte in May and then won the inaugural Brickyard 400. Elliott's lone victory was at Darlington in the fall, and stood at the end of the 1990s as his latest success.

Irvan and Geoff Bodine each won three times. Irvan's came at Richmond, Atlanta, and Sonoma in the spring, but he missed the final 11 races of the season after suffering life-threatening injuries during practice at Michigan in August. Irvan was second in points, 27 behind and considered the only driver capable of staying with Earnhardt down the stretch. Bodine's victories came in the summer at Pocono and Michigan, and in the fall at North Wilkesboro. Jimmy Spencer won the mid summer restrictor-plate races at Daytona Beach and Talladega. Dale Jarrett won the fall Charlotte race amid talk (correct, it turned out) that he'd soon leave Joe Gibbs Racing to replace the injured Irvan at Robert Yates Racing. Sterling Marlin opened the season by winning the first of his two consecutive Daytona 500s.

The 1994 rookie class included eight drivers: Jeff Burton and his brother, Ward; Indy car driver John Andretti; former Busch Series champions Steve Grissom and Joe Nemechek; Mike Wallace (the middle of the three racing Wallace brothers); short-track and Automobile Racing Club of America star Loy Allen; and Kentucky native Jeremy Mayfield.

In one of the closest battles in years (the top five were separated by 36 rookie points), Jeff Burton won the honor over Grissom, Nemechek, Andretti, Wallace, Ward Burton, Mayfield, and Allen. Andretti made news on May 29 by finishing 10th in the Indy 500, then using two helicopters and a private jet to get to the Charlotte Motor Speedway in time to run the Coca-Cola World 600. Alas, he crashed out to a 36th-place after 220 of the 400 laps.

A footnote to Earnhardt's record-tying seventh Winston Cup: Members of the media who follow NASCAR on a regular basis were only too happy to point out what Earnhardt himself said time and time again after winning the 1994 title:

"We might be tied with seven Winston Cups, but Richard Petty is still The King and will always be The King," Earnhardt said. "It just bumfuzzles me to be mentioned in the same sentence with Richard. It blows my mind, boggles my senses, gives me cold chills. He's one of the men who made racing what it is, and I'm just fortunate enough to have come along at the right time.

"People are always asking whether I expected to win seven championships when I started. I tell 'em I didn't expect to win even one since I had no idea I'd ever be at this level more than a year or two. To me, this is all just unbelievable."

The legendary Junior Johnson earned the final win as an owner with driver Bill Elliott at Darlington in September 1994. Johnson's impressive career as a driver is matched by his performance as a team owner. From 1966 to 1995, he won 838 races with Darrell Waltrip, Bobby Allison, Terry Labonte, and many others.

Junior Johnson—The Last American Hero

Novelist Tom Wolfe wrote a masterful *Esquire* feature on Junior Johnson, calling him the last American hero. Nobody with any knowledge of racing will argue that point.

Johnson was born in 1931 and reared in North Carolina's hardscrabble Wilkes County, near the Blue Ridge Mountains. Like so many other mountain men, he thought nothing of brewing and distributing moonshine. And, like so many others, he was caught and sent to prison.

His legend grew in part because of that notoriety. He had debuted in the 1953 Southern 500 at Darlington and made four more starts in 1954. He won two poles and five races in 1955, but was locked up for part of 1956 and 1957. He returned with a vengeance, winning six races and finishing eighth in NASCAR's 1958 points.

During a 313-start career Johnson won 47 poles and 50 races, finished 98 others among the top 10, and raised "creative engineering" (cheating) to an art form. He won the 1960 Daytona 500, the 1962 and 1963 fall races at Charlotte, the 1963 summer race at Atlanta, and the 1963 spring race at Darlington. His last start produced a fifth place at Rockingham, North Carolina, in October of 1966.

But he wasn't about to abandon what had made him moderately rich and very famous. Even as he raced his last season, Johnson was fielding cars for Darel Dieringer, Curtis Turner, Fred Lorenzen, Bobby Isaac, and Gordon Johncock. His first victory as an owner came with Dieringer at North Wilkesboro Speedway in 1967.

All told, he took 32 drivers to 838 races between 1966 and 1995. Cale Yarborough won 55 races and three Winston Cups with Johnson, and 43 of Darrell Waltrip's 84 victories and his three titles also came in Johnson's cars. Among his other drivers: LeeRoy Yarbrough, Bobby Allison, Neil Bonnett, Terry Labonte, Sterling Marlin, Geoff and Brett Bodine, Jimmy Spencer, and Bill Elliott.

The last of his 139 owner victories was with Elliott in the Mountain Dew Southern 500 at Darlington in September of 1994. Elliott started ninth in the Budweiser-sponsored No. 11 Ford and led three times for 21 of 367 laps, including the final 13. "It overheated the last half of the race," he said afterward. "I had no idea it would last. But why back off? I'd rather blow up leading than blow up running in the back."

Ol' Robert Glenn couldn't have said it better himself.

2nd

Car No.: 6
Make & Model:
 Ford Thunderbird
Team Owner:
 Jack Roush
Wins: 2
Top 10: 20

Mark Martin

Mark Martin, five-time winner the previous season, came to Charlotte Motor Speedway's The Winston all-star race with high hopes. All that crashed to earth during the event's second 30-lap segment, when Martin, Ernie Irvan, Dale Earnhardt, and Rusty Wallace—all front-runners in the early going—tangled in the first turn. The tally sheet for the race showed Martin in 16th place, earning just $18,000 out of the million-dollar pot. Aside from The Winston, Charlotte was cruel to Martin in 1994, allowing him 32nd place in May and 39th place in October—worst finish of the year for the season runner-up. Aside from his disappointment at Charlotte, Martin had a very strong season. He proved his road course mettle by taking the pole and winning the race at Watkins Glen. He also won the season finale at Atlanta. Martin posted 20 top 10s, and that dogged consistency carried him to second place in the championship.

Rusty Wallace

3rd

As in 1993, Rusty Wallace was unbeatable on the short tracks, and he put another notch in an eight-win campaign with a victory in September's Goody's 500 at half-mile Martinsville Speedway, giving Wallace a sweep of the season races on NASCAR's shortest track. From 1993 into 1995, Wallace won five of six races at Martinsville and finished second in the sixth. This time around, Wallace led 281 laps, including the last 67, and beat Ernie Irvan to the finish line by nearly half a second. Wallace also earned $98,800 in Unocal bonus money for winning from the pole.

Car No.: 2
Make & Model: Ford Thunderbird
Team Owner: Roger Penske
Wins: 8
Top 10: 20

4th

Car No.: 25
Make & Model:
 Chevrolet Lumina
Team Owner:
 Rick Hendrick
Wins: 0
Top 10: 18

Ken Schrader

Ken Schrader tacked up one of his nine top fives in 1994 and one of his best runs ever on a road course at Watkins Glen in August, finishing fourth behind Mark Martin, Ernie Irvan, and Dale Earnhardt. Notably, he came in ahead of more-noted road racers such as Ricky Rudd and Terry Labonte. Schrader surprised some by taking the outside pole (one of two such starts for the veteran in 1994), and although he did not lead, he never was far out of contention. The Glen run symbolized a steady season for Schrader, who showed 18 top 10s and only two DNFs.

Ricky Rudd

5th

The era of "independent" owner-drivers was in full swing in 1994, and Ricky Rudd, over six years in the business, was consistently the best. The 1994 season was Rudd's first after leaving Rick Hendrick's mammoth operation, and fifth in points with a victory at New Hampshire made believers out of many. The Bristol race in April was his worst of the season, a multi-car wreck parking him after 187 laps. He finished 32nd in the Food City 500; only three times the rest of the season did he finish out of the top 20. Rudd took home just $6,625, hardly enough for tires.

Car No.: 10
Make & Model: Ford Thunderbird
Team Owner: Ricky Rudd
Wins: 1
Top 10: 15

Car No.: 21
Make & Model:
 Ford Thunderbird
Team Owner:
 Wood Brothers
Wins: 0
Top 10: 16

6th

Morgan Shepherd

One-of-a-kind Morgan Shepherd was 52 years old at the time of 1994's Food City 500 at Bristol and in the steadiest ride of his long and colorful career, with the legendary Wood Brothers of Virginia. Shepherd and the Woods had won together at Atlanta the previous March, and workhorse Shepherd bid to do better in 1994, with a fifth in the Daytona 500 and a second at Atlanta. Bristol was middling, with Shepherd dragging home 18th, 43 laps behind winner Dale Earnhardt. Shepherd persevered, however, to finish sixth in points, the high-water mark of his career.

7th

Car No.: 5
Make & Model:
 Chevrolet Lumina
Team Owner:
 Bill Hagan
Wins: 3
Top 10: 14

Terry Labonte

Labonte's career revived after joining Rick Hendrick in 1994, replacing Ricky Rudd in No. 5 and bringing along sponsor Kellogg's. He bounced back from 18th in points (better than it should have been) with Billy Hagan in 1993 to seventh (just about par) with Hendrick in 1994. Overlooked as a road racer, Labonte has been at least the equal of Ricky Rudd, Rusty Wallace, Geoff Bodine, and others noted for their left-right ability. At the 2.4-mile Watkins Glen course in August, Labonte started 10th and finished sixth, with all three Hendrick cars finishing in the top 10.

Car No.: 24
Make & Model: Chevrolet Lumina
Team Owner: Rick Hendrick
Wins: 2
Top 10: 14

Jeff Gordon

Jeff Gordon, still just 21, grew wings in 1994, paving the way for greater things with his first two career victories, at Charlotte's Coca-Cola 600 and, of course, at the historic inaugural Brickyard 400 at Indianapolis in August. Some of NASCAR's more extreme circuits, such as Bristol, still perplexed him, but his stratospheric racing IQ enabled him to catch on quickly. One such learning experience came in April at Bristol, where he and Mark Martin were caught in a typical Bristol crunch, with Gordon finishing 22nd after starting fourth. He had led three times for 68 laps.

8th

Darrell Waltrip

Some compared it to Jackie Robinson walking out onto the baseball field in 1947—stock cars at Indianapolis Motor Speedway? The dream came true in August 1994, and Darrell Waltrip, NASCAR's shining star of the 1980s and pioneer owner-driver of the 1990s, joined a parade of NASCAR's best at the finish line. Jeff Gordon won, with Brett Bodine an improbable second. Behind them were the big names: Bill Elliott, Rusty Wallace, Dale Earnhardt, and Waltrip, who again rose to the occasion. Waltrip had 13 top fives in 1994, and his sixth-place earned him $82,600, a winner's share at most other stops.

Car No.: 17
Make & Model: Chevrolet Lumina
Team Owner: Darrell Waltrip
Wins: 0
Top 10: 13

9th

10th

Bill Elliott

Bill Elliott already was planning his exit from Junior Johnson's group with intent to go on his own with sponsor McDonald's, but he and Johnson had one last trick up their sleeves. Elliott, whose Ford was overheating much of the afternoon, came out of final pit stops like a scalded cat, ambushed Dale Earnhardt with 24 laps to go, and won the grand old Southern 500 at Darlington Raceway. In typical possum fashion, Elliott started ninth, led early, then dropped back to let his boiling radiator breathe until the time was right. The classic strategy earned Bill the last of his six wins with Johnson.

Car No.: 11
Make & Model: Ford Thunderbird
Team Owner: Junior Johnson
Wins: 1
Top 10: 12

11th

Car No.: 15
Make & Model: Ford Thunderbird
Team Owner: Bud Moore
Wins: 0
Top 10: 9

Lake Speed

Lake Speed's curious career bounced him back and forth from independent to hired shoe. In 1994, Speed was in the most secure spot of his racing life, driving Bud Moore's No. 15 with backing from Ford Quality Care. Ford and its subsidiaries carried Moore along for 20 years, and he and Speed had a decent season in 1994, with a third at Bristol in April and a fourth at Atlanta in November. The Rockingham race in October was about average, with Speed qualifying poorly (41st), then racing to 10th at the end. Lake thus picked up 31 positions, no easy feat.

12th

Car No.: 30
Make & Model:
  Pontiac Grand Prix
Team Owner:
  Chuck Rider
Wins: 0
Top 10: 9

Michael Waltrip

For Michael Waltrip and long time boss Chuck Rider, 1994 was about as good as it got. Michael urged the Pennzoil Pontiacs to nine top 10s and 12th in points, his best championship effort to that time. One of those top 10s came at Dover in June, where Mikey guided the Pennzoil ship home seventh, just behind brother Darrell. Both were a lap down, with only the top five—Rusty Wallace, Ernie Irvan, Ken Schrader, Mark Martin, and Jeff Gordon—holding on to the lead lap. Michael's best run of the year (third) came at one of his best tracks, Talladega, in the spring.

13th

Ted Musgrave

Quiet, steady Ted Musgrave caught a career break in 1994, when, at the urging of Mark Martin, owner Jack Roush handed the Chicago native the wheel of his No. 16. Musgrave had performed commendably for the second-line Ulrich-DeWitt team the previous three seasons. Ted responded with eight top 10s and 13th in final points. The Brickyard 400 at historic Indianapolis Motor Speedway in August provided Musgrave with moments he won't forget: He led briefly during the first green-flag stops, and that's in the record book forever; he also finished 13th after starting 37th, and scored a (to-then) career-high payday of $52,800.

Car No.: 16
Make & Model: Ford Thunderbird
Team Owner: Jack Roush
Wins: 0
Top 10: 8

Sterling Marlin

Owner Larry McClure scored right off the line with driver Sterling Marlin, hired to replace Ernie Irvan, who had bolted to Robert Yates. In the season-opening Daytona 500, Marlin seized the lead from Irvan with 21 laps to go, giving McClure his second 500 trophy. McClure and Marlin both were superspeedway demons, but Marlin followed up strongly at Rockingham the next week, leading 22 laps in the Goodwrench 500 and finishing second, albeit 5 seconds behind winner Rusty Wallace. Sterling stumbled, however, after the robust start, finishing 19th, 24th, and 34th in the next three events.

14th

Car No.: 4
Make & Model: Chevrolet Lumina
Team Owner: Larry McClure
Wins: 1
Top 10: 11

15th

Kyle Petty

After finishing fifth in points the previous two seasons, Kyle Petty and the Sabco team had hoped for more or better in 1994. The departure of crew chief Robin Pemberton (replaced by Jim Long) changed the picture somewhat, but despite a wreck at Daytona, Kyle pressed at the edge of the top 10 through the season's first half. Martinsville in April was not one of the team's better tries, with a variety of misfortunes leaving him 26th at the finish line. The 1994 season marked the first time since 1989 that Petty won neither a race nor a pole; his best run was fourth at North Wilkesboro in April.

Car No.: 42
Make & Model: Pontiac Grand Prix
Team Owner: Felix Sabates
Wins: 0
Top 10: 7

16th

Car No.: 18
Make & Model: Chevrolet Lumina
Team Owner: Joe Gibbs
Wins: 1
Top 10: 9

Dale Jarrett

Dale Jarrett, pumped after his strong start in 1993, fell face-down at the start of 1994 and never really recovered the rest of the season. Engine failure kept him from defending his Daytona 500 title, and a sustained streak of horrible luck allowed him only four top 10s to early fall, the best being fourth places at Darlington and Charlotte. The June race at Dover was typical, with Jarrett struggling to 29th, 76 laps behind winner Rusty Wallace. Jarrett finished strong, however, winning at Charlotte in October and finishing top 10 in four of the last six races. It came out late fall that he would leave the Joe Gibbs team to join Robert Yates.

17th

Car No.: 7
Make & Model:
 Ford Thunderbird
Team Owner:
 Geoff Bodine
Wins: 3
Top 10: 10

Geoff Bodine

Tire War II between Goodyear and Hoosier peaked at the time of the inaugural Brickyard 400, and Geoff Bodine was Hoosier's flag-carrier. That set up one of the most dramatic single on-track events of 1994. The Hoosier-shod cars were faster but less numerous, and Bodine (pictured in the Brickyard 400) had the lead at halfway of the race. Off Turn 4, brother Brett, running second on Goodyear tires, spun his brother out; Geoff crashed and finished 39th. The incident brought up allegations of deep sibling rivalries, not to mention the one between the tire companies. Bodine, in his second year as owner-driver, won three races in a wildly inconsistent season.

Car No.: 1
Make & Model: Ford Thunderbird
Team Owner: Richard Jackson
Wins: 0
Top 10: 10

18th

Rick Mast

Honest Virginian Rick Mast continued to labor along with owner Richard Jackson, with 18th in points marking one of the better campaigns in their six-year association. The team ran Hoosier tires much of the year, leading to Mast's surpassing career highlight—the pole at the first Brickyard 400, stock-car racing's debut at fabled Indianapolis Motor Speedway. At Dover (seen here), Mast got caught in a mid-race wreck and retired with 98 laps to go. Rick came heartbreakingly close to his first career victory in fall of 1994, at Rockingham, where he hounded Dale Earnhardt to the finish, losing by just over a second.

Car No.: 20
Make & Model: Ford Thunderbird
Team Owner: Kenny Bernstein
Wins: 0
Top 10: 6

19th

Brett Bodine

Brett Bodine survived the decade of the 1990s by being quick on his feet and alert for opportunity. By 1994, the clock had run down on Kenny Bernstein's NASCAR effort, and Bodine, wheel man for five years, was looking elsewhere. By the end of the season, he had clinched a deal with Junior Johnson, with long-term consequences. Martinsville always has been one of Brett's best tracks, back to Modified days. The flat half-mile was not kind to him in 1994, giving him 24th place in the Hanes 500 in April (shown here), and 30th in the Goody's 500 in September.

20th

Todd Bodine

Through the 1990s, Todd Bodine was the man at the door, never quite in the room and never quite out, as he bounced back and forth between steady work in the Busch Series and opportunities in Winston Cup. One such opportunity arose mid year in 1993, when Bodine, youngest of the three brothers, was hired by Butch Mock's No. 75 team; he continued through 1994 with fair success, making better-than-average runs at Daytona, Martinsville, New Hampshire, and fall Atlanta. At Indianapolis in August, he finished ninth and accepted the role of family mediator after older brothers Geoff and Brett tangled on-track.

Car No.: 75
Make & Model: Ford Thunderbird
Team Owner: Butch Mock
Wins: 0
Top 10: 7

21st

Car No.: 22
Make & Model: Pontiac Grand Prix
Team Owner: Bill Davis
Wins: 0
Top 10: 14

Bobby Labonte

Owner Bill Davis had broken into the game with sponsor Maxwell House and driver Bobby Labonte. By the end of 1994, both were gone, with the coffee brand declining to renew and Labonte consequently joining Joe Gibbs Racing in the chain of events that followed Ernie Irvan's injuries at Michigan. Labonte was a better qualifier than finisher in 1994, perhaps due in part to trying to force the cars. He qualified top 10 eight times but finished top 10 just twice, with sixth at Bristol (April) and fifth at Michigan (August). He is shown here trying to hold back Sterling Marlin at Rockingham in October.

22nd

Car No.: 28
Make & Model:
Ford Thunderbird
Team Owner:
Robert Yates
Wins: 3
Top 10: 15

Ernie Irvan

A brilliant season came to an abrupt end at Michigan Speedway in August, when Irvan crashed in morning practice, his injuries leaving him close to death. Doctors described Irvan's recovery as a miracle, and his return to racing left them shaking their heads in wonder. Irvan had won three races and led in points until a wreck at New Hampshire in July dropped him to second, behind Dale Earnhardt. The 1994 year was Irvan's first in Robert Yates' No. 28, and he fulfilled the horsepower. At Martinsville in April, he led 75 laps late and finished less than a half-second behind Rusty Wallace.

23rd

Bobby Hamilton

After Kenny Wallace's unfortunate strike out as a rookie in 1993, owner Felix Sabates drafted dogged Bobby Hamilton, who had lurked on the fringes for several years, for 1994, with stopgap sponsorship from Kendall Oil. Although results were not spectacular (Hamilton managed just one top 10, at Bristol in April), Bobby was steady, and his work ethic and car know-how cemented his role as Cup regular. Hamilton moved on after this one season with Sabates to Petty Enterprises' famous No. 43. At Rockingham in February (seen here, with Bobby Labonte on the outside), Hamilton crashed out and finished 38th.

Car No.: 40
Make & Model: Pontiac Grand Prix
Team Owner: Felix Sabates
Wins: 0
Top 10: 1

Car No.: 8
Make & Model: Ford Thunderbird
Team Owner: Stavola Brothers
Wins: 0
Top 10: 3

24th

Jeff Burton

Bright, congenial Jeff Burton was the easy choice for Rookie of the Year in 1994, consistently showing his face at the window as car owners looked about for the next winner. Burton, who turned 27 in 1994, rose from the Busch Series to take the Stavola Brothers' ride and fulfilled the promise with two fourth-places, at Atlanta and Pocono. His best demonstration may have been The Winston show at Charlotte in May. Burton ran fourth in the Winston Open qualifier, then picked his way from 16th to sixth in the all-star race that followed.

Harry Gant

Harry Gant may have been the smartest racer in history in that he knew when to stop. Racing success was always something of a surprise to Gant, and he had enough else in the works, including home construction, his steakhouse, and his family, to keep him fully occupied at 54. He'd matched a record in 1992 by winning four races in a row, and he'd raced with, and beaten, the best in the business. Gant raced quietly in 1994, and no one begrudged him that a bit. His eighth place at Darlington in April was one of seven top 10s as he said good-bye.

Car No.: 33
Make & Model: Chevrolet Lumina
Team Owner: Leo Jackson
Wins: 0
Top 10: 7

25th

26th

Car No.: 23
Make & Model:
Ford Thunderbird
Team Owner:
Travis Carter
Wins: 0
Top 10: 1

Hut Stricklin

Hut Stricklin spent just one season with Junior Johnson before being dished off to the R.J. Reynolds offshoot team owned by Travis Carter—the controversial "Smokin' Joe's" No. 23. Stricklin fared no better in the Camel car, failing to qualify at Richmond in March and slipping from 24th to 26th in points. At Watkins Glen in August (shown here), Stricklin and Carter just were not in it, with Hut finishing 30th, four laps down. By the end of the season, Stricklin, protégé of Bobby Allison's Alabama Gang, was out of a job. He tied on early the next season with Kenny Bernstein.

Joe Nemechek

Joe Nemechek, 1992 Busch Series champion, made his debut as Winston Cup rookie in 1994, with Larry Hedrick's up-and-coming team. He finished 27th in points and third in a surprisingly tough rookie race, behind Jeff Burton and Steve Grissom. Nemechek always seemed to have a trick up his sleeve at the restrictor-plate tracks, but he did not have a chance to show his hand in the two races at Talladega. He finished last with engine failure in April's Winston 500, then fell out of July's DieHard 500 (shown here) with a faulty distributor, finishing 35th.

27th

Car No.: 41
Make & Model: Chevrolet Lumina
Team Owner: Larry Hedrick
Wins: 0
Top 10: 3

Car No.: 29
Make & Model: Chevrolet Lumina
Team Owner: Gary Bechtel
Wins: 0
Top 10: 3

Steve Grissom

Owner Gary Bechtel had money to burn as heir to one of the world's largest construction companies, and he burned some part of it in running his No. 29 Diamond Ridge team, largely without sponsorship, for several years. Bechtel went full-time into Winston Cup in 1994, the unsponsored car painted in company colors, and Alabama native Steve Grissom, promising 1993 Busch Series champion, was hired to drive. The effort was slow-starting, with Grissom failing to qualify for the Daytona 500 and making the top 10 just three times. Grissom finished 23rd at Darlington in September (shown here) and was 28th in points.

28th

29th

Car No.: 27
Make & Model: Ford Thunderbird
Team Owner: Junior Johnson
Wins: 2
Top 10: 4

Jimmy Spencer

Jimmy Spencer's short tenure with Junior Johnson in 1994 produced dramatically mixed results. Hard-driving Spencer won the first two races of his Winston Cup career, at Daytona and Talladega in July. Two weeks after the Talladega win, Spencer crashed in the inaugural Brickyard 400 at Indianapolis, finishing last and breaking his shoulder, leaving him unable to start subsequent races at Watkins Glen and Bristol. Spencer also won the pole at North Wilkesboro in the fall, but overall, results were dreadful, with Johnson planning his exit after 40 years in the sport. Both Spencer and sponsor McDonald's were gone after 1994.

30th

Derrike Cope

Derrike Cope, 1990 Daytona 500 winner, was looking for answers in 1994. He began the season in owner Cale Yarborough's No. 98, finishing 21st in the Daytona 500 and continued to struggle through the first half, both in qualifying and in races. Mercurial Yarborough cut Cope loose after the New Hampshire race in July, and Cope, after three races for upstart T. W. Taylor, landed with Bobby Allison's team at Watkins Glen. Performance picked up from there, with Cope starting third and finishing seventh in the finale at Atlanta. Through it all, Cope somehow finished 30th in driver points.

Car No.: 98
Make & Model: Ford Thunderbird
Team Owner: Bobby Allison
Wins: 0
Top 10: 2

Chapter 6

1995

The Legend Begins

JEFF GORDON CLAIMS INAUGURAL TITLE

It wasn't that close. Not by any stretch of the imagination. No way, no how. They could have raced and raced until the cows came home, but nothing would have changed. That's how good Jeff Gordon, crew chief Ray Evernham, owner Rick Hendrick, and the No. 24 DuPont Chevrolet Monte Carlo team were during the 1995 Winston Cup season.

The final margin might suggest otherwise, but this championship was settled long before the season finale at Atlanta in mid-November. Just 25 and a full-time Cup driver for three years, Gordon dominated the 31-race schedule. He led everyone in poles (eight) and victories (seven). He was No. 1 in races led (29) and times led (96), and he led 1,730 more miles and 1,037 more laps than second-ranked Dale Earnhardt.

Those numbers are why most knowledgeable NASCAR-watchers chalk up Gordon's measly 34-point

Jeff Gordon

After two starbursts in 1994, the Jeff Gordon era commenced for real in 1995, with Gordon winning poles at Rockingham and Richmond and the races at Rockingham and Atlanta (shown here), where Jeff started third. Those were the first of nine poles and the seven victories that carried him to his first Winston Cup championship and NASCAR's first $4 million-plus season. Chevrolet's new Monte Carlo model replaced the six-year-old Lumina, giving the Chevy men better aero-downforce at tracks such as Atlanta. Gordon dominated all day but had to fight off Bobby Labonte at the end by .19 of a second.

Car No.: 24
Make & Model: Chevrolet Monte Carlo
Team Owner: Rick Hendrick
Wins: 7
Top 10: 23

championship margin as an aberration. After all, he'd taken the lead at New Hampshire in July and steadily built it to 309 points. Only a series of uncharacteristic late-season gaffes allowed Earnhardt and his No. 3 Goodwrench Chevrolet team to crawl back within shouting distance.

Gordon's 147-point lead going into the Atlanta finale was more than enough to ensure his first Cup. "We had an awesome year," he said shortly before the start of the 1996 season, "but nothing came easy. Dale staged a great late-season comeback and almost caught us. He was relentless in the last six races, winning twice, finishing top five twice and top 10 in the other two. The best we could do in those six races was third at North Wilkesboro [where Earnhardt was ninth]. We knew he'd never give up and he didn't. It was harder than it looked."

Fellow Chevrolet driver Sterling Marlin finished third, his best ranking before or since. Ford drivers Mark Martin and Rusty Wallace were fourth and fifth, followed by Chevy star Terry Labonte, Ford drivers Ted Musgrave, Bill Elliott and Ricky Rudd, then Chevy driver Bobby Labonte. The Labontes were the first brothers to finish top 10 in points since two sets did it 43 years earlier: the

Flocks (Tim and Fonty) were first and fourth, and the Thomases (Herb and Donald) were second and ninth.

The lead Hendrick Motorsports team had something of a roller coaster spring. Gordon led much of the season-opening Daytona 500 before a pit incident knocked him back to a lap-down 22nd. He won the following weekend at Rockingham, but was an engine-related DNF 36th at Richmond. He won at Atlanta, but was a wreck-related DNF 32nd two weeks later at Darlington. He won at Bristol, was second to Earnhardt at North Wilkesboro, third at Martinsville, second to Martin at Talladega, and third at Sonoma the first weekend in May. After 10 of the year's 31 races, Gordon was third in points, but only six behind Martin and 15 behind Earnhardt.

Gordon started the middle third of the season much like he had at Daytona Beach three months earlier. He ran well at Charlotte on Memorial Day weekend, but ended up 33rd after falling out with suspension problems. He was sixth in the next race at Dover, then blew a likely victory at Pocono (he finished 16th) by missing a shift while leading on a late-race restart. Many will think the 14 consecutive top 10s between that Pocono mistake and the

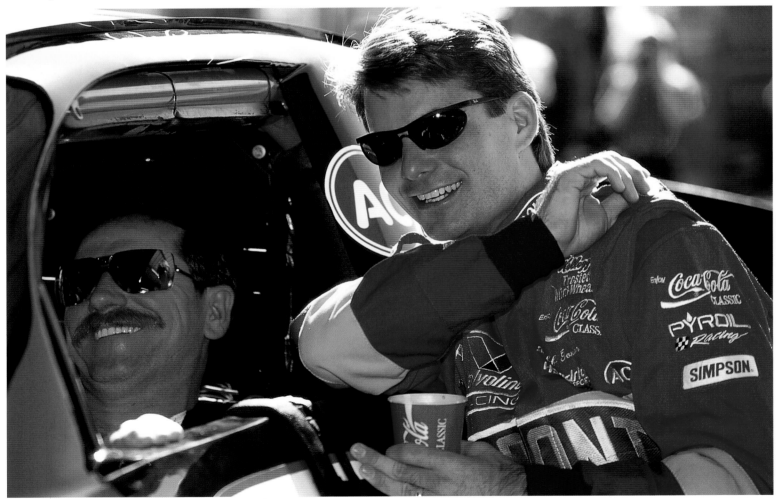

Dale Earnhardt and Jeff Gordon share a laugh in Phoenix at the Dura Lube 500. In only his fourth year on the circuit, Gordon grabbed the points lead in July and held it the rest of the way. Earnhardt made a valiant challenge late in the season before falling 34 points shy.

October race at Charlotte were the key to Gordon's championship season.

In his mind, though, the spring race at Rockingham was the key to the Rainbow Warriors' season. He won the pole at Rockingham and led 329 of the 492 laps, easily winning over Bobby Labonte, Earnhardt, Rudd, and Dale Jarrett. "We started fourth in the Daytona 500 and had led 61 laps before a bad stop put us behind," Gordon said. "It was just one of the many things that can happen in racing. But instead of wallowing in misery, the team came back with a vengeance. We won Rockingham and two of the next four, and were on our way. That bad stop in the 500 pulled us together; it showed this team's character, showed how determined it was not to let anything get us down."

The team quickly recovered after Gordon's mistake at Pocono. He was second in Michigan, won the mid summer race at Daytona Beach, then took the points lead for good by winning eight days later at Loudon. He started piling up the top 10s and points: second to Jarrett in Michigan, eighth at Talladega, sixth in the Brickyard 400 at Indy, third at Watkins Glen, third in Michigan, then sixth in the summer night race at Bristol. After 22 of 31 races, his lead was 176 points over Marlin. And after Gordon won the Labor Day weekend race at Darlington, almost everyone in the garage was conceding him the Cup.

He and Evernham did nothing to prove the competition wrong: sixth at Richmond, first at Dover, and seventh at Martinsville. Their third-place finish the first weekend in October at North Wilkesboro built their lead to 302, with just four races remaining. That spread was easily enough to withstand their erratic finishes of 30th (Charlotte), 20th (Rockingham), fifth (Phoenix), and 32nd (Atlanta) to close the season. Earnhardt did all he could—second at Charlotte, seventh at Rockingham, third Phoenix, and first at Atlanta—but it wasn't quite enough.

The new champ said he had no idea his first championship would come so soon in his Cup career. (Not to mention coming over a seven-time champion who had won four of the five previous titles.) "We never guessed when the season opened we could win it," Gordon said at the time. "Back then, our goals simply weren't set that high. We always try to do our best at every race, but I don't think anybody expected to win the Winston Cup in our third season. We thought it might take about five years, so I still can't believe we did it this quickly."

As things turned out, 1995 was Earnhardt's last great season in the 1990s. His victories came at North Wilkesboro and Sears Point in the spring, at Indianapolis in the summer, and at Martinsville and Atlanta in the fall. He and crew chief Andy Petree also had six runner-ups, five thirds, a fourth, two fifths, and four other top 10s.

Sterling Marlin had the best finish of his career in 1995, ending up third behind Gordon and Earnhardt. He started the year off right with a victory at Daytona—his second consecutive Daytona 500— and then took two more checkered flags on the year.

They won poles at Atlanta in the spring, Daytona Beach in the summer, and Richmond in the fall, and closed the season with 10 consecutive top 10 finishes, nine of them top fives.

But the Richard Childress–owned team had a spell of mid season problems that likely cost them the Cup. (It would have been Earnhardt's eighth, Childress' seventh, and Petree's third.) They were 35th in Michigan in June, 22nd at Loudon and 20th at Pocono in July, then 23rd at Watkins Glen and 35th at Michigan in August. Gordon scored 465 more points than Earnhardt in those five races, a deficit not even the Intimidator could overcome.

Marlin's third-place finish in the No. 4 Kodak Chevrolet was a stunner. The second-generation driver had never finished better than seventh in points and had only three top 10s in nine full seasons. But he and crew chief Tony Glover quickly showed they meant business, winning the season-opening Daytona 500 and the spring race at Darlington. Their other victory was in the summer at Talladega, where Marlin got his only pole of the season.

He backed his three-victory performance with a pair of second-place finishes, three fourths, and a fifth for team owners Larry McClure and Charles Morgan. He finished between sixth and 10th in a series-high 13 races, and dropped out of only one race. In almost every category, 1995 was the best season of Marlin's oft-erratic career.

Fourth-place Martin and team owner Jack Roush extended to seven their consecutive top 10s. They won at Talladega in the spring, Watkins Glen in the summer, and North Wilkesboro and Martinsville on back-to-back weekends in the fall. He and crew chief Steve Hmiel also had a second, four thirds, a fourth, three fifths, and nine other finishes between sixth and 10th in their No. 6 Valvoline Ford. Martin won poles at Bristol in the spring, and at New Hampshire, Watkins Glen, and Bristol in the summer.

Wallace had another solid season—his ninth top 10 in the past 10 years, including the 1989 Winston Cup. His fifth place with crew chief Robin Pemberton and owner Roger Penske came via victories at Martinsville in the spring and Michigan in the summer. He was second in four races, third in six others, fourth in two others, and fifth once. He was between sixth and 10th in four races, but also had 10 finishes of 20th or worse. He closed strong: 10 top-five finishes in the last 13 races to come from seventh in points.

Terry Labonte won the spring race at Richmond, the first of two summer races at Pocono, and the summer night race at Bristol in a Chevrolet. Ted Musgrave was 0-for-31 in his Ford, but ran consistently enough (seven top fives, 13 top 10s) to finish a career-best seventh. Elliott also was 0-for-31 in a Ford (at the time, only his second winless effort in 13 seasons), and had only four top fives and 11 top 10s. Rudd won the fall race at Phoenix in a Ford and Bobby Labonte got his first three career victories,

Ted Musgrave didn't win a single race in 1995, but his consistency and seven top-five finishes catapulted the Ford driver to a career-best seventh in the standings.

Bobby Labonte and brother Terry were both in the top 10 in 1995, with a pair of one-two finishes at the Coca-Cola 600 in May and the GM Goodwrench 400 in August. Bobby's one other victory was at Michigan in June.

winning at Charlotte on Memorial Day weekend, then both of the summer races in Michigan in a Chevrolet.

Much of Gordon's success—indeed, Earnhardt's as well—was laid at the feet of the new Chevy Monte Carlo. After years of campaigning the Lumina model, designers and builders at General Motors presented NASCAR with the "new generation" Monte Carlo. It was an immediate hit, winning 17 of 30 poles (fall qualifying at Martinsville was rained out) and 21 of 31 races. Chevys took the first three points positions, plus sixth and 10th. (Rookie of the Year Ricky Craven and runner-up Robert Pressley also drove new Monte Carlos.)

The season's other two victories went to Pontiac drivers not among the top 10 in the final ranking. Kyle Petty started 37th, avoided a massive early-race pileup and went on to win the summer race at Dover. And a major scoring dispute and questionable calls by officials at Rockingham couldn't keep Ward Burton and team owner Bill Davis from winning their first race in the fall. (Davis opened the season with Randy LaJoie, switched to Jimmy Hensley at mid season, and used Wally Dallenbach for one race before hiring Burton for the August race at Bristol.)

Speaking of which . . .

Terry Labonte's last-turn, last-lap victory that night featured the year's most controversial and exciting finish. After running into almost everyone but the pace-car driver, Earnhardt saved his best—worst?—shot for the finish. Labonte passed Jarrett for the lead with 68 laps remaining, then began to carefully run out the string. But heavy traffic was a factor, allowing Earnhardt to catch up in Turn 3 on the last lap. He gave Labonte a shot exiting Turn 4, then another perhaps 50 yards from the checkered flag.

The second lick turned Labonte directly into the outside concrete wall. But Earnhardt's assault had come a split-second too late. Labonte was close enough to the line to take the checkered flag just ahead of Earnhardt. "I just kept the wheels pointing forward the best I could," Labonte said beside his battered car in Victory Lane. "I was sideways at the line, but I knew I'd gotten there first. I'm not especially happy about it, but I'd be a lot less happy if he'd turned me and then beaten me."

For that precise scenario, Labonte would have to wait four years.

The Softer Side of NASCAR

At the time, few people within NASCAR would have imagined a motorcycle ride becoming one of the most popular and meaningful events on the Winston Cup calendar. Of course, most people within NASCAR seriously underestimated Kyle Petty.

In March of 1995, at Darlington, South Carolina, the grandson of Lee Petty and son of Richard Petty revealed plans for the inaugural Kyle Petty Charity Ride Across America. He invited NASCAR drivers, team owners, crewmen, and officials to ride motorcycles from California to North Carolina in the week after the Winston Cup race at Sonoma. They would leave San Jose on Monday after the race and reach Charlotte a week later.

The idea was to raise funds for the Winston Cup Racing Wives Auxiliary. The Auxiliary accepted tax-deductible donations from riders and sponsors and passed along a sizable portion to children's hospitals and camps for children with special needs. Riders and passengers made per-mile, per-day, or full-ride pledges in return for fuel, food, and lodging during the 3,500-mile trip.

Kyle and his wife, Pattie, organized the ride after realizing how many NASCAR competitors and fans had motorcycles. For years, the Pettys had ridden to races and public appearances, and simply toured for fun and education. The previous fall, when several fans asked to accompany them to Phoenix, they saw a way to combine cross-country touring with fund-raising for the Auxiliary.

The inaugural ride left San Jose and headed southward to near Los Angeles for the first overnight. Riders spent the second and third nights in Las Vegas and Phoenix before making a grueling 750-mile run to Odessa. The fifth stopover was in Dallas, followed by overnights in Memphis and Knoxville. The ride ended with a glorious reception near the Charlotte Motor Speedway on Monday, May 15.

The handful of riders who made the entire trip nicknamed themselves the "Odessa Gang" in memory of the ride's toughest leg. Hundreds of riders signed on for shorter legs, each making a charity donation to join the Pettys, Harry Gant, Dick Brooks, Geoff Bodine, Michael Waltrip, NASCAR executives Mike Helton and Gary Nelson, and team owners Bill Davis, Robert Yates, and Felix Sabates.

One story speaks volumes about the ride: A businessman from northern California called his office from Las Angeles that first night to say he was going to North Carolina. He'd be back to work in a couple of weeks. As of 2002, he'd done every ride.

2nd

Car No.: 3
Make & Model: Chevrolet Monte Carlo
Team Owner: Richard Childress
Wins: 5
Top 10: 23

Dale Earnhardt

Dale Earnhardt made Jeff Gordon work for his first championship, finishing top 10 in the final 10 races and lower than fifth in just two of those. He sounded a keynote at Indianapolis in August (seen here), where Earnhardt got a fine pit stop under the race's single caution (Lap 133 of 160) and beat Rusty Wallace to the finish by .37 of a second. Gordon had been 22 when he won the first Brickyard 400 in 1994; Earnhardt, 44, joked that he had become the first *man* to win the Speedway's stock-car show-case. Earnhardt closed with a win at Atlanta, cutting Gordon's final margin to 34 points.

3rd

Car No.: 4
Make & Model:
Chevrolet Monte Carlo
Team Owner:
Larry McClure
Wins: 3
Top 10: 22

Sterling Marlin

Rival engine men wondered aloud at the power produced by Morgan-McClure engine man Runt Pittman on the big tracks. Especially suspicious to many was the high-pitched exhaust whine from the Kodak No. 4 car, although nothing improper ever was found. The result, however, was a second consecutive Daytona 500 victory for Sterling Marlin, which propelled him into the points hunt through two-thirds of the year. Marlin, who started third, beat Dale Earnhardt to the finish by more than half a second. He became only the third man to win back-to-back Daytona 500s, joining Richard Petty (1973–1974) and Cale Yarborough (1983–1984).

4th

Car No.: 6
Make & Model:
  Ford Thunderbird
Team Owner:
  Jack Roush
Wins: 4
Top 10: 22

Mark Martin

The 1995 season was another almost for Mark Martin, the best racer not to win a championship in the decade. Notoriously slow starting, Martin and the Jack Roush team got the jump in 1995, finishing top 10 in all but one of the first 10 races, with a victory at Talladega. At New Hampshire in July, Martin won the pole and paced the first half of the race, only to watch from third place as Jeff Gordon pulled another one out of the hat. Martin also closed strong, with back-to-back victories at North Wilkesboro and Charlotte, but four finishes of 35th or worse in between cost him a chance to contend.

5th

Car No.: 2
Make & Model:
  Ford Thunderbird
Team Owner:
  Roger Penske
Wins: 2
Top 10: 19

Rusty Wallace

Rusty Wallace had a new crew chief in 1995, with Robin Pemberton taking over from Buddy Parrott, who had guided the team to 18 victories the previous two seasons. Wallace was steady, but not spectacular, in 1995, earning two victories—at Martinsville and Richmond, as usual. Wallace actually equaled his number of top 10s in 1994 with 19, but he fell two spots in points to fifth. At Rockingham in February (shown here), usually one of his better races, Wallace did not lead and fell out 41 laps from the finish with a broken engine. Both races at The Rock were condensed to 400 miles in 1995.

6th

Car No.: 5
Make & Model: Chevrolet Monte Carlo
Team Owner: Rick Hendrick
Wins: 3
Top 10: 17

Terry Labonte

Rick Hendrick was the only owner to field three cars in 1995. Although Jeff Gordon, driving Hendrick's No. 24, quickly became the superstar, Terry Labonte, in his second year driving Hendrick's original No. 5, made one of his more-memorable campaigns, winning a single-season, career-high three races, at Richmond, Pocono, and Bristol. He also earned bragging rights around the shop by finishing best among the three Hendrick cars in the Daytona 500. Labonte started 11th and finished ninth, one position ahead of teammate Ken Schrader, with Gordon trailing in 22nd, a lap down. Hendrick's shops had helped to develop the new Chevy Monte Carlo.

7th

Car No.: 16
Make & Model:
 Ford Thunderbird
Team Owner: Jack Roush
Wins: 0
Top 10: 13

Ted Musgrave

Ted Musgrave began to fulfill the confidence shown in him when, at Mark Martin's suggestion, owner Jack Roush hired him to drive No. 16 in 1994. In 1995, Musgrave raked in seven top fives and 13 top 10s, enabling him to rise as high as fourth in points by mid summer. The dream died down the stretch, however, with Ted managing just two top 10s in the final 14 races. Darlington in September was part of the late-season pattern. Musgrave started 28th but fought into the top 10 before his engine quit with 17 laps to go; Ted finished 22nd. Second-places at Martinsville and Pocono were his best.

8th

Bill Elliott

Bill Elliott, always independent-minded, jumped at the opportunity to be owner and driver upon leaving Junior Johnson after 1994. It seemed to be a match made in heaven—clean-cut, popular Elliott and sponsor McDonald's, which followed him from Johnson's camp to the new venture. Long time Georgia associate Charles Hardy was listed originally as co-owner. Elliott did not win in 1995, but results were encouraging, as he rang up fourths at Indianapolis (leading the most laps) and Atlanta. He qualified second at Watkins Glen in August and hung in to finish 11th. Seen widely as an oval specialist, Elliott runs well on the road courses.

Car No.: 94
Make & Model: Ford Thunderbird
Team Owner: Bill Elliott
Wins: 0
Top 10: 11

Ricky Rudd

In his second season as owner-driver, Rudd cut it close in extending his streak of consecutive seasons with at least one victory to 13. He finally claimed a trophy at Phoenix in the fall, the next-to-last stop on the circuit. Rudd had high moments, including the win, poles at Sears Point and Charlotte, and the richest season of his 20-year career, with $1,337,703 won. Six DNFs derailed his run, but he was stout through the fall, only twice finishing out of the top 10 from Darlington on. The Rockingham race in February kindled hope; he started second and finished fourth.

9th

Car No.: 10
Make & Model: Ford Thunderbird
Team Owner: Ricky Rudd
Wins: 1
Top 10: 16

Bobby Labonte

Labonte signed on with Joe Gibbs Racing for 1995, replacing Dale Jarrett, who had accepted the wheel of Robert Yates' Texaco No. 28. Labonte's polite move from Bill Davis Racing was the right one at the time, and Bobby, 31, came out from under the shadow of older brother Terry with the first three victories of his career, the first coming in the glamorous Coca-Cola 600 at Charlotte in May. Labonte also won twice at Michigan, one of his favorite tracks. The race at the .625-mile North Wilkesboro track in October (shown here) was forgettable, with Bobby starting 22nd and finishing 18th.

10th

Car No.: 18
Make & Model: Chevrolet Monte Carlo
Team Owner: Joe Gibbs
Wins: 3
Top 10: 14

11th

Car No.: 21
Make & Model: Ford Thunderbird
Team Owner: Wood Brothers
Wins: 0
Top 10: 10

Morgan Shepherd

Although nearing the end of his four-year stand with the Wood Brothers, Morgan Shepherd continued to give honest effort, finishing 11th in points in 1995. Shepherd's best runs included a second place at New Hampshire, a third at Talladega in April, and a fourth at Talladega in July. The October race at Rockingham was shortened from 500 to 400 laps for the first time, and 400 miles were more than enough for Shepherd and crew, with Morgan struggling to 18th place, two laps down. Shepherd fell just short of a million dollars in 1995, winning $966,374.

12th

Car No.: 30
Make & Model:
  Pontiac Grand Prix
Team Owner:
  Chuck Rider
Wins: 0
Top 10: 8

Michael Waltrip

Like old pal Kyle Petty with Felix Sabates, Michael Waltrip had been considered a fixture at the Bahari team, owned by auto-parts entrepreneur Chuck Rider. Waltrip had helped Rider get off the ground as an owner in 1988, but his winning personality and pleasant ways with sponsors were not enough to make the cars run better than they were. Pontiac also introduced a new body in 1995, although without the drama of the Chevy Monte Carlo controversy. Initially tail-heavy, the car got better as NASCAR allowed modifications. At Rockingham in February, Waltrip finished 17th, about average.

Dale Jarrett

13th

What looked in 1994 to be a career move became very much a burden to Dale Jarrett through most of 1995. Jarrett had left Joe Gibbs for the chance of a lifetime—driving horsepower-king Robert Yates' No. 28, made famous by Davey Allison and Ernie Irvan. Irvan, out with injuries through most of 1995, was visible on the sidelines, and Jarrett's failure to win through the first half of the year made the pressure unbearable. Jarrett found sweet vindication in winning the Pocono race in July. His fifth place at Rockingham in February (shown here) was his best until the Pocono win.

Car No.: 28
Make & Model: Ford Thunderbird
Team Owner: Robert Yates
Wins: 1
Top 10: 14

Car No.: 43
Make & Model: Pontiac Grand Prix
Team Owner: Richard Petty
Wins: 0
Top 10: 10

Bobby Hamilton

Bobby Hamilton made yet another step up the ladder in 1995, leaving the ill-starred Felix Sabates No. 40 team for Petty Enterprises' legendary No. 43, the car made famous by Richard. When Petty retired after 1992, the team floundered with unlucky successors such as Rick Wilson, Wally Dallenbach, and John Andretti before deciding on plucky Hamilton for 1995. Success did not come immediately; Hamilton's best finish was second at Dover in the fall, and the Pettys' losing streak, dating to 1983, continued. Qualifying was encouraging, however, with Hamilton starting second at Richmond and Indianapolis. The engine quit at Rockingham (shown here) in February.

14th

15th

Derrike Cope

Derrike Cope actually had his best season of the 1990s as chauffeur of Bobby Allison's No. 12 in 1995—even better than 1990, the year he won two races, including the Daytona 500. Cope finished 15th in points with a second-place run at Phoenix and a total of eight top 10s. At Phoenix, Cope led until Ricky Rudd, on fresher tires, ran him down with 11 laps to go. Jim Fennig, later with Mark Martin, was crew chief for the group. The Darlington race in March was one of the team's better efforts, with Cope starting 13th and finishing fifth. A long, hot summer followed, though, before the late-year rally.

Car No.: 12
Make & Model: Ford Thunderbird
Team Owner: Bobby Allison
Wins: 0
Top 10: 8

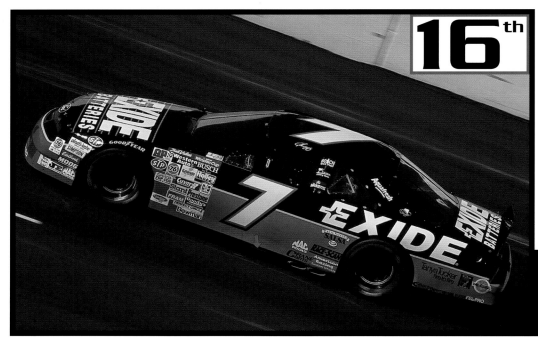

16th

Car No.: 7
Make & Model: Ford Thunderbird
Team Owner: Geoff Bodine
Wins: 0
Top 10: 4

Geoff Bodine

Geoff Bodine had capitalized on the success of Hoosier tires during Tire War II in 1994. With Hoosier gone in 1995, Bodine no longer had the "unfair advantage" he'd demonstrated at several stops the previous season. He won no poles, and he failed to win a race for the first time since 1987. The flip side was that Bodine reduced his DNF count from an astonishing 15 to just five, and he actually improved one place in points, to 16th. Meanwhile, however, Bodine was swatting hornets as owner-driver, with sponsor Exide announcing it would leave at the end of the year. Geoff was 13th at Darlington in March (shown here).

17th

Car No.: 25
Make & Model:
  Chevrolet Monte Carlo
Team Owner:
  Rick Hendrick
Wins: 0
Top 10: 10

Ken Schrader

Ken Schrader would not call .526-mile Martinsville Speedway one of his best tracks. Yet Schrader pulled out one of his best finishes of 1995 at the flat Virginia oval in April, nudging to sixth at the finish. Only a third at Ponoco, a fourth at Richmond, and a sixth at Daytona in July covered the spread. Owner Rick Hendrick had thrown some force behind No. 25, acquiring sponsorship from Budweiser, which became free when Junior Johnson went out of business after 1994. The results were unpleasant for all, with Schrader showing only 10 top 10s, nine DNFs, and tumbling from fourth to 17th in points, Schrader's worst of the decade.

18th

John Andretti

Michael Kranefuss, former worldwide chief of Ford's motor sports operations, and partner Carl Haas formed the No. 37 team for 1995, with sponsorship from Kmart. Haas, who had fielded Kmart cars for John Andretti's uncle Mario and cousin Michael, brought the sponsorship, and John was a natural fit. From a distance, the No. 37 team looked like an all-star group. Versatile Andretti had paid his stock-car dues, Kranefuss and Haas were proven warriors, and Tim Brewer, formerly with Junior Johnson, was crew chief. But the gears never seemed to mesh, and Andretti's best finish was fourth at Michigan in June.

Car No.: 37
Make & Model: Ford Thunderbird
Team Owner: Michael Kranefuss
Wins: 0
Top 10: 5

Car No.: 17
Make & Model: Chevrolet Monte Carlo
Team Owner: Darrell Waltrip
Wins: 0
Top 10: 8

19th

Darrell Waltrip

Darrell Waltrip, 48 in 1995, remained determined to build a contending team and to return to winning form, and results were just encouraging enough to keep his hopes alive. Waltrip continued to make changes within his Western Auto–sponsored team, and with veteran Pete Peterson in charge, Waltrip described the team's latest incarnation as a "bunch of Marines, the guys who will get in there and do what it takes." Waltrip scored a season-best third at Bristol and added fourths at Martinsville and Talladega, gaining the top 10 in points. From there, the effort stumbled, and Waltrip, finishing 19th, looked to reorganize again.

20th

Brett Bodine

This was the last go-round for legendary Junior Johnson, winner of six Winston Cup championships as the series' top car owner and power broker in the 1970s and 1980s. Johnson's famous No. 11, driven to championships by Cale Yarborough and Darrell Waltrip, was a shadow by 1995, with Brett Bodine taking the wheel and Lowe's taking over from Budweiser as sponsor. Although performance was middling, Bodine and Johnson apparently had reached agreement early-on for Bodine to buy the remains of the organization after the season. Bodine, always careful with equipment, ran steadily in the teens and 20s, with two top 10s.

Car No.: 11
Make & Model: Ford Thunderbird
Team Owner: Junior Johnson
Wins: 0
Top 10: 2

21st

Car No.: 1
Make & Model:
  Ford Thunderbird
Team Owner:
  Richard Jackson
Wins: 0
Top 10: 3

Rick Mast

Rick Mast and Richard Jackson continued to plow an increasingly barren furrow in 1995. With brother Leo's retirement from racing after 1994, Richard found himself operating more and more on his own, although sponsor Skoal remained steadfast. The Jackson team, which won at Talladega with Phil Parsons in 1988 with much the same resources, was an example of NASCAR's increasing gap between the haves and the have-nots. Mast managed three top 10s, including eighth places at Indianapolis and North Wilkesboro (shown here) and a ninth place at Phoenix. The highlight was the pole at Dover in September, but nine DNFs, mostly engine failures, were costly.

Ward Burton

Ward Burton's 22nd-place in points in 1995 was deceptive, with the 33-year-old speedster enduring a split season. Ward began the year with owner Alan Dillard, who had graduated him from the Busch Series in 1994. The Dillard team encountered trouble mid year, and Ward drove the last nine races of the season for Bill Davis. Results for both Burton and Davis immediately improved, with Ward scoring his first win, and the first for Davis, at Rockingham in October. Burton was Davis' fourth chauffeur in a difficult year; the win led Davis' wife Gail to exclaim, "We've got ourselves a *driver.*"

22nd

Car No.: 22
Make & Model: Pontiac Grand Prix
Team Owner: Bill Davis
Wins: 1
Top 10: 6

23rd

Lake Speed

Lake Speed, winner at Darlington in 1988, joined Harry Melling, patron of the Elliotts in their glory days, in a rejuvenation project for both in 1995. Considering the circumstances, Speed and Melling did not do badly, with Lake turning up top 10s at Charlotte and Darlington and finishing 23rd in points. Hormel's Spam brand adorned the cars in 1995, giving Melling his first steady sponsorship since the departure of the Elliotts and Coors in 1991. Melling had strung along since then, running limited schedules in 1992, 1993, and 1994, before Speed (also listed as general manager) helped stabilize the package in 1995.

Car No.: 9
Make & Model: Ford Thunderbird
Team Owner: Harry Melling
Wins: 0
Top 10: 2

Ricky Craven

Ricky Craven and owner Larry Hedrick were riding a rising curve through 1995. Craven replaced Joe Nemechek, who decided to go out on his own, and won Rookie of the Year in Hedrick's Chevrolets, out pointing Robert Pressley. Hedrick, chief of a car auction in Statesville, North Carolina, had built toward success and needed the one big break, and Craven's sure-handed freshman season appeared to give the team a sound jump point. Craven's best finish was seventh at Michigan in August, but he surprised many with strong qualifying efforts, such as third place at Charlotte in May. The season was worth $597,054, Hedrick's best yet.

24th

Car No.: 41
Make & Model: Chevrolet Monte Carlo
Team Owner: Larry Hedrick
Wins: 0
Top 10: 4

Dick Trickle

Driver Dick Trickle and owner Bud Moore both had seen better days by 1995. War hero Moore, 71, who had won the NASCAR championship with Joe Weatherly in 1962, also had schooled the likes of Buddy Baker, Dale Earnhardt, and Ricky Rudd. He picked up veteran Trickle after Lake Speed left in 1994. Trickle, 54, with a thousand victories on Midwestern short tracks, went full-time in Winston Cup in 1989, winning Rookie of the Year, the second-oldest in Cup history. He had bounced around a good bit since. By the end of the year, Moore faced the loss of his long time backing from Ford, and his association with Trickle lasted just one year.

25th

Car No.: 15
Make & Model: Ford Thunderbird
Team Owner: Bud Moore
Wins: 0
Top 10: 1

26th

Car No.: 23
Make & Model: Ford Thunderbird
Team Owner: Travis Carter
Wins: 0
Top 10: 4

Jimmy Spencer

Jimmy Spencer had racked up two victories with Junior Johnson in 1994, and although the Johnson team was wildly inconsistent, Spencer was convinced mid season that he and Johnson would prosper together in the long run. In 1995, however, Johnson handed Spencer to R.J. Reynolds and veteran owner/crew chief Travis Carter. Under Carter's steady hand, consistency improved, and even with no victories, Spencer rose from 29th to 26th in points, with only two DNFs. Carter and R.J. Reynolds also helped reinforce Jimmy's increasing maturity, with Mr. Excitement coming under rein.

27th

Car No.: 29
Make & Model:
  Chevrolet Monte Carlo
Team Owner: Gary Bechtel
Wins: 0
Top 10: 4

Steve Grissom

Owner Gary Bechtel spent money freely, even importing premium crew chief Buddy Parrott for a spell, but could not seem to dig in, despite an encouraging start. Driver Steve Grissom finished seventh in the Daytona 500 and sixth the next time out at Rockingham (shown here), placing the team squarely in the top 10 in points. Grissom, however, failed to qualify the next week at Richmond, dealing his season a fatal blow. Grissom thereafter ran sixth at Darlington and fifth at North Wilkesboro, but Parrott left mid spring and the team fell into a hole it couldn't escape. From July Daytona on, Grissom only once finished better than 22nd.

28th

Joe Nemechek

Florida's Joe Nemechek was used to doing things his way. After a strong rookie run with Larry Hedrick in 1994, Nemechek decided to test his own destiny. Acquiring sponsorship from Burger King, he formed his No. 87 team for 1995 and set sail. Nemechek survived the crucial, four-race opening gantlet for rookie teams in fair shape, then tripped at Bristol and Talladega, failing to qualify. That set the whole program back on its heels. Joe did reasonably well the rest of the year, with four top 10s in qualifying (including third at New Hampshire) and a fourth place at Dover in September.

Car No.: 87
Make & Model: Chevrolet Monte Carlo
Team Owner: Joe Nemechek
Wins: 0
Top 10: 4

Robert Pressley

Pressley, product of a long time racing family in western North Carolina, was Leo Jackson's choice to replace legend Harry Gant in No. 33. In a way, that was Pressley's misfortune. Toward the end of the year, Jackson gradually yielded control of the team to protégé Andy Petree, who became owner for 1996, and Petree had other ideas. Pressley ran as a rookie in 1995, his first full season after a solid career in the Busch Series. Never afraid of speed, Pressley put up notable numbers in time trials, qualifying second at Martinsville and New Hampshire, fourth at Richmond, and fifth at summer Daytona. Race results did not follow.

29th

Car No.: 33
Make & Model: Chevrolet Monte Carlo
Team Owner: Leo Jackson
Wins: 0
Top 10: 1

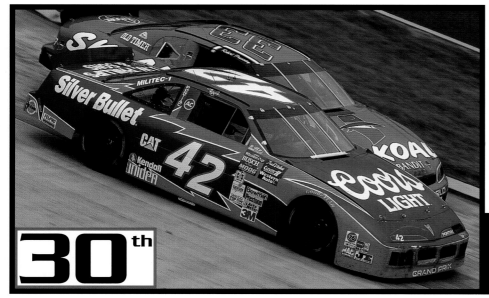

30th

Car No.: 42
Make & Model: Pontiac Grand Prix
Team Owner: Felix Sabates
Wins: 1
Top 10: 5

Kyle Petty

Kyle Petty and long time car owner Felix Sabates took a wild ride in 1995. Shrewd Petty picked off a victory amid Goodyear's tire crisis at Dover in June—after starting 37th. Over the long haul, however, 10 DNFs cost him any chance to contend, and his fading fortunes in points left Kyle without a starting spot at Martinsville in September. From August on, the team finished better than 24th only twice. Qualifying was equally erratic, with seven top 10s (including thirds at spring Bristol and fall Dover) weighted down with nine provisionals. Barry Dodson, trophy-winner with Rusty Wallace in 1989, was crew chief.

Chapter 7

1996

A Flash from the Past

TERRY LABONTE RETURNS TO TOP FORM

Almost every magazine and newspaper touting the 1996 NASCAR Winston Cup season mentioned the same half-dozen title contenders. The previews spoke of seven-time champion Dale Earnhardt, defending champion Jeff Gordon, 1989 champion Rusty Wallace, consistent top-10 finishers Mark Martin and Ricky Rudd, and two-time defending Daytona 500 winner Sterling Marlin.

If anyone who claimed to know anything about NASCAR was giving Terry Labonte a chance, he was keeping that opinion pretty much to himself.

But 10 months, 31 races, and almost 11,750 miles later, there was Labonte, posing with the champion's trophy and almost sheepishly waving the index finger of his right hand. For the second time—the first was 1984 with owner Billy Hagan and crew chief Dale Inman—the quiet, understated Texan was king of the NASCAR hill.

And what a strange and eventful journey it was from Cup I to Cup II.

Labonte had quit Hagan in 1986 to drive three seasons for Junior Johnson. He'd driven for Richard Jackson

Terry Labonte

A measure of Terry Labonte's consistency is that, despite just one early-year victory (at North Wilkesboro), he led the points battle by 134 heading into the home-stretch. That was partly due to an amazing seven second-places and 12 other top fives. The team stumbled a bit, giving up the points lead at Dover, but Labonte rallied at Charlotte in October (shown here), leading the most laps on the way to his second win of the season, closing back to a dead heat with Jeff Gordon. Labonte took the lead with 27 (of 334) laps to go and pulled away from Mark Martin to the finish.

Car No.: 5
Make & Model: Chevrolet Monte Carlo
Team Owner: Rick Hendrick
Wins: 2
Top 10: 24

in 1990, then rejoined Hagan for three years. But fearful of that becoming a dead-end road, Labonte accepted Rick Hendrick's invitation to join Ken Schrader and Jeff Gordon at Hendrick Motorsports in 1994. The 12-year gap between his 1984 and 1996 Cups was the longest in NASCAR history. Talk about your overlooked long shots.

"When I won in 1984, I felt that with the team we had coming back we might just win it again the next year," Labonte said after accepting the 1996 Cup at Atlanta in November. "I never figured it would take 12 years. 'Next year' took a long time, but that's what makes my feelings about this time so much stronger. I didn't understand everything that went with being the 1984 champion, so I'll appreciate this one even more."

On the surface, his 1996 run with Hendrick and crew chief Gary DeHart wasn't especially impressive. He won only two races, the same as in 1984 and when the late Alan Kulwicki won the 1992 championship. (Bill Rexford in 1950, Ned Jarrett in 1961, and Benny Parsons in 1973 each won once, the fewest during any championship season.)

Labonte won at North Wilkesboro in the spring and at Charlotte in the fall. But his Kellogg's-backed No. 5 Chevrolet Monte Carlo was maddeningly consistent: seven runner-up finishes, five thirds, a fourth, six fifths, and three more finishes between sixth and 10th. He had four DNFs, but was still ranked top five in miles led, laps led, times led, races led, and miles completed.

"Obviously, we wanted to win more than just two races, but we were in position to probably win five others," Labonte said. "We led the most laps at Daytona Beach and Rockingham early in the year, but had problems in each race. We came out of those two [24th at Daytona Beach, 34th at Rockingham] 30th in points. That's the lowest I'd ever been in my career."

He didn't waste much time making up ground. He was eighth in the spring race at Richmond, second at Atlanta, fifth at Darlington, then second at Bristol before winning at North Wilkesboro in mid-April. That 400-lapper was his 513th consecutive start, tying Richard Petty's record. (He set the record a week later at Martinsville,

Twelve years and three owners after his first Winston Cup title, Terry Labonte was back on top in 1996 with Hendrick Motorsports. Consistency was the name of the game for Labonte's team, capturing 21 top-fives on the year.

where he finished 24th.) After eight of 31 races, Labonte was second in points, 25 behind Dale Jarrett.

He maintained his championship-level consistency from late spring deep into the summer: fourth at Talladega, fifth at Sonoma, third at Charlotte on Memorial Day weekend, second at Dover, seventh at Pocono, second at Michigan, second at Daytona Beach, then sixth a week later at Loudon. His run of top 10s ended at Pocono, where Labonte finished a lap-down 16th.

He was 24th a week later in the rain-shortened race at Talladega before rallying to finish third at Indianapolis early in August. He capped the summer portion of his championship season with a rush: second at Watkins Glen, third at Michigan, and fifth at Bristol. Despite that consistency—10 top fives and two more top 10s in 14 starts—Labonte went into the final third of the season leading Gordon by only 114 points.

Things began tightening up in the fall. Labonte was 26th and lost 90 points to race-winner Gordon at Darlington on Labor Day weekend. When he finished fifth to runner-up Gordon a week later at Richmond, Labonte's lead was down to four points after 24 races. Gordon took the lead by winning at Dover, where Labonte was 21st. They finished one-two (Gordon-Labonte) at Martinsville, building Gordon's lead to 81 points after 26 of 31 races.

Labonte's fortunes took another serious hit the following weekend. Gordon won and Labonte was fifth in the 72nd and last Winston Cup race scheduled at storied North Wilkesboro, North Carolina Speedway. With four races left, Gordon's lead stood at 111 points and not even the most fervent Labonte fan was holding out much hope.

But Labonte wasn't among them. His hopes were revived early in October at Charlotte, where he won, led the most laps, and finished the race within one point of 31st-finishing Gordon. Later that month, at Rockingham, Labonte went from one point behind to 32 ahead by finishing third, six spots ahead of Gordon.

Labonte's rally continued the following weekend at Phoenix. Despite qualifying 30th and racing with a broken hand suffered in a practice crash, he led twice for 61 laps and finished third. Gordon, finishing fifth, didn't lead and lost 15 more points. Labonte went into the season finale at Atlanta leading by 47 points, a 158-point swing in three races.

Atlanta was a truly memorable weekend for the Labonte family. Bobby qualified on the pole, led the most laps, and won the NAPA 500 over Jarrett and Gordon. Terry qualified third, led some laps and finished fifth, and that was more than enough to win the championship by 37 points. "If you'd brought in a movie

director," Terry said after the finale, "he couldn't have written a better script for this weekend. If I talked like my brother, I'd have called our shared victory lap 'way cool' like he did."

All told, four drivers swapped the points lead six times during 1996: Jarrett led after the first seven races; Earnhardt after the next eight; then Labonte after the 16th and 17th races. Gordon led after Talladega in July, then Labonte regained the lead through the Richmond race in September. Gordon took the lead at Dover, held it for four races and seemed destined for another Cup until Labonte beat him in three of the last four races—a total of 39 finish positions—to reign as champion.

Jarrett overhauled Earnhardt late in the summer and finished third in points, well behind the front two. Earnhardt was fourth and Martin fifth, followed by Rudd, Wallace, Marlin, Bobby Hamilton, and Ernie Irvan.

Bobby Hamilton squeaked in at ninth place in 1996, winning only one race—the first of his career—and notching two other top-fives.

Driving Robert Yates' No. 28 Ford, Ernie Irvan rebounded from the life-threatening injuries of two years earlier to crack the top 10 in 1996.

Rusty Wallace's silver Ford gets attention from the crew at Martinsville. Behind crew chief Robin Pemberton, Penske's Miller Lite team won five races in 1996.

Just as they had the previous season, Gordon and crew chief Ray Evernham led the tour in both poles (five) and race victories (10). Their poles came at Charlotte in the spring, then Dover, Pocono, Daytona Beach, and Indianapolis in the summer. They won races at Richmond, Darlington, and Bristol in the spring; Dover, Pocono, and Talladega in the summer; then Darlington on Labor Day weekend. The No. 24 DuPont Chevrolet team closed with a rush, winning on consecutive fall Sunday afternoons at Dover, Martinsville, and North Wilkesboro.

Gordon backed those stats with three seconds, four thirds, a pair of fourths, two fifths, and three finishes between sixth and 10th. But his downfall was dropping out of the spring races at Daytona Beach, Rockingham, and Talladega, and the summer races at Loudon and Indianapolis. (In retrospect, though, the 31st at Charlotte in the fall was the race that did him in.)

Jarrett and crew chief Todd Parrott won poles at Darlington and Phoenix in the fall. Their race victories came at Daytona Beach and Charlotte in the spring and at Indianapolis and Michigan in the summer. They finished second seven times, were third on four occasions, fourth in two races, and between sixth and 10th four times. Jarrett and his No. 88 Quality Care Ford led the standings through North Wilkesboro in mid-April and wasn't ranked below fourth all season.

Earnhardt's season opened with great promise: he won the pole and finished second to Jarrett in the Daytona 500. He and crew chief David Smith won the following weekend at Rockingham, then prevailed again at Atlanta two weeks later. Earnhardt led the standings after eight consecutive races (between Martinsville in April and Daytona Beach in July) before slipping back to fourth. In addition to two victories, he had three second-place finishes, three thirds, four fourths, a fifth, and four other results between sixth and 10th.

But their season turned sour in July at Talladega. There, while leading 312 miles into the DieHard 500, Earnhardt was involved in a massive front-stretch accident. His No. 3 Goodwrench Chevrolet flipped and rolled several times, and was hit by several cars as it slid on its roof. Earnhardt was lucky to escape with only cuts, bruises, and a broken sternum. Despite denials to the contrary, the frightening accident affected him deeply.

Witness: he dropped from second to fourth in points and had only one top 10 in the eight races immediately following the accident.

Martin's season was unlike anything he'd experienced during his nine-year association with team owner Jack Roush. He and crew chief Steve Hmiel won poles at Bristol in the spring, Pocono and Bristol in the summer, and Richmond in the fall. Despite that and four outside poles, the No. 6 Valvoline Ford didn't win a race. It was Martin's first winless season since he and Roush teamed up in 1988. They finished 14 races among the top five (including four runner-up finishes) and nine more between sixth and 10th.

Top-five drivers won 18 of 31 races and drivers ranked sixth through 10th won 11 of the other 13. Rudd won at Rockingham in the fall, Wallace at Martinsville and Sonoma in the spring, then at Michigan, Pocono, and Bristol in the summer. Marlin won at Talladega in the spring and Daytona Beach in the summer. Hamilton got his career breakthrough victory at Phoenix in the fall, and Irvan won at Loudon in the summer and Richmond in the fall. Eleventh-ranked Bobby Labonte (in the finale at Atlanta) and 17th ranked Geoff Bodine (Watkins Glen in the summer) were the other two winners.

Former ASA and Busch Series champion Johnny Benson had an easy run to Rookie of the Year. He was, in fact, the only rookie in 27 of the year's 31 races, making it easy for the rookie points system and the panel of voters. (Stacy Compton made one start and Randy MacDonald three.) Early in his career, Benson had also been ASA and Busch Series Rookie of the Year.

For not the first time in its history, NASCAR found itself defending its points system. Critics pointed out that Gordon had three times as many front-row starts and five times as many victories—but still finished second in points, 37 behind. (He and Labonte had an equal number of top fives and top 10s, but Gordon had two more DNFs, 5-3.)

Neither driver allowed himself to become embroiled in the contretemps. They had (as Hendrick pointed out early the next season) started the 1996 season knowing exactly how the points system worked. "It's the system NASCAR has used for years," he said, "and I imagine it'll be the system they use for years to come.

"Both those guys had great seasons, and the championship wasn't decided until the last race of the year. I'm sure Jeff was disappointed to win 10 races and still finish second. I'm just as sure that Terry wished he could have won more than two races. But he couldn't trade the Winston Cup for three or four or five more victories. I'm positive of that."

NASCAR Thunder in Japan

It might surprise many NASCAR fans to learn that their beloved all-American sport has some international connections. In July of 1952, the Grand National tour (later, Winston Cup) ran 200 laps on a half-mile dirt track in Niagara Falls, Ontario, Canada. Six years later, Richard Petty made the first of his 1,177 starts in a 100-lap race on a third-mile track in Toronto.

Those road trips were easy (after all, teams were already in upstate New York) compared to the next time NASCAR sent its teams abroad. In November of 1996, at the Suzuka Circuitland in Japan, 23 Americans and four Japanese ran the Suzuka Special 100 before more than 40,000 fans. The exhibition race two weeks after the Cup finale covered 100 laps on the famous 1.89-mile road course 300 miles south of Tokyo.

The field was impressive: Dale Earnhardt, Jeff Gordon, Terry Labonte, Rusty Wallace, and Dale Jarrett represented 14 existing or future championships. Michael Waltrip, David Green, Wally Dallenbach, Johnny Benson, Bobby Hillin, Robby Gordon, Ernie Irvan, and Sterling Marlin also represented Winston Cup. Mike Skinner, Ron Hornaday, and Rick Carelli were there from the Craftsman Truck Series, and Butch Gilliland, Lance Hooper, Scott Gaylord, Larry Gunselman, Dan Obrist, Joe Bean, and the legendary Hershel McGriff represented several West Coast–based series.

Pole-winner Wallace led 84 laps to win $130,940 and bragging rights over Earnhardt, Gordon, Labonte, Dallenbach, Benson, Hillin, Skinner, Carelli, and Gilliland. The top-finishing Japanese driver was 15th-place Keiichi Tsuchiya, the last driver on the lead lap. Teams raced 50 laps, then the top eight were inverted for the second 50-lap heat. Gordon won the first segment, then spent the second 50 laps trying to catch up.

The trip was a massive logistical undertaking. Teams delivered their car and support equipment to the West Coast in mid summer for surface transit to Japan. Reams of customs and tariff paperwork piled up as NASCAR handled all the travel, food and lodging, passports, tours, ground transportation, and financial arrangements for 300 people. The Winston brand of R.J. Reynolds supported the trip (and two subsequent trips) in hopes of cutting into Marlboro's huge advantage in the Far Eastern cigarette market.

But NASCAR was all for it, too. And why not? After all, millions of its fans drive Japanese-built cars. It is, to be sure, an ever-shrinking globe, and there are corporate alliances and personal friendships waiting to be forged.

2nd

Car No.: 24
Make & Model: Chevrolet Monte Carlo
Team Owner: Rick Hendrick
Wins: 10
Top 10: 24

Jeff Gordon

Indianapolis' Brickyard 400 helped propel Jeff Gordon to stardom in 1994. In 1996, it may have cost him the championship. Gordon started from the pole at the fabled speedway (seen here) but was caught in a wreck among lapped cars early in the race, finishing 37th. He rallied to take the points lead in September, but an overheating problem at Charlotte, caused by a cracked cylinder head, left him 31st. Gordon finished just 37 points behind champion Terry Labonte, and 10 or 12 places better in either race would have given him sufficient points to overtake the leader.

3rd

Car No.: 88
Make & Model: Ford Thunderbird
Team Owner: Robert Yates
Wins: 4
Top 10: 21

Dale Jarrett

Upon the return of Ernie Irvan to No. 28, owner Robert Yates accommodated stand-in Dale Jarrett with a team of its own, the No. 88 Ford Quality Care group. The move paid off immediately, with Jarrett and rookie crew chief Todd Parrott winning the Daytona 500 right out of the box. Jarrett easily outran frustrated pole-winner Dale Earnhardt, who complained NASCAR had "given Ford the candy store" in allowing engine improvements over the winter. Jarrett also added glamorous victories at Charlotte, the Brickyard, and Michigan, leading to his best-ever points finish (third) and nearly $3 million in prize money.

4th

Dale Earnhardt

Dale Earnhardt, 45, ripped off early victories at Rockingham and Atlanta (shown here) to get an early grip on the points lead. He did not win again, and a devastating crash at Talladega in July hurt him more than he knew at the time. At Atlanta, Earnhardt started 18th but had the lead by Lap 49. He and Terry Labonte had the cars to beat, with Earnhardt taking the lead on Lap 300 (of 328) and beating Labonte by better than 4 seconds. The old Atlanta oval (1.522 miles) was one of Earnhardt's best tracks. His 1996 win there was his eighth, breaking a career tie with Cale Yarborough.

Car No.: 3
Make & Model: Chevrolet Monte Carlo
Team Owner: Richard Childress
Wins: 2
Top 10: 17

Car No.: 6
Make & Model: Ford Thunderbird
Team Owner: Jack Roush
Wins: 0
Top 10: 23

5th

Mark Martin

Mark Martin, who had won four times in 1995, endured a puzzling 1996, going winless for the first time since his debut year with Jack Roush in 1988. Martin had a new crew chief in 1996, with old pal Jim Fennig taking hands-on duties from Steve Hmiel, and the team tried some chassis modifications, but there really was no good explanation. Martin did not have a *bad* year, although he started slow. He came on with a rush from August on, scoring three second-places and four thirds in the last 13 races. At Rockingham in October (shown here), Mark started fourth and finished seventh.

6th

Car No.: 10
Make & Model: Ford Thunderbird
Team Owner: Ricky Rudd
Wins: 1
Top 10: 16

Ricky Rudd

Ricky Rudd's record streak of winning seasons, dating to 1983, was on the line by October 1996, his third year as owner-driver. He kept it alive with a bizarre finish at Rockingham (shown here), winning for the 14th-straight year. Rudd became exasperated with his pit crew, replacing two men on the spot with members of another team. When that didn't work, Rudd and crew chief Richard Broome skipped their last tire stop entirely, took a huge lead, and coasted to victory over Dale Jarrett. Rudd had one of his best seasons ever in 1996, with 16 top 10s and only one DNF.

7th

Car No.: 2
Make & Model:
  Ford Thunderbird
Team Owner:
  Roger Penske
Wins: 5
Top 10: 18

Rusty Wallace

Rusty Wallace, now in his second season with Ford, was strong as always on the short tracks, collecting victories at spring Martinsville (seen here) and summer Bristol. He also won at Sears Point and added big-track victories at Michigan and Pocono. But all was not entirely well, as Rusty and team president Don Miller continued to wrestle with their engine program, moving personnel in and out. Wallace had six DNFs in 1996, most of them engine-related, negating the five victories and leaving him seventh in points. At Martinsville, Rusty outran Ernie Irvan and Jeff Gordon.

8th

Car No.: 4
Make & Model:
  Chevrolet Monte Carlo
Team Owner:
  Larry McClure
Wins: 2
Top 10: 10

Sterling Marlin

The name Sterling Marlin brings to mind the big, fast tracks, where, as Marlin said, he could "put the pedal down and let 'er eat." Runt Pittman, Morgan-McClure's engine magician, continued to supply power at the restricted tracks, and Sterling responded with victories at Talladega in April (shown here) and Daytona in July. The team was only fair elsewhere, with 10 top fives counterweighted with six DNFs, but Sterling nevertheless made his second-best points finish of the decade. In the reprise at Talladega in July, Sterling was caught in the big wreck (Lap 117) which also took out Dale Earnhardt and Terry Labonte.

Bobby Hamilton

Bobby Hamilton, hired on by declining Petty Enterprises in 1995, helped stabilize the organization in 1996, and Hamilton's victory at Phoenix in November was one of the very heartening events of the season. Hamilton had been closing in on success, finishing third on the flat half-mile at Martinsville in September. On the loopy, flat mile at Phoenix, Hamilton held off Mark Martin and Terry Labonte (driving with a broken wrist) to give Petty Enterprises its first win since 1983—Richard's 200th. The Phoenix win was Hamilton's first, and it helped him to ninth in points, his (and Petty's) best of the decade.

Car No.: 43
Make & Model: Pontiac Grand Prix
Team Owner: Richard Petty
Wins: 1
Top 10: 11

Car No.: 28
Make & Model: Ford Thunderbird
Team Owner: Robert Yates
Wins: 2
Top 10: 16

Ernie Irvan

The story of Robert Yates' No. 28 car was the drama of the decade, and Ernie Irvan, nearly killed at Michigan in August 1994, opened another act by returning full-time to the car in 1996, completing a medical miracle. The highlights, of course, were Irvan's first post-return victory at New Hampshire in July and a follow-up win at Richmond in September, eliminating doubts about Irvan's fitness to race. Normally excellent on the road courses, Irvan encountered off-course trouble at Sears Point in May, finishing 42nd, 13 laps down. Irvan and teammate Dale Jarrett finished one-two at New Hampshire.

Bobby Labonte

In his second year with Joe Gibbs Racing, Bobby Labonte began to establish a reputation as a cool, steady competitor, winning at least one race each year with Gibbs through the 1990s. The team, led by Jimmy Makar, continued to form around Labonte, 32, in 1996. Bobby's one victory came at Atlanta in November, bringing on a memorable celebration with Bobby as race winner and older brother Terry as season champion—Terry clinching by finishing fifth. At the New Hampshire race in July (shown here), Bobby qualified third but ran into trouble midway, finishing 31st.

Car No.: 18
Make & Model: Chevrolet Monte Carlo
Team Owner: Joe Gibbs
Wins: 1
Top 10: 14

12th

Car No.: 25
Make & Model:
Chevrolet Monte Carlo
Team Owner:
Rick Hendrick
Wins: 0
Top 10: 10

Ken Schrader

Ken Schrader turned 41 in 1996 and was in his eighth year with Hendrick Motorsports. He had won three races with Hendrick (none since 1991) and had slipped in points in 1995 (from fourth to 17th). The 1996 season opened with a bang, Schrader finishing a strong third (behind Dale Jarrett and Dale Earnhardt) in the Daytona 500. Unfortunately for Kenny, that was the best the team could do, with nine other top 10s adding up to 12th in the final standings. In September, Schrader finally made up his mind to leave the No. 25 team and sign on for 1997 with Andy Petree.

13th

Car No.: 99
Make & Model:
Ford Thunderbird
Team Owner:
Jack Roush
Wins: 0
Top 10: 12

Jeff Burton

Jack Roush drafted Jeff Burton out of the faltering Stavola team and put him to work with his new, Exide-sponsored No. 99 team for 1996, under Buddy Parrott's tutorship. Burton, hard-working and methodical, quickly earned Roush's respect and by mid year was considered close to par with veteran Mark Martin in the organization. It took Burton a year to learn how to win within the Roush system, although he scored highly by finishing fifth in the Daytona 500 (pictured here). Burton's best run of the year came in September at Richmond in his native state, where he ran a strong third behind winner Ernie Irvan and Jeff Gordon.

14th

Michael Waltrip

By the end of 1995, Michael Waltrip and Chuck Rider, his boss for eight years, agreed it was time for a change. Michael and Rider's Bahari team had been a steady, mid range team through the early 1990s but had never won. Likeable Waltrip quickly was adopted by old friends Eddie and Len Wood—the younger Wood brothers, now increasingly in charge of the ancient family operation. Michael responded with a cameo victory in The Winston all-star game, but his best finish in a real race was fifth. At Darlington in April (seen here), Waltrip finished 29th, 16 laps down.

Car No.: 21
Make & Model: Ford Thunderbird
Team Owner: Chuck Rider
Wins: 0
Top 10: 11

15th

Car No.: 23
Make & Model: Ford Thunderbird
Team Owner: Travis Carter
Wins: 0
Top 10: 9

Jimmy Spencer

Spencer and the Travis Carter/R.J. Reynolds team showed marginal improvement in 1996, rising to 15th in points with nine top 10s and a best of fourth. Carter's cars continued to carry the controversial Joe Camel logo, and some believed R.J. Reynolds preferred that its No. 23 cars stay just visible enough (which was very likely, with the purple-and-yellow paint on the No. 23 Fords), and not too much in the foreground, with U.S. government rulings on tobacco advertising then pending. Spencer was pretty much in the background at Martinsville in September, finishing a quiet 19th, three laps down.

16th

Car No.: 16
Make & Model: Ford Thunderbird
Team Owner: Jack Roush
Wins: 0
Top 10: 7

Ted Musgrave

After a brief brush with championship racing in 1995, Ted Musgrave tumbled in 1996, displaced somewhat by the arrival of Jeff Burton into the Jack Roush stable. From seventh in points in 1995, Musgrave fell to 16th in 1996, and results declined after a third place at Richmond in March, Musgrave's best of the season. The spring Darlington race (shown here) was encouraging, with all three Roush cars showing in the top 10—Mark Martin sixth, Musgrave seventh, and Burton 10th. Musgrave's Family Channel/Primestar sponsorship was one of the early information-age trade-ins with NASCAR, representing a movement which lasted into the next decade.

Car No.: 7
Make & Model:
Chevrolet Monte Carlo
Team Owner: Geoff Bodine
Wins: 1
Top 10: 6

Geoff Bodine

Geoff Bodine, always up his own tree, set a singular course at Watkins Glen in August and stuck to it. The result was his first victory since the Hoosier invasion of 1994 and his last of the decade. Bodine had decided beforehand to make just two pit stops in the 90-lap race, the natural interval coming at 35 laps. He thus skipped a pit stop during an early caution; with the rest of the leaders pitting. Seldom has a set battle plan played so easily into one man's hands. Bodine needed only two pit stops and coasted to an easy victory over Terry Labonte and Mark Martin.

Car No.: 1
Make & Model:
Pontiac Grand Prix
Team Owner:
Richard Jackson
Wins: 0
Top 10: 5

Rick Mast

U.S. Tobacco, long time sponsor of the Richard Jackson team, drew in its horns somewhat in 1996, backing only the No. 33 team of Leo Jackson/Andy Petree. Richard Jackson (Leo's brother) and long time driver Rick Mast replaced their U.S. Tobacco offerings by picking up partial sponsorship from Hooters, which had had starburst successes with Alan Kulwicki (1992 championship) and Loy Allen (1994 Daytona 500 pole), but Richard's team gradually became unhooked. Mast gave it all he had, finishing a best of fourth at Martinsville in September. Jackson began to cut back after 1996, and Mast had a new situation in 1997.

19th

Car No.: 75
Make & Model: Ford Thunderbird
Team Owner: Butch Mock
Wins: 0
Top 10: 5

Morgan Shepherd

After four decent years with the Wood Brothers, Morgan Shepherd, who turned 55 in October 1996, landed with Butch Mock's No. 75 team, replacing hard-luck Todd Bodine. Shepherd had driven for Mock during Butch's previous Rahmoc incarnation in 1989; Mock had fielded winning cars for Neil Bonnett in the 1980s. The new association with Shepherd was not particularly fruitful, with Morgan managing five top 10s and 19th in points for hopeful sponsor Remington. North Wilkesboro (shown here) was Morgan's "home" track; he grew up 20 miles from the old oval. He finished 27th, four laps down, in April.

20th

Ricky Craven

Ricky Craven's 1996 season began brightly, with third places at Rockingham and Darlington (pictured here), and he also brought home two pole trophies. The young man from Maine and genial car owner Larry Hedrick were on their way up. A frightening crash at Talladega in April changed the picture, and Craven also was caught in a bad wreck at Charlotte in May. They could have been contenders, Craven and Hedrick, but events conspired against them. Toward the end of the year, Craven decided to accept an offer from *Hendrick* Motorsports, leaving Hedrick to fish on his own.

Car No.: 41
Make & Model: Chevrolet Monte Carlo
Team Owner: Larry Hedrick
Wins: 0
Top 10: 5

21st

Johnny Benson

Replacing Michael Waltrip in Chuck Rider's No. 30 cars was Johnny Benson, 1995 Busch Series champion. Even with the adjustment to a new team, new tracks, and new machinery, Benson was one of the year's pleasant surprises. He won the pole in March at Atlanta (the team's first since 1991), then in the summer pulled off fifth place at Pocono and seventh at Michigan, down the road from his home in Grand Rapids. Benson ended up 21st in points and earned Rookie of the Year. At Charlotte in May (shown here), Benson was victim of a violent crash in Turn 2. More shaken than hurt, he finished 38th.

Car No.: 30
Make & Model: Pontiac Grand Prix
Team Owner: Chuck Rider
Wins: 0
Top 10: 6

22nd

Car No.: 8
Make & Model:
Ford Thunderbird
Team Owner:
Kenny Bernstein
Wins: 0
Top 10: 1

Hut Stricklin

Drag-racing star Kenny Bernstein cashed out of NASCAR after 1995, and driver Hut Stricklin, career in limbo, signed on with the Stavola Brothers' team. The cars were no better than average, but Hut exceeded expectations a few times, most notably at Darlington's Southern 500, where he led the most laps before yielding to Jeff Gordon at the finish. The second place at Darlington was Stricklin's best of the season. Martinsville (seen here) had not been one of Hut's good tracks, and in the September race at the old half-mile, he finished 25th, eight laps behind winner Gordon.

23rd

Car No.: 9
Make & Model:
Ford Thunderbird
Team Owner: Harry Melling
Wins: 0
Top 10: 2

Lake Speed

Things got neither better nor worse for Lake Speed and the Melling Racing team in 1996. Speed, 47, collected two top-10 finishes, just as he had in 1995. Wrecks and other misfortunes, however, resulted in nine DNFs. In the final counting, Speed was 23rd in points, exactly where he had finished the year before. Speed, a former world karting champion, was a skilled road-racer, although he never really had the equipment to show it. At Sears Point in May (shown here), Speed drove to 16th place, on the lead lap, which probably was about as well as the car could do.

24th

Brett Bodine

Brett Bodine followed older brother Geoff's lead in 1996, becoming owner-driver. He inherited (for a reported $4.5 million) the remains of Junior Johnson's No. 11 team, and the Lowe's sponsorship, as Johnson retired after 1995. The team had not been that good in 1995, and with restructuring and debt retirement, it struggled through 1996. Bodine, however, did a better-than-expected job just making it through his first year, with one top 10, only three DNFs, and 24th place in points. The New Hampshire race in July was about average, with Brett finishing a safe 16th, one lap down.

Car No.: 11
Make & Model: Ford Thunderbird
Team Owner: Brett Bodine
Wins: 0
Top 10: 1

Car No.: 15
Make & Model: Ford Thunderbird
Team Owner: Bud Moore
Wins: 0
Top 10: 3

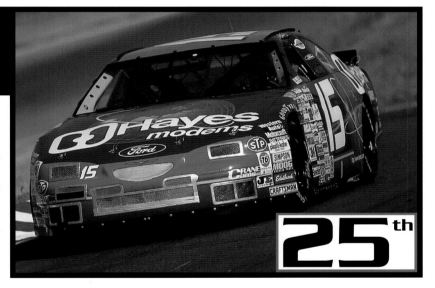

25th

Wally Dallenbach Jr.

Both driver Wally Dallenbach and owner Bud Moore were scrambling in 1996, with Dallenbach trying to rescue his career and Moore hoping to stay in business, after the departure of long time backer Ford. Dallenbach, out of a job after 1995, went to Daytona in Moore's unsponsored No. 15 and made the race, helping clinch a deal with Hayes, maker of computer modems. That did not help much, although Wally, excellent as usual on road circuits, ran third at Sears Point in May. He had only two other top 10s, however, and at the end of the year Moore mothballed the team for lack of sponsorship.

26th

Jeremy Mayfield

Jeremy Mayfield kept a smile on his face during a very unusual 1996 season. He began the season with Cale Yarborough's team, which had new sponsorship from RCA, and results appeared to improve. Mayfield ran fourth at Martinsville, best of his career and Yarborough's best since 1987, then added his first career pole at Talladega in July. But due to a web of personality difficulties, Mayfield went to Michael Kranefuss' Kmart team in September, in what amounted to a straight swap for driver John Andretti. On the road course at Sonoma, California, in May (seen here), Jeremy came in 32nd, a lap down.

Car No.: 98
Make & Model: Ford Thunderbird
Team Owner: Cale Yarborough
Wins: 0
Top 10: 2

27th

Car No.: 42
Make & Model: Pontiac Grand Prix
Team Owner: Felix Sabates
Wins: 0
Top 10: 2

Kyle Petty

Through most of the 1990s, Kyle Petty, driving for Felix Sabates, had been at least a threat, winning six races and finishing fifth in points in 1992 and 1993. By 1996, Kyle's eighth year with the Cuban tycoon, he and the team had lost direction. The 42 team reduced their DNF count from 10 to four, but Petty managed just two top-10 finishes, fewest of his Winston Cup career, which dated to 1981. At North Wilkesboro in April, Petty brought his battered Pontiac home 30th, six laps down. By fall, Petty revealed he would leave Sabates to rejoin the family operation in 1997.

Car No.: 81
Make & Model: Ford Thunderbird
Team Owner: Filbert Martocci
Wins: 0
Top 10: 2

28th

Kenny Wallace

After his failed rookie try with Felix Sabates in 1993, Wallace returned to the Busch Series with owner Filbert Martocci and had notable success. With sponsor Square D, Martocci and Wallace moved in the direction of Winston Cup and entered full-time in 1996. That may have been a case of too much too soon, as the Martocci team never really seemed to get to its feet, with two top 10s, nine DNFs, and 28th place in points. Wallace had a decent weekend at Darlington in the spring, qualifying seventh and bringing the car home 17th, two laps down. Note contact marks on Darlington's infamous third-turn wall.

Car No.: 17
Make & Model: Chevrolet Monte Carlo
Team Owner: Darrell Waltrip
Wins: 0
Top 10: 2

29th

Darrell Waltrip

Darrell Waltrip, at 49, had slowed a step or two, especially on the bigger tracks, but he continued to insist that once he got his team and cars in order, he still had it in him to win. There may have been something in that, but by 1996, Waltrip seemed unable to put all the right parts together. He finished the year with just two top 10s and in 29th position in points, the worst of his career. Waltrip's best runs, as always, came on the short ovals, and at Bristol in August (shown here), Waltrip came in 11th, first car a lap down.

Car No.: 94
Make & Model: Ford Thunderbird
Team Owner: Bill Elliott
Wins: 0
Top 10: 6

30th

Bill Elliott

Bill Elliott's season came crashing down when an airborne wreck at Talladega in April left him with a broken hip, requiring surgery and rehabilitation. Bill missed the next seven races. This kind of misfortune seemed to mark Bill's career as owner-driver; every time he'd seem to have the team pointed straight, he'd come across a patch of rocky road. Elliott isn't likely to boast about his results at half-mile Martinsville, but the April race in 1996 was encouraging. Bill qualified third, his best of the season, and made the best of a brutal afternoon in finishing 13th, three laps down.

Car No.: 37
Make & Model: Ford Thunderbird
Team Owner: Jeremy Mayfield
Wins: 0
Top 10: 3

John Andretti

Andretti came to the newly formed Michael Kranefuss team in 1995 with high hopes, but by 1996 internal trouble led to personnel shake ups, with crew chief Tim Brewer going over the side in the summer. From there, Andretti could do little more than watch the clock, and after the Richmond race in September he was "traded" to Cale Yarborough's team for driver Jeremy Mayfield. In 22 races with Kranefuss, Andretti failed to finish 10 times, making for a miserable season. The Sears Point race in May was one of the team's better days, with John finishing 11th.

Chapter 8

1997

Taking Flight

JEFF GORDON NOTCHES ANOTHER ONE

By 1997, there was little doubt that driver Jeff Gordon, crew chief Ray Evernham, and team owner Rick Hendrick were onto something special. At the time they had 15 poles and 19 NASCAR Winston Cup victories in only 124 starts spanning four seasons. Among their more impressive victories: a Brickyard 400, a Coca-Cola 600, a DieHard 500, two Pepsi Southern 500s, and five short-track triumphs.

So it was no surprise when Gordon went into his fifth season favored to win another championship. And why not? He had improved from 14th as a rookie to eighth in his second year, then won his first title in 1995. Despite even-better stats in 1996, he finished second to Hendrick Motorsports teammate Terry Labonte.

In many respects, Gordon outdid himself en route to the 1997 Winston Cup. Let us count the ways:

He won his first Daytona 500, leading a one-two-three sweep of Hendrick-owned Chevrolet Monte Carlos featuring teammates Terry Labonte and Ricky Craven. It

Jeff Gordon

Could life get better for Jeff Gordon? No question. Gordon opened 1997 by winning the Busch Clash and the Daytona 500, and the season shot upward from there. Gordon collected 10 victories for the second year in a row and won his second series championship at 26. The Daytona 500 (shown here) was beyond imagination. With car owner Rick Hendrick stricken with leukemia and in legal difficulty, Gordon led a one-two-three sweep of Hendrick cars across the finish line under caution, with Terry Labonte second and Ricky Craven third. Not even NASCAR could have written that script.

Car No.: 24
Make & Model: Chevrolet Monte Carlo
Team Owner: Rick Hendrick
Wins: 10
Top 10: 23

was the first one-two-three finish by the same organization in Daytona 500 history;

He won the inaugural 500-miler at the California Speedway near Fontana. It was the first major NASCAR victory in his home state and the first Cup race in southern California since the 1988 mid summer event at Riverside;

He got his first road-racing victory, winning at Watkins Glen in August. He'd been top five in four previous road races before winning on the only kind of track he'd failed to conquer;

He became only the second driver (the first was Bill Elliott in 1985) to win the Winston Million bonus. He did it by winning the Daytona 500 in February, the Coca-Cola 600 at Charlotte in May, and the Labor Day weekend Pepsi Southern 500 at Darlington;

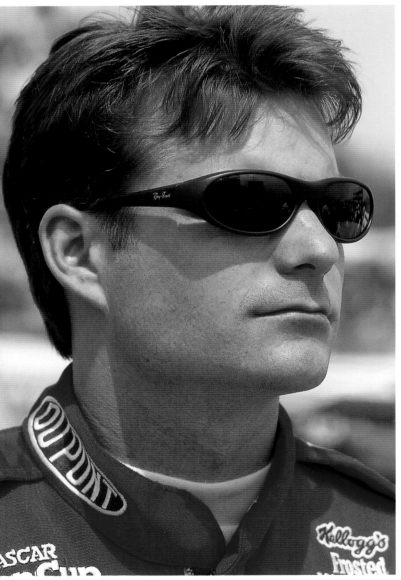

With 10 wins, including the first two races of the season at Daytona and Rockingham, Jeff Gordon claimed his second championship of the decade in 1997.

He had a pair of two-race winning streaks and never lost more than four straight until a seven-race skid that closed the season. He had three top fives and another top 10 during that spell so it wasn't exactly like he was stinking up the joint. All told, he won a pole, three outside poles, 10 races, had a dozen more top fives and another finish between sixth and 10th;

He won his second Winston Cup, beating Dale Jarrett by 14 points in the fourth-closest (at the time) finish in NASCAR history. Those 14 points were the closest anyone had been to Gordon since he took the lead by winning at Darlington over Labor Day weekend;

And, not insignificantly, he topped the $6 million mark in official NASCAR and R.J. Reynolds Inc. earnings. Not only was he the first driver to top $6 million, he's also the only driver to go over $4 million in a season.

"Winning on short tracks, medium-sized speedways, superspeedways, and a road course makes this a special year," Gordon said during the 1997 awards banquet in New York City. "Winning the championship on top of that makes it a career year. Losing to Terry in 1996 only made this team stronger. We've run for the Cup late in the season with nothing to lose [1996] and now we've run for the Cup late in a season with a lot to lose [1997]. We faced some bad luck and adversity this year, but came through it a stronger and better team. I guess that's why our motto is, 'Refuse to Lose'."

Gordon's season began with his first victory in the Daytona 500. It was an uplifting weekend for Hendrick, who stayed back home in North Carolina because of treatment for leukemia. He watched on TV as Gordon gave him his third Daytona 500 victory as an owner, coming after Geoff Bodine in 1986 and Darrell Waltrip three years later.

Gordon won a week later at Rockingham, was fourth at Richmond the week after that, finished a career-worst 42nd at Atlanta, and was third at Darlington. He crashed hard to a DNF 30th in the inaugural race at Texas, rallied to win Bristol and Martinsville on back-to-back weekends in April, was second on the road course at Sonoma, and fifth at Talladega. He capped the spring portion of the schedule by winning the Memorial Day weekend night race at Charlotte. He was second in points after Charlotte.

For Gordon, the middle third of the season opened with a 26th at Dover, a victory at Pocono, fifth at Michigan, first at Fontana, 21st in the mid summer race at Daytona Beach, 23rd at Loudon, second at Pocono, then fourth at Indianapolis. He won at Watkins Glen, was second at Michigan, and a wreck-related DNF 35th in the August night race at Bristol. After 22 of 32 races, Gordon was still second in points, this time 13 behind Mark Martin.

Gordon took the lead for good by winning the Labor Day weekend race at Darlington. (Martin finished eighth and dropped to second in points, 25 behind.) The victory brought a $1 million bonus from R.J. Reynolds, a reward for having won the Daytona 500, Coca-Cola 600, and Pepsi Southern 500. Gordon and Ford driver Jeff Burton roughed each other up the final two laps, each trying to win NASCAR's oldest race and one trying to win an extra million. "To me, the thing about this is accomplishing something that only one other person has ever done," Gordon said afterward. "This is just unbelievable."

Six days later, he built his lead by winning at Richmond, where Martin was ninth. Gordon kept building by winning and leading the most laps at Loudon in September, then was seventh at Dover, fourth at Martinsville, and fifth at Charlotte in early October. When he left that 500-miler 125 points ahead of Martin, most NASCAR-watchers figured his third Cup was virtually assured.

Everything seemed to be going Gordon's way. He was a wreck-related 35th at Talladega, but Martin was a wreck-related 30th. Gordon was fourth at Rockingham (two positions ahead of Martin), then closed the 1997 season with 17th places at Phoenix and Atlanta. (Martin was sixth at Phoenix and third at Atlanta.) Gordon's late-season struggles allowed Jarrett to close from well behind to within 14 points at the finish.

The margin is deceiving because Gordon either finished top five (22 times in 32 starts) or outside the top 10 (nine times). Among his poor finishes: 42nd at Atlanta and 30th at Fort Worth in the spring; and 26th at Dover, 21st at Daytona Beach, 23rd at Loudon, and 35th at Bristol in the summer. The late-season swoon saw his points lead shrink from 125 to 14 points in just four races.

Jarrett's seven-victory season for Robert Yates and the No. 88 Quality Care Ford team was more steady than spectacular. He won at Atlanta and Darlington in the spring, then at Pocono and Bristol in the summer. He was strong in the fall: victories in the night race at Richmond, then Charlotte and Phoenix. He went into the finale at Atlanta down by 77 points, but his runner-up finish behind Bobby Labonte wasn't enough to overhaul Gordon.

In finishing second, Jarrett didn't have as many top fives as Gordon (22 to 20), but each had 23 top 10s. Of no small consequence is this stat: Gordon had 10 more lap-leader bonus points than Jarrett, 155 to 145. A lap or two here or there by one or both drivers likely would have produced an altogether different champion.

The heartbreak story of the title chase was Martin and the Jack Roush No. 6 Valvoline team. Martin hung tough all year, bouncing between second and third place five times in the spring and early summer. He was No. 1 after the August night race at Bristol, but went into Phoenix eight races later down by 125 points. His seventh at Phoenix brought him to within 87 with one race remaining—but he was third and not second. (The 29-point difference between one-two and two-three remains the closest one-two-three finish in Cup history.)

The surprise driver of the year—hands down, no question about it—was Jeff Burton. He won three races in his

Jeff Burton won the inaugural race at Texas Motor Speedway in April, one of three checkered flags for Burton's Roush-owned Ford in 1997.

second year with owner Jack Roush and his No. 99 Exide Ford team. Burton had more top fives than in his previous 90 career starts *combined* and won more money than in his previous three full Cup seasons. He finished fourth in points, but never was a serious championship contender.

He won the inaugural Texas race in the spring, then New Hampshire in the summer, and got a gift at Martinsville in the fall. Rusty Wallace was going to win the 500-lapper until jumping a late-race restart. When officials black-flagged Wallace for a stop-and-go penalty, Burton inherited the lead for only the second time all afternoon. After leading the most laps, a seething Wallace finished a disappointing and somewhat controversial 15th.

Earnhardt was fifth in points, his seventh top five in the past eight years. He was winless—his first 0-fer showing since 1981—but had seven top fives and nine finishes between sixth and 10th for Richard Childress and his No. 3 Goodwrench Chevrolet team. Nobody knew it yet, but fifth would be Earnhardt's best finish for the rest of the 1990s.

Bill Elliott was 0-for-32 in 1997, with only five top-fives on the year. He finished eighth in total points but remained a fan favorite.

Sixth-ranked Terry Labonte won the fall race at Talladega and had 19 other top-10 finishes for Rick Hendrick. His younger brother, seventh-ranked Bobby, won the finale near Atlanta and had 17 other top 10s for coach-turned-owner Joe Gibbs. Bill Elliott was 0-for-32 (only 14 top-10 finishes) in his own cars, ninth-ranked Rusty Wallace won the spring race at Richmond for Roger Penske, and 10th-ranked Ken Schrader had only seven top 10s for owner Andy Petree.

Four victories went to drivers outside the final top 10. Ernie Irvan (14th in the standings) won the first Michigan race; Bobby Hamilton (16th) won the fall race at Rockingham; Ricky Rudd (17th) won the summer races at Dover and Indianapolis (by far, the biggest victory of his career); and John Andretti (23rd) won the mid summer race at Daytona Beach.

The Rookie of the Year campaign was fairly one-sided. Mike Skinner qualified for 31 races, won two poles, and had three top 10s for team owner Richard Childress. That easily topped the efforts of brothers Jeff and David Green, and Indy car refugee Robby Gordon. Skinner was the first "graduate" of NASCAR's Craftsman Truck Series to move up and get a quality Cup ride.

NASCAR continued to expand its schedule and add races. Two new tracks came aboard in 1997, each with one race. The 1.5-mile, high-banked Texas Motor Speedway

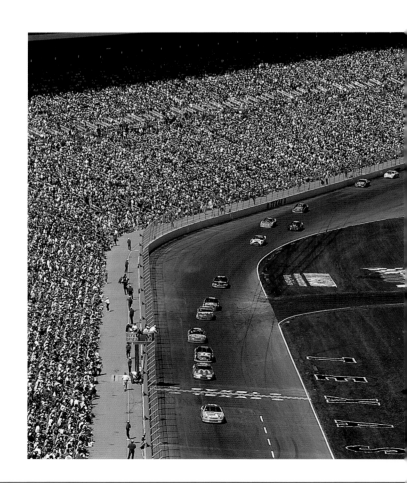

near Dallas–Fort Worth had a spring date. The 2-mile California Speedway at Fontana had a mid summer date. And 1997 also saw New Hampshire International Speedway at Loudon add a fall race.

Bruton Smith's inaugural Cup date in Texas and Bob Bahre's fall Cup date in New Hampshire came at the expense of North Wilkesboro. Smith and Bahre each bought 50 percent of the track, then closed it down and moved its dates to their larger, more profitable tracks.

There was an off-the-track tragedy even before the season began. On January 14, five weeks before the Daytona 500, T. Wayne Robertson died in a boating accident during a hunting trip into southern Louisiana. The 48-year-old was president of Sports Marketing Enterprises, a major division of R.J. Reynolds Tobacco Co. His department supported the Winston brand's sponsorship of NASCAR and National Hot Rod Racing Association (NHRA) racing, and the Vantage brand's affiliation with the Senior Professional Golf Association Tour event.

Robertson helped create the 1985 Winston Million program and The Winston all-star race, and the NHRA's Winston Invitational all-star race in 1989. He also organized the inaugural Winston Cup Preview, an annual pre season show bringing cars, drivers, and fans together in Winston-Salem, North Carolina. Proceeds from the preview go to the nearby Brenner's Children's Hospital.

Every day and in every way, NASCAR still misses him.

Bruton Smith's 1.5-mile Texas Motor Speedway opened with the Interstate Batteries 500 on April 6, 1997. This state-of-the-art racing facility would host a number of racing events in the central Texas market.

Bruton Smith's New Texas Track

Bruton Smith has never learned to slow down and proceed with caution. He ran wide-open in 1959 and 1960 while he and Curtis Turner (with help from the Teamsters Union) built and opened Charlotte Motor Speedway one step ahead of their creditors. After surviving several financial crisises in the 1960s, the ever-innovative businessman resurfaced in the early 1970s and began turning Charlotte Motor Speedway into a 1.5-mile showplace of motor sports, housing, and business.

But the man is nothing if not ambitious. For him, ruling one kingdom simply wasn't challenging enough. In the early 1990s he began buying, refurbishing, and expanding some of the country's best-known, privately owned speedways. In addition to Charlotte, his holdings grew to include Atlanta, Bristol, Las Vegas, and Sears Point. (The other NASCAR tracks of the time were owned by International Speedway Corp., Penske Motorsports, or by families too loyal to the France family to sell to Smith.)

Even *that* buying spree didn't satisfy Smith. In 1995 he broke ground on a 1.5-mile, Charlotte-look-alike track north of the Dallas-Fort Worth area. Even though NASCAR hadn't guaranteed any race dates, he nevertheless aimed to open in the spring of 1997. To ensure he had something to run, he bought half-interest in the venerable North Wilkesboro (North Carolina) Speedway, then promptly announced plans to move its 1997 spring race to Texas Motor Speedway.

Later, with NASCAR's "encouragement," Bob Bahre bought the other half-interest in North Wilkesboro Speedway. With the track's spring date bound for Texas, it was no shock when Bahre said he'd move its 1997 fall date to his New Hampshire International Speedway. (Although the men share ownership of the closed-down track, they hardly consider themselves partners.)

Traditionalists mourned the loss of North Wilkesboro, one of two tracks (the other is Martinsville Speedway) that hosted NASCAR races in 1949. Pragmatists, however, argue that North Wilkesboro was close to Martinsville, Bristol, and Charlotte, and that the marketplace couldn't support four tracks, each with spring and fall races only weeks apart.

Texas Motor Speedway was one of two tracks that opened in 1997. The 2-mile, Penske-owned California Speedway opened in June, two years after groundbreaking. The site at Fontana is close to Ontario, former home of the 2.5-mile Ontario Motor Speedway that hosted NASCAR and Indy-car races from 1970 through 1980. Fontana filled the desperate need of southern California fans for something to replace Riverside (California) International Raceway, which had closed in 1988.

Car No.: 88
Make & Model:
Ford Thunderbird
Team Owner:
Robert Yates
Wins: 7
Top 10: 23

2nd

Dale Jarrett

Dale Jarrett's 1997 season would have been good enough for a championship in about any other year. In his second year with Robert Yates, and with equipment and manpower to match his determination, Jarrett knocked out seven victories and three poles, and his points total was higher than that of any champion since 1987. Unfortunately for Jarrett, Jeff Gordon was a shade better, although Jarrett finished just 14 points behind with a strong finish. At Martinsville in the fall (seen here), Jarrett finished 16th, stalling his fast start. He finished 27th or worse in three of the next four races, and that was costly.

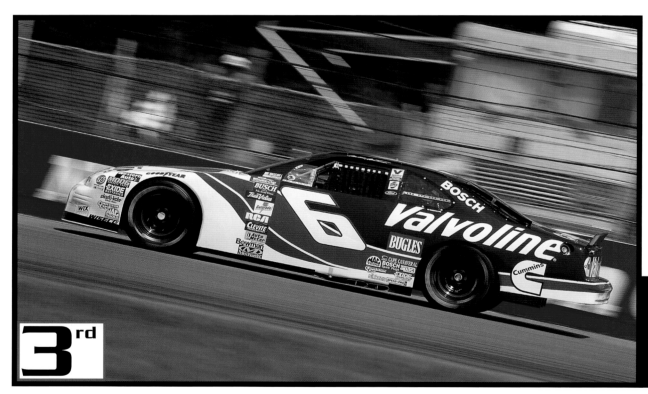

Car No.: 6
Make & Model:
Ford Thunderbird
Team Owner:
Jack Roush
Wins: 4
Top 10: 24

3rd

Mark Martin

Mark Martin's puzzling losing streak, which lasted all of 1996, came to an end at Sears Point in May. The streak had grown to 42 races before Mark's dominating run at the northern California road course. Martin led all but eight of the 74 laps and beat Jeff Gordon home by more than half a second. As if to convince himself the worst was over, Martin followed the next week by winning at Talladega. He added trophies at Michigan in August and Dover in September, and ended up just 29 points behind winner Jeff Gordon in one of the closest three-way battles in history.

Car No.: 99
Make & Model:
Ford Thunderbird
Team Owner:
Jack Roush
Wins: 3
Top 10: 18

4th

Jeff Burton

Virginia's Jeff Burton delivered quickly on the promise he'd shown in 1996, his first year with owner Jack Roush. Jeff deftly handled the challenges of the controversial new Texas track for his first career victory, then added victories on the tight flat tracks at New Hampshire (July) and Martinsville (September). Suddenly, Burton and the No. 99 team were forces to be reckoned with. Young Frank Stoddard was graduated to crew chief, with Buddy Parrott moving to general manager, and old buddies Stoddard and Burton clicked right off. At New Hampshire (shown here) Burton beat Dale Earnhardt by more than 5 seconds.

Car No.: 3
Make & Model:
Chevrolet Monte Carlo
Team Owner:
Richard Childress
Wins: 0
Top 10: 16

5th

Dale Earnhardt

Like Mark Martin the year before, Earnhardt weathered a strange dry spell through all of 1997, this in his first year with superstar crew chief Larry McReynolds, hired away from Robert Yates. The losing streak eventually reached 59 races before Earnhardt broke it with the victory he'd coveted for 20 years, the Daytona 500, in 1998. Despite the drought, Earnhardt recorded four second-places and not a single DNF, keeping him a respectable fifth in points. Two of Earnhardt's two-spots were behind young Jeff Burton, at New Hampshire and at fall Martinsville (shown here). This also was the year of Earnhardt's strange black out at Darlington, never fully explained.

6th

Terry Labonte

Although not as dominating as in the previous year's race, Terry Labonte and crew shrewdly maneuvered to second place in the Daytona 500 (seen here), bracketed by teammates Jeff Gordon (winner) and Ricky Craven (third place). Labonte thus bid to repeat as champion, and he led in points to mid summer. Disasters at Pocono and Indianapolis, then a horrible streak in September, knocked him off the top perch and out of contention. His one win came at Talladega in October, where he led all but eight of the last 65 laps. Terry drafted by Ken Schrader with two laps to go to seal the win.

Car No.: 5
Make & Model:
Chevrolet Monte Carlo
Team Owner:
Rick Hendrick
Wins: 1
Top 10: 12

7th

Car No.: 18
Make & Model: Pontiac Grand Prix
Team Owner: Joe Gibbs
Wins: 1
Top 10: 18

Bobby Labonte

Despite a switch to Pontiac bodies in 1997, Labonte and crew remained solid and steady and continued to gain, improving from 11th to seventh in points. Labonte needed a whole season to find his one victory, at Atlanta in the season finale (repeating his feat of 1996), but he backed that up with three seconds, five other top fives, and only one DNF. He also won three poles. Labonte started fourth at Phoenix in October (pictured) but struggled to 23rd, two laps down. Bobby earned his single biggest payday to date by finishing second at Indianapolis in August, cashing a check for $242,275.

8th

Bill Elliott

Bill Elliott basically had to write off 1996 after crippling injuries from his crash at Talladega. He started off right in 1997, nearly winning the Daytona 500 before being ambushed by a pack of Hendrick Chevrolets at the finish, but his year went flat thereafter until July. Elliott was as low as 17th in points before pulling out of the dive with a sixth place at New Hampshire (seen here), starting a streak of five-straight top 10s. He won the pole at Richmond in September, and despite a broken clutch which left him 36th in the closer at Atlanta, Elliott ended up eighth in points.

Car No.: 94
Make & Model: Ford Thunderbird
Team Owner: Bill Elliott
Wins: 0
Top 10: 14

Rusty Wallace

An unbelievable plague of engine failures contributed to 11 DNFs for Rusty Wallace in 1997 as the team searched vainly for reliable power. Wallace, in the course, recorded just one victory (at Richmond in March) and continued to slide down the ladder from his decade-high of second in points in 1993—third, fifth, seven, and ninth in the following years. Wallace also qualified poorly in 1997, needing five provisionals, the first coming at the Atlanta race (shown here) in March. Atlanta affirmed a pattern of misfortune, with Wallace getting caught in a wreck on Lap 268 (of 328), finishing 31st.

Car No.: 2
Make & Model: Ford Thunderbird
Team Owner: Roger Penske
Wins: 1
Top 10: 12

9th

Ken Schrader

Ken Schrader suddenly made up his mind he'd had enough of the Hendrick Motorsports camp late in 1996, so he joined budding car owner Andy Petree, who had inherited the old Leo Jackson/Harry Gant team in 1996. All things considered, the new combination worked pretty well. Schrader did not win, but two fourth places in the fall (Talladega and Phoenix) and two poles (both at New Hampshire) were encouraging, and Schrader gave Petree his best points finish of the decade, 10th. Schrader was respectable at Darlington in the fall, starting fifth and finishing 10th.

10th

Car No.: 33
Make & Model: Chevrolet Monte Carlo
Team Owner: Andy Petree
Wins: 0
Top 10: 8

11th

Johnny Benson

Any doubts about Johnny Benson's talents disappeared in 1997, when Benson guided Chuck Rider's crumbling No. 30 team to 11th in points, after finishing 21st the year before, in his rookie season. It took Benson a few more years to find the right opportunity, but he had made his statement. Benson's best run came at Indianapolis in August, where he ran among the leaders all day and finished seventh. He also won the pole at Michigan two weeks later. Bristol in April (seen here) was not so good. Benson started 33rd, got caught in a wreck on Lap 149, and finished 31st, his worst of the year.

Car No.: 30
Make & Model: Pontiac Grand Prix
Team Owner: Chuck Rider
Wins: 0
Top 10: 8

Car No.: 16
Make & Model:
Ford Thunderbird
Team Owner:
Jack Roush
Wins: 0
Top 10: 8

12th

Ted Musgrave

As usual, the summer tracks were Ted Musgrave's best. He scored sixth at Pocono, fourths at Michigan and California, and second Pocono, sixth at Watkins Glen, and third in the August reprise at Michigan. That made for a great middle third of the season. The first third and the last third were what nailed his shoes to the floor, with only one finish better than 11th through April and only one better than ninth from mid-August on. That one came at Richmond in September (shown here), one of Ted's better tracks. He needed a provisional to start, but he dug in for ninth at the finish.

13th

Jeremy Mayfield

Mayfield, who joined the Michael Kranefuss team late in 1996, served his first full season in 1997 and continued to show a fine balance of: a) taking care of equipment, and b) running to the front. In 28 of the 32 races, Mayfield finished better than he started, with improvements such as 21st to sixth at Daytona, 32nd to ninth at Bristol, 29th to seventh at Martinsville, 25th to fourth at Dover, and 27th to fifth at Pocono. Of course, part of that was that the team did not qualify all that well. At Richmond in September (seen here), Jeremy qualified 16th and finished 10th.

Car No.: 37
Make & Model: Ford Thunderbird
Team Owner: Michael Kranefuss
Wins: 0
Top 10: 8

Ernie Irvan

Beneath the joy accompanying Ernie Irvan's return to racing in 1996, after major injuries in 1994, were underlying personality conflicts. Team owner Robert Yates, under pressure from several directions, revealed in August that Irvan was out and rookie Kenny Irwin was in for 1998. It wasn't that Irvan did badly. Despite a slow start, he finished second at Atlanta, then won from 20th place at Michigan in June. He also won poles for the prestigious Brickyard 400 at Indianapolis in August and at Talladega in October. At Daytona (seen here) he got caught in the Lap 189 wreck which also took out Dale Earnhardt and decided the race.

14th

Car No.: 28
Make & Model: Ford Thunderbird
Team Owner: Robert Yates
Wins: 1
Top 10: 13

Kyle Petty

Kyle Petty was called home in 1997. After nine years with Felix Sabates, Petty welcomed sponsorship from Mattel and took a step back toward the family operation by forming his pe2 team (the "pe" an obedient reference to Petty Enterprises). After a dreadful 1996, Petty seemed to bloom with his own group, which he had assembled by hand. Kyle came on strong toward the end of 1997, with a third at Dover, ninth at Charlotte, seventh at Talladega, ninth at Phoenix, and sixth at Atlanta. At Darlington in the spring (seen here), Kyle started 28th, wrecked, and finished 33rd.

15th

Car No.: 44
Make & Model: Pontiac Grand Prix
Team Owner: Richard Petty
Wins: 0
Top 10: 9

Car No.: 43
Make & Model:
 Pontiac Grand Prix
Team Owner: Richard Petty
Wins: 1
Top 10: 8

16th

Bobby Hamilton

Bobby Hamilton had put Petty Enterprises back in the record books with his victory at Phoenix in 1996. He pulled off another late-season wonder for the Pettys at Rockingham, the team's "home" track, in October 1997, taking the points from another long shot, Ricky Craven, 16 laps from the finish and beating Dale Jarrett by nearly a second. Hamilton added two poles (June Pocono and Phoenix), but he drifted backward in points. Gear failure cost him a shot at Richmond in September (seen here). On good terms, Hamilton left the Pettys after 1997 to join superspeedway master Morgan-McClure.

Car No.: 10
Make & Model:
 Ford Thunderbird
Team Owner:
 Ricky Rudd
Wins: 2
Top 10: 11

17th

Ricky Rudd

Ricky Rudd scored two victories in 1997 (the most for him since 1987), including the lucrative Brickyard 400 at Indianapolis in August (shown here), but the writing had begun to appear on the wall for the Tide-sponsored independent. He increasingly had to put his eggs in one basket, such as Indianapolis, where he won on strategy and mileage, while shorting his efforts elsewhere. Rudd was eighth in points after Indy, then took a nose dive, finishing 28th or worse in seven of the last nine events. At Indy, where he won a career-high $571,000, Rudd beat Bobby Labonte by .18 of a second.

18th

Michael Waltrip

Michael Waltrip and the Wood Brothers—the *new* Wood Brothers—tried again in 1997 and hit on a little bit less than they had in their debut the year before. The younger Woods, Eddie and Len, came out cautiously from under the shadow of founding father Glen Wood and his Hall of Fame brother, Uncle Leonard, and attempted to maneuver the group into the 20th century, if not the 21st. Michael, one of the clan of infield kids (which also included Eddie and Len and Kyle Petty), fit in fine and probably did as well as anyone could have. You'd have to say the Wood boys did too, considering the circumstances.

Car No.: 21
Make & Model: Ford Thunderbird
Team Owner: Wood Brothers
Wins: 0
Top 10: 6

Car No.: 25
Make & Model: Chevrolet Monte Carlo
Team Owner: Rick Hendrick
Wins: 0
Top 10: 7

Ricky Craven

The 1991 NASCAR Busch North champion and 1994 Busch Grand National runner-up started out his promising Winston Cup career with the Larry Hedrick team. He drove to 24th and 20th in the championship in 1995 and 1996. In 1997, Craven earned his dream ride with one of the sport's top teams, Hendrick Motorsports, driving the No. 25 Chevrolet. Craven nailed down an impressive third behind his teammates Terry Labonte and Jeff Gordon at the Daytona 500 to complete a Team Hendrick sweep of the top 3 positions. He followed it up with a third at the October Rockingham race. Unfortunately, Craven's season was cut short by a vicious crash while practicing for the inaugural event at Texas Motor Speedway. During that year, he posted 5 top-5 finishes.

19th

Jimmy Spencer

Jimmy Spencer got off to an awful start in 1997, finishing no better than 22nd through the first six races. The Travis Carter/R.J. Reynolds team had spotty success through the middle third of the season, with seventh places at Talladega and Pocono and fifth on the new California speedway in June. The cars got faster in the fall, at least for qualifying, with Spencer starting ninth at Charlotte, third at Talladega, and second at Phoenix. The races, however, reverted to disaster, with Jimmy making better than 24th just once in the final seven tries. Due to new federal regulations, this was the last year for Joe Camel.

20th

Car No.: 23
Make & Model: Ford Thunderbird
Team Owner: Travis Carter
Wins: 0
Top 10: 4

21st

Car No.: 41
Make & Model:
 Chevrolet Monte Carlo
Team Owner: Gary Bechtel
Wins: 0
Top 10: 6

Steve Grissom

Dogged Steve Grissom, out of a job after Gary Bechtel's team dissolved into chaos, hung around the garages weekly and was there when Larry Hedrick needed a driver with the departure of Ricky Craven. Grissom started with a bang, qualifying No. 2 (next to Mike Skinner) at the Daytona 500. He crashed out early, however. Then, at Rockingham the next week, Grissom qualified a respectable seventh before struggling to 24th, two laps down. He sprinkled in a few good runs, with the cars generally teens at best, finishing fourth at both New Hampshire races and fifth at Martinsville.

22nd

Car No.: 7
Make & Model:
 Ford Thunderbird
Team Owner:
 Geoff Bodine
Wins: 0
Top 10: 10

Geoff Bodine

Geoff Bodine had managed to string along the team he bought from the estate of Alan Kulwicki in 1993, somehow finding sponsorship deals as late as January. QVC, a cable merchandising channel, appeared on the cars in 1997, but the money wasn't adequate, and Bodine finally pitched in the towel in August, selling to businessmen Jim Mattei and John Porter. Bodine, meanwhile, had a wildly inconsistent year. He failed to qualify for three major races—Charlotte, summer Daytona, and the Brickyard—yet finished second at Watkins Glen and set a speed record at reconfigured Atlanta in the fall, topping 197 miles per hour, best-ever on a "non-restricted" track.

23rd

John Andretti

Cale Yarborough's diamond-in-the-rough in 1997 was engine man Tony Santanicola, who quietly had mastered the restrictor plates. That helped boost John Andretti to his first career victory at Daytona in the summer, plus a pole at spring Talladega and the outside pole at Talladega in the fall. Andretti also gained his other two top fives at Talladega, with a fourth in May and a third in October. That could have made for an encouraging year, but results were no better than fair elsewhere. At Richmond in September (shown here), Andretti started 23rd and finished 32nd. As sponsor RCA pulled the plug, John went job hunting.

Car No.: 98
Make & Model: Ford Thunderbird
Team Owner: Cale Yarborough
Wins: 1
Top 10: 3

Ward Burton

Older brother Ward Burton was the first of the Burtons to win, in 1995, but the next was a long time in coming, and 1997 rated as a big disappointment for driver and team. Ward started out fair enough, with eighth in the Daytona 500 and seventh at Texas (where brother Jeff won his first). Summer, however, was a disaster, with Ward finishing 26th or worse in eight straight races. Hope rose toward the end of the year, with Burton running seventh at Richmond (seen here), then following with a pole at Martinsville and three top-10 finishes in the homestretch.

24th

Car No.: 22
Make & Model: Pontiac Grand Prix
Team Owner: Bill Davis
Wins: 0
Top 10: 7

25th

Sterling Marlin

What once had been a potent combination—driver Sterling Marlin and the Morgan-McClure team—had lost steam by 1997, for reasons not clear. Marlin kept his grip at Daytona, finishing fifth in the 500 and fourth in the Pepsi 400 (qualifying second). Elsewhere, the team was only middling, with Marlin needing provisionals to start at Martinsville in April and at New Hampshire in September. Sterling started ninth at Darlington in March (shown here) but sputtered to 32nd at the finish, 15 laps off the pace. The team tumbled from eighth to 25th in points, Sterling's worst of the decade.

Car No.: 4
Make & Model: Chevrolet Monte Carlo
Team Owner: Larry McClure
Wins: 0
Top 10: 6

Darrell Waltrip

By 1997, Darrell Waltrip began to admit that either: a) he wasn't the driver he used to be, or b) that his attempt to carry the load as owner and driver wasn't working. Nevertheless, Waltrip, now 50, held his own, improving three positions in points. He finished a strong fifth at Sears Point in May and at the time was top 15 in points. But his season went in the tank starting at Bristol in the fall, and he hit bottom in failing to qualify for the Charlotte race in October, his first-ever DNS. The March race at Atlanta (pictured here) marked his qualifying high point; he started third and finished 16th.

26th

Car No.: 17
Make & Model:
  Chevrolet Monte Carlo
Team Owner: Darrell Waltrip
Wins: 0
Top 10: 4

Car No.: 36
Make & Model:
  Pontiac Grand Prix
Team Owner: MB2
Wins: 0
Top 10: 2

27th

Derrike Cope

Derrike Cope was the somewhat-surprising choice to handle the new No. 36 Mars candy entry for 1997. Cope's star had dimmed since his Daytona 500 victory in 1990, and he had spent the past four years with the teams of Cale Yarborough and Bobby Allison. The new Mars team, officially MB2 (after the last names of its three owners), reportedly was well funded. Given the usual start-up pains, Cope did not do badly, and the team appeared to be gaining toward the finish, with Cope scoring a season-best fifth at Atlanta in November. By that time, MB2 already had decided on a new driver for 1998.

Joe Nemechek

After a two-year try as owner-driver, Joe Nemechek realized the dollars weren't there, and he yielded to an offer from multimillionaire Felix Sabates for 1997, forming a complicated three-car operation. Kyle Petty, Sabates' driver for eight years, left after 1996, and Felix suddenly found himself with Robby Gordon and Coors, Nemechek and BellSouth, and Wally Dallenbach, running part-time for First Union. The move did not pay off immediately, with DNQs at Atlanta and Sears Point. He turned that around quickly, winning his first career pole at the California inaugural and adding another at Pocono. He also had outside poles at Martinsville, Michigan, and Indianapolis.

28th

Car No.: 42
Make & Model: Chevrolet Monte Carlo
Team Owner: Felix Sabates
Wins: 0
Top 10: 3

29th

Car No.: 11
Make & Model: Ford Thunderbird
Team Owner: Brett Bodine and Andy Evans
Wins: 0
Top 10: 2

Brett Bodine

Brett Bodine pulled together one of his last-minute sponsorship deals entering 1997, bringing aboard Close Call, a phone-card provider. But Bodine, like others in the owner-driver boat, realized by mid year that he would need help, and he took on investor Andy Evans as partner. Given the tumult, it's a wonder Bodine did as well as he did. He was steady all year; unfortunately, he was steady in the middle or mid back of the pack. He scored two top 10s, at Bristol and Sears Point, but he failed to qualify for the Rockingham race in October. His winnings came to just under $1 million.

Mike Skinner

Mike Skinner had gained the confidence of owner Richard Childress, and won the inaugural Craftsman Truck championship in 1995. Childress graduated him to Winston Cup in 1997 as teammate to legend Dale Earnhardt, and Skinner, never afraid of speed, tore into his new job by winning the pole for the Daytona 500, one of only two rookies to do so in the 1990s. He also won the pole for the summer race at Daytona. It became apparent, however, that Skinner had a lot to learn in the big series. His best finish was sixth at Pocono, and he missed the show at Charlotte in October.

30th

Car No.: 31
Make & Model: Chevrolet Monte Carlo
Team Owner: Richard Childress
Wins: 0
Top 10: 3

Chapter 9

1998

A Season for the Ages

JEFF GORDON WINS THE CUP; DALE EARNHARDT TAKES DAYTONA 500

The most compelling image to emerge from the entire 1998 NASCAR Winston Cup season had absolutely nothing to do with Jeff Gordon's impressive run that delivered his third championship. Rather, it had everything to do with the racing community's emotional reaction to Dale Earnhardt's victory in the season-opening Daytona 500 in Daytona Beach.

After coming so agonizingly close—so heartbreakingly close so many times—the seven-time Cup champion finally had the trophy he'd chased the hardest since his 1979 rookie season. And truth be told, nobody, save perhaps 500 runner-up Bobby Labonte and third-place Jeremy Mayfield, begrudged "The Intimidator" his long-awaited moment in the sun.

Jeff Gordon

Jeff Gordon's 1998 was the most remarkable single season in modern NASCAR history, as he demonstrated not only mastery, but dominance, at every type of track on the circuit. Especially notable was his conquest of the road courses, traditionally thought to be difficult for oval-trackers to tame. In 1998, Gordon surpassed previous road-racing experts Ricky Rudd, Rusty Wallace, Mark Martin, and Geoff Bodine by winning at Sears Point and Watkins Glen (shown here)—his second in a row at the Finger Lakes trail. Gordon started from the pole and ran down Mike Skinner with four laps to go, winning by 3.4 seconds.

Car No.: 24
Make & Model: Chevrolet Monte Carlo
Team Owner: Rick Hendrick
Wins: 13
Top 10: 28

For Jeff Gordon, 1998 was truly a season to remember. In previous seasons, drivers had won the championship with a modicum of race victories. For example, Hendrick teammate Terry Labonte won two races along with his 1996 Winston Cup championship. In contrast, Gordon was competitive at almost every track, winning 13 of 33 races, and posting 26 top-fives for a second-straight Winston Cup title.

"I guess this means you people will have to come up with some new questions," Earnhardt told the media after opening the 1998 season by winning the 500 in his 20th try. "All I've heard from y'all for the past 10 or 12 years is, 'When are you gonna win the Daytona 500?' Well, I've won the thing, so y'all had better start thinking of something else to ask me."

Then he got serious—or, as serious as he ever gets with the media. "You can't imagine how good this feels," he said. "You can't imagine the relief I feel in winning this race and getting the monkey off my back. I was afraid I might never win it. To be so close so many times and not win it makes you wonder if it's meant to be."

It was the tour's most popular outcome since Dale Jarrett won the 1993 Daytona 500 for new owner Joe

Gibbs. So popular, in fact, the media responded by spontaneously suspending its age-old rule against cheering in the press box. As Earnhardt slowly drove down pit road toward Victory Lane, every crewman on every team lined up to touch his outstretched left hand. Nobody was even remotely put off when he momentarily interrupted his trip and cut some donuts in the trioval grass.

While the 500 rightfully belonged to Earnhardt, the rest of the season belonged to Gordon and his No. 24 DuPont Chevrolet Monte Carlo team. Just 27, "Wonder Boy" won his second consecutive title, his third overall, and the fourth in a row for team owner Rick Hendrick and Hendrick Motorsports. (Gordon won the Cup in 1995, teammate Terry Labonte in 1996, then Gordon again in 1997 and 1998. It was the first time any owner had won four consecutive championships.)

But unlike the previous year, when Gordon won the title by only 14 points in the year's last race, there was absolutely no doubt about this one. Gordon won seven

poles and 13 races, tying the modern-era, single-season victory record set by Richard Petty in 1975. And how dominating was Gordon's season? Rusty Wallace was second with four poles and Mark Martin was second with seven victories. In fact, Gordon won as many races as top-five finishers Martin, Dale Jarrett, Rusty Wallace, and Jeff Burton combined.

"Every driver starts every season hoping to run well and contend for the championship, but I don't think anybody realistically expects to have the kind of season we did," Gordon said at the 1998 awards banquet in New York City. "We never imagined it could be this good. The competition is too tough week-in and week-out to expect anything like this. The crew worked hard and gave me great equipment, and a lot of things went our way. We were blessed, truly blessed with how the season went."

It wasn't until Fontana in the spring that Gordon got his first pole. He backed it three weeks later near Charlotte, then two weeks after that at Richmond. He also

For the sixth year in a row, Rusty Wallace was among the top 10 in points in 1998. Wallace was a model of consistency during the season. He won one race, had 15 top-fives, 21 top-10s, and just two DNFs on his way to fourth place in the final standings.

Mark Martin and the Roush team won an impressive seven races in 1998 and had an additional 15 top-five finishes to accumulate nearly 5,000 Winston Cup points—but that was good enough for only second place behind Gordon. It was his third runner-up finish for the decade.

won poles at Pocono, Sonoma, and Watkins Glen in the summer, and Loudon in the fall. He was on the outside pole four times: Bristol in the spring, then Dover, Loudon, and Pocono in the summer.

He and crew chief Ray Evernham were somewhat inconsistent in the first third of the 33-race season. They finished 16th in the season-opening Daytona 500, won a week later at Rockingham, were 17th in the inaugural race at Las Vegas, 19th at Atlanta, and second at Darlington before winning the spring race at Bristol. After six starts, Gordon trailed Wallace and Jeremy Mayfield in the standings.

The Rainbow Warriors fared better in the next six races: 31st at Texas, then eighth at Martinsville, fifth at Talladega, fourth at Fontana, first in the Memorial Day weekend race at Charlotte, then third at Dover the last Sunday in May. The victory at Charlotte and third place at Dover pushed Gordon into the points lead, 45 ahead of Mayfield after a dozen races. He stayed there for only two races, falling back to second when Mayfield beat him by 31 positions (sixth to 37th) at Richmond.

It was during the summer portion of the schedule that Gordon kicked into his Cup-clinching mode. (With, of course, a handful of stumbles along the way.) He won the pole and was running well until contact with Wallace left him an unhappy DNF 37th at Richmond in June. He came back to finish third a week later in Michigan, then was second at Pocono before his easy victory at Sonoma that put him back atop the points, this time to stay. He was third at Loudon then put together a four-race winning streak: Pocono the last Sunday in July, Indianapolis the first weekend in August, Watkins Glen the second Sunday in August, then Michigan the third Sunday of the month.

Gordon ended the June-July-August stretch of the schedule by finishing fifth in the Saturday night race at Bristol and another victory at Loudon. Despite that sensational run—six victories, four top fives and one DNF in 11 starts—he led Martin by only 67 points heading into the final third of the season. "That's the way it is out here," Gordon said. "It's so hard to build a big lead and get away from anybody. I'm sure Mark and his people will be there right to the last weekend."

In truth, it didn't take long for Gordon to remove all suspense and put a hammerlock on another Cup. He won the Labor Day weekend race at Darlington, where Martin lost 132 points with an engine-related DNF 40th. Gordon was second at Richmond (one finish position ahead of Martin), then second to Martin at Dover the third weekend in September. He was second at Martinsville (Martin was third) and fifth at Charlotte, where Martin won and gained 25 almost-meaningless points.

Gordon was second at Talladega, where Martin was 34th and virtually conceded the title. With four races left, Gordon's lead had grown to 238 points over Martin. Even so, the 24 team didn't let up. Gordon won the rescheduled (from July because of wildfires) second race at Daytona Beach, where Martin was 16th. The champion-to-be was seventh a week later at Phoenix (Martin was second), then clinched the Cup a week later by winning at Rockingham, where Martin was fourth. With nothing to lose or gain, Gordon won the rain-shortened season finale at Atlanta the second weekend in November.

His final 364-point margin over Martin is remarkable considering they were only 67 points apart after Round 23 at Loudon the last weekend in August. In the last 10 races, though, Gordon beat Martin seven times by 93 total finish positions. Martin's advantage over Gordon in the other three races was only 10 points.

"I really can't believe this," Gordon said after winning his 13th race at Atlanta. (The finale began late because of rain, was interrupted several times, stopped after 221 of 325 laps, and didn't end until after midnight.) "I can't believe this season, but I also can't believe the kind of career I've had. We did more this year than anyone on this team would have expected. I've already had a much better career than I ever dreamed."

In almost any other season, Martin's three-pole, seven-victory performance would have won the Cup. In fact, his 4,964 points as runner-up were more than any champion's since Cale Yarborough's 5,000 points in 1977 and Gordon's 5,328 in 1998. (Gordon and Martin ran 33 races in 1998, three more than Yarborough did in 1977.)

He won poles at Darlington in the spring and at Dover and Rockingham in the fall. Driving Ford's controversial new Taurus model—controversial because street versions have four doors and the NASCAR version has only two—he won at Las Vegas, Fort Worth, and Fontana in the spring; in Michigan and at Bristol in the summer; then at Dover and Charlotte in the fall. He backed those victories with six runner-up finishes, four thirds, three fourths, two fifths, and four finishes between sixth and 10th in the Jack Roush–owned No. 6 Valvoline Ford.

Despite finishing third in points, Dale Jarrett never was a serious championship contender. (In all fairness, though, who else was?) He won poles at Las Vegas in the spring and Darlington over Labor Day weekend. His victories in the Robert Yates–owned, No. 88 Quality Care Ford were at Darlington and Dover in the spring, then not again until Talladega in the fall. Jarrett had 16 other top-five finishes (among them, five seconds and six thirds) and three finishes between sixth and 10th.

Fourth-ranked Wallace and the No. 2 Miller Ford team owned by Roger Penske faded from title contention after being second until the spring race at Talladega. He won poles at Bristol in the spring, at Dover and Bristol in the summer, then Darlington in the fall. His lone victory was at Phoenix in the fall, a race shortened by rain from 312 to 257 laps. It truly was a forgettable year: only two of Wallace's 14 other top fives were second places and he finished outside the top 10 a dozen times.

It wasn't much of a year for Burton and the Roush-owned, No. 99 Exide Ford, either. He didn't win a pole, and his only victories came at Loudon in the summer and Richmond in the fall. Burton managed to finish top five in points based on four runner-up finishes, two thirds, five fourths, five fifths, and five more finishes between sixth and 10th.

Sixth-ranked Bobby Labonte won three poles and 500-mile races at Atlanta and Talladega in the spring. Mayfield won a pole and got his breakthrough victory in the first of two summer races at Pocono. Earnhardt didn't win any poles, but had his precious Daytona 500 trophy to keep him warm. Terry Labonte won at Richmond in the summer, and Hamilton won one pole and the spring race at Martinsville. Ricky Rudd was the only winner not to finish top 10 in points. His courageous victory in the fall race at Martinsville extended his annual winning streak to 16 years.

The Rookie of the Year battle wasn't much of a fight. Kenny Irwin started 32 of 33 races, won the pole for the finale at Atlanta, had one top five, and five top 10s. Kevin LePage was second in the final Rookie of the Year stats, starting 27 races with a best finish of sixth. Jerry Nadeau and Steve Park were the only other full-schedule rookies. Nadeau had a mediocre season and Park's was cut short (17 races) by serious injuries suffered in a vicious crash near Atlanta in the spring

NASCAR continued to add races to its already over-crowded schedule. The 1998 addition was Las Vegas Motor Speedway, a 1.5-mile, moderately banked, multi-use facility north of the Strip. It was the fifth new speed-way to join the tour in the 1990s, following New Hampshire International Speedway (1993), Indianapolis Motor Speedway (1994), and the Texas Motor Speedway and California Speedway in 1997.

Little did anyone know what was on the schedul-ing horizon.

Despite suffering heat exhaustion and second-degree burns on parts of his body when his cool suit failed, Ricky Rudd drove his No. 10 car to an astonishing victory in the NAPA 500 at Martinsville.

Ricky Rudd Perseveres Through a Heatwave

Ricky Rudd has always been one of NASCAR's upper-level "fringe" drivers. Despite being a consistent top 10 runner most of his career, he's never won more than four poles and two races in any season. He's been top 10 in points 17 times, including second place behind Dale Earnhardt in 1991.

Crafty and workmanlike, his greatest claim to Winston Cup fame remains his 16-year winning streak. From 1983 through 1998, he won at least once every year for Richard Childress, Bud Moore, Kenny Bernstein, Rick Hendrick, and himself. None of those 20 victories was nearly as difficult as the NAPA 500 at Martinsville Speedway.

To many NASCAR-watchers, it was the most coura-geous performance they'd ever seen.

Sunday, September 27 was unseasonably warm at the half-mile track. Like most drivers, Rudd wore a "cool suit" that circulated water next to his skin. At their best, the suits enable drivers to endure unbearable heat. It's a dif-ferent story when something happens and the water turns hot—like what happened to Rudd.

He qualified his No. 10 Tide-backed Ford Taurus sec-ond-fastest for the 500-lap, 263-mile race. Pole-sitter Ernie Irvan led Laps 1–14 before Rudd led Laps 15–63. He stayed top 5 all day, leading three more times for 149 more laps. But every trip around was an ordeal.

He realized early-on that his suit wasn't working and he might not last 500 laps. Crew chief Jim Long recruited Hut Stricklin for relief, but Rudd chose to stay put while the car was competitive. The crew did its job, drenching Rudd with cold water and dumping ice into his seat dur-ing every stop.

"It was like sitting on a hot iron," Rudd said later. "I would have gotten out, but the car was running so good and I didn't want to lose a lap making a driver change. I never thought I'd pass out or anything like that, but it was unbelievably hot. Without question, the hottest I've ever been in a racecar."

Rudd was pulled from the car, laid out, and given IV fluids. He was treated in Victory Lane for cramps, heat exhaustion, and second-degree burns on his back and but-tocks. He recovered enough to do the traditional post-race media interviews.

When someone asked if winning was worth it, Rudd nodded. "The only thing that kept me going," he said, "was knowing I could win. I woulda hated to go through this and not win."

2nd

Car No.: 6
Make & Model: Ford Taurus
Team Owner: Jack Roush
Wins: 7
Top 10: 26

Mark Martin

Mark Martin put up his strongest title bid of the decade, and probably the most frustrating. Seven victories and six second places would have been more than enough in any other year; four of those second places, however, were behind Jeff Gordon, leading car owner Jack Roush to cry foul in August, claiming Gordon and team were using treated tires, a claim NASCAR dismissed. At Bristol in August (shown here), Martin was in command, leading the last 181 laps and beating Jeff Burton by 2.2 seconds. Gordon, who did not lead all night, finished fifth. At the time, Martin stood just 67 points behind Gordon.

3rd

Car No.: 88
Make & Model: Ford Taurus
Team Owner: Robert Yates
Wins: 3
Top 10: 22

Dale Jarrett

Dale Jarrett took a bulldog hold on third place at mid summer and never let it go, although the leaders gradually pulled away. Engine failure at Martinsville in September ended his title bid, leaving him 470 points behind. After a slow start, Jarrett had begun to climb through the pack by the time of the Dover race end of May (pictured here). He won on the concrete mile by stretching mileage and tires, thus beating Jeff Burton to the flag by more than half a lap. This was Jarrett's second 1998 win, the first coming at Darlington in March.

4th

Rusty Wallace

Although Rusty Wallace's 1998 season looked modest on paper (one victory, two second-places), his Penske Racing team had cured its 1997 engine trouble, reducing DNFs from 11 to two. Wallace thus posted a points finish comparable to his big-number years, 1993 and 1994. Always formidable on the flat, shorter tracks, he scored his one victory at Phoenix in November. He was points leader through mid spring, and finished a steady sixth at Martinsville in April (shown here), the last man on the lead lap. Engine failure at California two weeks later dropped him out of the points lead.

Car No.: 2
Make & Model: Ford Taurus
Team Owner: Roger Penske
Wins: 1
Top 10: 21

5th

Jeff Burton

Jeff Burton cemented his gains of 1997 and became recognized as a genuine rival to the established stars. The best example of Burton's willingness to do battle came at Richmond in September (seen here), where Burton bumped and scratched with Jeff Gordon to win by a bumper length, a popular "hometown" victory for the Virginian. The week before at Darlington, Gordon had fought off Burton over the closing laps. Burton also won at New Hampshire, and he added four second-places and 12 other top 10s. Young Frank Stoddard succeeded Buddy Parrott as race-day crew chief for Burton this season, Parrott becoming general manager.

Car No.: 99
Make & Model: Ford Taurus
Team Owner: Jack Roush
Wins: 2
Top 10: 23

6th

Car No.: 18
Make & Model:
Pontiac Grand Prix
Team Owner: Joe Gibbs
Wins: 2
Top 10: 18

Bobby Labonte

Bobby Labonte and the Joe Gibbs team continued to edge northward in 1998, gaining one spot to sixth in points behind two victories and 18 total top 10s. As usual, Bobby was at his best on the big, fast tracks such as Atlanta and Michigan, and he notched his first-ever restrictor-plate victory at Talladega in April. Fords dominated in the debut race at Las Vegas (shown here), with only Dale Earnhardt's Chevrolet intruding on a top-14 sweep by the Ford's new Taurus models. Labonte, in a Pontiac, started 11th but finished 19th, a lap down. He and Ward Burton had the best Pontiacs, with Ward finishing 18th.

7th

Car No.: 12
Make & Model:
Ford Taurus
Team Owner:
Roger Penske
Wins: 1
Top 10: 16

Jeremy Mayfield

With Roger Penske buying into the Michael Kranefuss team and a new alliance formed with Rusty Wallace's team, Jeremy Mayfield got his first taste of the Winston Cup points lead, holding the top spot through much of May and June. He also plucked his first Cup victory at Pocono in June, holding off late-race challenger Jeff Gordon by .340 of a second. That was the highlight, as Mayfield stumbled thereafter with four-straight finishes of 18th or worse, including Indianapolis, where a wreck left him 42nd. Mayfield found one of his 12 top fives at Dover (seen here), where he came home fifth.

Dale Earnhardt

On his 20th try, Dale Earnhardt caught and held the one prize which had eluded him for 20 years, the Daytona 500 (seen here). The race ended under caution, with Earnhardt leading the last 61 laps, and a respectful parade comprising Bobby Labonte, Jeremy Mayfield, Ken Schrader, and Rusty Wallace followed him across the finish line. The victory, with crew chief Larry McReynolds, also ended Earnhardt's 59-race losing streak, dating to March 1996. Fortune deserted him afterward, however. Dale did not win again, he sagged to eighth in points, and he changed crew chiefs mid year.

8th

Car No.: 3
Make & Model: Chevrolet Monte Carlo
Team Owner: Richard Childress
Wins: 1
Top 10: 13

Terry Labonte

Other teams continued to surpass 1996 champion Terry Labonte, who counted 14 finishes out of the top 10 in 1998. As with Dale Earnhardt, Labonte's season started with a highlight, as he and brother Bobby swept the front row for the Daytona 500. He also survived for victory in the controversial, wreck-marred finish at Richmond in June. Terry and team could not seem to find traction the rest of the way, however, with a sixth at Martinsville in September his best of the second half. At Indianapolis in August (seen here), Labonte started eighth and finished ninth, leading two laps during a pit break.

9th

Car No.: 5
Make & Model: Chevrolet Monte Carlo
Team Owner: Rick Hendrick
Wins: 1
Top 10: 15

10th

Bobby Hamilton

Hamilton, sensing opportunity, took the Morgan-McClure ride for 1998. Hamilton promised to win a short-track race for speedway king McClure, and McClure and the team promised to win a big-track race for bullring specialist Hamilton. Hamilton kept his end of the bargain quickly, beating Ted Musgrave by 6.4 seconds at Martinsville in April. McClure, whose team had lost the horsepower edge it held in the early 1990s, could not return the favor. Still, Hamilton kept the team around the top 10 all year. At Sears Point in June, Hamilton finished a strong second to Jeff Gordon, leading 17 laps near the end.

Car No.: 4
Make & Model: Chevrolet Monte Carlo
Team Owner: Larry McClure
Wins: 1
Top 10: 8

11th

John Andretti

John Andretti had driven briefly for Petty Enterprises in 1994. He signed on full-time in 1998, with some noting the irony of an Andretti driving for a Petty. The season was encouraging, with John twice finishing third and achieving his best-ever points finish, 11th. The Rockingham race in February (shown here) was about average for the team. Andretti started ninth, avoided trouble, and finished 13th without leading. In a season dominated by Jeff Gordon, Mark Martin, and Dale Jarrett, Andretti's best results came at Sears Point in June and at New Hampshire in August. He also scored eight other top 10s.

Car No.: 43
Make & Model: Pontiac Grand Prix
Team Owner: Richard Petty
Wins: 0
Top 10: 10

12th

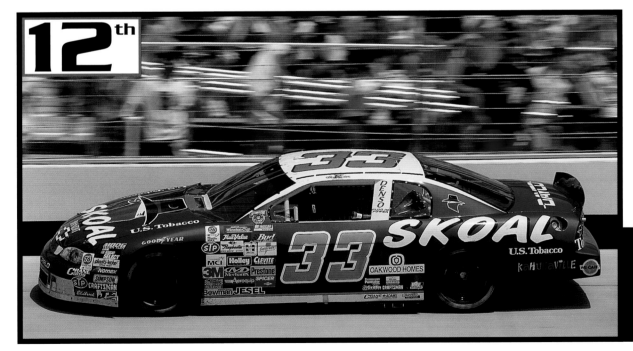

Car No.: 33
Make & Model:
  Chevrolet Monte Carlo
Team Owner:
  Andy Petree
Wins: 0
Top 10: 11

Ken Schrader

In his second season with owner Andy Petree, Ken Schrader held his own, recording 10 top 10s and 12th in points—about what he had done the previous three seasons. Rugged Schrader played with pain at Daytona, steering to fourth place in the Daytona 500 despite a cracked sternum he suffered in a wreck during the qualifying heats. Three fourth places were the best Schrader and the team could do, the other two coming in the races at Richmond in June and September. The Dover race in May (shown here) was not notable, with Schrader starting 25th and finishing 15th. He was ninth in points at the time.

13th

Car No.: 40
Make & Model: Chevrolet Monte Carlo
Team Owner: Felix Sabates
Wins: 0
Top 10: 6

Sterling Marlin

Smiling Sterling Marlin traded in the bright yellow of Kodak and Morgan-McClure for the blue and gold of Coors and Felix Sabates in 1998. After a dismal 1997, Marlin returned to his level with a very consistent run. With the series increasingly competitive, Marlin failed to qualify for the Atlanta race in March, his first-ever DNQ. On the other hand, Sterling failed to *finish* just one race all year. He ended with six top 10s, the best being seventh places at (surprisingly) the two road-course races. At Darlington in March (shown here), Marlin steered to a steady 14th place, two laps down.

Jimmy Spencer

The changing face of tobacco advertising, after the 1997 class-action settlement agreement, brought Jimmy Spencer and the Travis Carter team a new look in 1998, with plain, red-and-white Winston packaging replacing the garish Joe Camel colors. Meanwhile, results improved a bit and could have been better had Spencer not broken his shoulder in a crash at the Brickyard in August; Spencer yielded to reason and took the next two races off. Jimmy, who loves restrictor-plate racing, was second at Talladega in April, his best. After seventh place at Las Vegas in March (seen here), he was fourth in points.

Car No.: 23
Make & Model: Ford Taurus
Team Owner: Travis Carter
Wins: 0
Top 10: 8

14th

Chad Little

Chad Little caught an unexpected break in 1998, with sponsor John Deere looking to counter rival Caterpillar's high-dollar effort and ending up in the fold of Jack Roush. Little, who had hitchhiked through Winston Cup since 1988, formed a Busch Series partnership with high-school buddy Mark Rypien and had acquired the John Deere deal in 1995; the team tried to make a go alone in Cup in 1997 before accepting Roush's offer. The result was Chad's best year ever, 15th in points with a second place at Texas. At Rockingham in February (shown here), Chad finished 21st, two laps down.

15th

Car No.: 97
Make & Model: Ford Taurus
Team Owner: Jack Roush
Wins: 0
Top 10: 7

16th

Ward Burton

Although increasingly in the shadow of younger brother Jeff, Ward Burton patiently abided the building efforts of car owner Bill Davis. Davis, with a keen eye for talent, corralled up-and-coming crew chief Tommy Baldwin toward the end of the year, and he and Ward clicked. Burton tallied a strategic second place at Charlotte in October (his best since his initial win at Rockingham in 1995) and gained to 16th in points. The team made just four other top 10s, but progress was evident. At Rockingham (pictured here; one of his best tracks), Ward started 14th and finished 11th.

Car No.: 22
Make & Model: Pontiac Grand Prix
Team Owner: Bill Davis
Wins: 0
Top 10: 5

17th

Car No.: 21
Make & Model:
 Chevrolet Monte Carlo
Team Owner: Wood Brothers
Wins: 0
Top 10: 5

Michael Waltrip

The 1998 season brought pretty much more of the same to Michael Waltrip and the Wood Brothers. One less top 10 (five this year) and one less DNF (three) equaled a one-place gain in points, to 17th. This season, the ancient Wood Brothers team came more and more under the control of Jack Roush, with a marketing partnership the first link. Toward fall, Mikey and the Woods came to an understanding that their partnership was not working, and Waltrip began looking elsewhere. At Watkins Glen (seen here), Waltrip ran out of fuel on the last lap—a terrible thing to happen on a 2.45-mile course—and finished 28th.

Bill Elliott

What looked like a good business decision backfired on Bill Elliott in 1998. In trying to build his team to a two-car powerhouse, he entered a partnership with former Super Bowl quarterback Dan Marino and what looked like strong sponsorship from FirstPlus, a finance company for which Marino did promotions. Promising youngster Jerry Nadeau took the wheel. By mid-year, FirstPlus had backed out, and Elliott was left with distracting headaches. Perhaps as a result, Elliot tumbled to 18th in points with five top 10s and seven DNFs. He finished 38th at New Hampshire in August after a wreck.

18th

Car No.: 94
Make & Model: Ford Taurus
Team Owner: Bill Elliott
Wins: 0
Top 10: 5

Ernie Irvan

Put out by Robert Yates after 1997, Ernie Irvan found a home with the sophomore MB2 team, and he gave the No. 36 car a creditable run. Irvan rang some high notes, winning three poles (including Indianapolis for the second year in a row) and building momentum with seven top 10s through the second half. Unfortunately, Irvan again was shaken in a crash at Talladega and, given that he was lucky to be alive after Michigan in 1994, he took the rest of the year off. Although the team expressed confidence in Irvan, he came more and more to be seen as damaged goods, even in his own eyes.

Car No.: 36
Make & Model: Pontiac Grand Prix
Team Owner: MB2
Wins: 0
Top 10: 11

19th

20th

Johnny Benson

After a two-year Winston Cup break-in with Chuck Rider, Benson accepted an offer from Jack Roush to drive for Roush's new, General Mills–sponsored team in 1998. What looks good on paper sometimes is too good to be true, and that seemed to be the case for Benson through his first season with Roush, with many suspecting the No. 26 cars were R&D chariots for his No. 6 and No. 99 teams. It wasn't all that bad; Benson scored three top fives, his most ever, but he fell to 20th in points. The Bristol race in March (shown here) was his best of the year, as he drove to fifth place.

Car No.: 26
Make & Model: Ford Taurus
Team Owner: Jack Roush
Wins: 0
Top 10: 10

21st

Car No.: 31
Make & Model: Chevrolet Monte Carlo
Team Owner: Richard Childress
Wins: 0
Top 10: 9

Mike Skinner

No longer a rookie, Mike Skinner, driver for Richard Childress and teammate of Dale Earnhardt, was expected to win, and no one expected to win more than Skinner did. Skinner, however, took a wild ride in 1998. He and Earnhardt swapped crew chiefs mid year, with Kevin Hamlin taking over the No. 3 and Larry McReynolds managing the No. 31. McReynolds' arrival brought improvement, with Skinner scoring top fives at Indianapolis, Watkins Glen, and in the fire-delayed Pepsi 400 at Daytona. The races at Pocono in the summer (shown here) were forgettable, with Skinner finishing 29th and 30th.

22nd

Car No.: 10
Make & Model: Ford Taurus
Team Owner: Ricky Rudd
Wins: 1
Top 10: 5

Ricky Rudd

The big deal was the streak, and Ricky Rudd, despite his worst points season ever, managed to extend it by winning at Martinsville in September, despite being nearly roasted alive in the car. Seating expansion had made the half-mile bowl into a giant aluminum solar collector, and on a hot day, Rudd nearly gave out. He dug deep to beat Jeff Gordon by half a second. Rudd's winning streak thus reached 16 years, the longest in history. Rudd, however, made just four other top 10s, and his five-year dream of controlling his destiny as car owner began to look less and less realistic.

Ted Musgrave

In his fifth year with Jack Roush, Ted Musgrave began to chafe, and with sponsorship of the No. 16 team only chancy, he left the Roush stable after Watkins Glen in August. Musgrave hadn't had a bad year with Roush, with a second at Martinsville in April and three other top 10s through 20 races, but apparently rancor ran deeper than results. Musgrave served as sub for five other teams the rest of the year, and actually recorded a top five for the fading Elliott-Marino team (after Jerry Nadeau's discharge) at Phoenix. No one doubted Musgrave could drive, but his temperament came into question.

Car No.: 16
Make & Model: Ford Taurus
Team Owner: Jack Roush
Wins: 1
Top 10: 5

23rd

Car No.: 17
Make & Model: Chevrolet Monte Carlo
Team Owner: Darrell Waltrip
Wins: 0
Top 10: 2

Darrell Waltrip

The world blew up for veteran champion Darrell Waltrip in 1998. After the departure of sponsor Western Auto the previous winter, Waltrip displayed the colors of Speedblock, a building and landscaping product, at Daytona. That deal went nowhere, and by March, Waltrip tossed in the towel, selling his eight-year-old team to wildcatter Tim Beverley. Waltrip's high times came almost immediately, with old rival Dale Earnhardt choosing him to sub for injured Steve Park in Earnhardt's No. 1 car. Waltrip had the best race of his late career at California, where he finished fifth. When Park returned, Waltrip drove for Beverley the rest of the year.

24th

Brett Bodine

Once again, Brett Bodine cobbled together sponsorship to make payroll and keep his No. 11 team alive. The patron this time was Paychex, a payroll-services firm from upstate New York, and the company carried Bodine through another year. The season was typical for Brett: he made all the races and had just two DNFs. But he failed to make the top 10 for the first time since ever. Although rising purses increased Bodine's season take to nearly $1.3 million (his first million-plus season), the increase hardly covered increasing costs. Brett, however, was making a living, with an eye toward better.

25th

Car No.: 11
Make & Model: Ford Taurus
Team Owner: Brett Bodine and Andy Evans
Wins: 0
Top 10: 0

Joe Nemechek

Joe Nemechek assured his survival in Winston Cup by pitching in with Felix Sabates in 1997, but results failed to improve much in 1998. Racing is Nemechek's business, and with his own Busch Series team he knocked out two victories in 1998. On the Cup side, Nemechek missed the show at Bristol in March, then qualified second and finished fourth the next week at Texas, both season-bests. Joe also added up his first million-dollar season in 1998, banking $1,343,991, doubling his previous best. Martinsville in September (shown here) was a write-off; Joe finished 40th with a broken engine.

26th

Car No.: 42
Make & Model:
  Chevrolet Monte Carlo
Team Owner: Felix Sabates
Wins: 0
Top 10: 4

27th

Car No.: 7
Make & Model:
  Ford Taurus
Team Owner: Geoff Bodine
Wins: 0
Top 10: 5

Geoff Bodine

Geoff Bodine's 1993 dream went haywire in 1998, as the owner-driver vogue of the mid-1990s dramatically faded. Bodine acquired the No. 7 team in 1993 and held it together for five years. Loyal crew chief Paul Andrews departed after 1996. For 1998, Bodine took on investor Jim Mattei and international electronics giant Philips. Mattei quickly became partner, then owner, and Bodine was out at the end of the year. Bodine, a true racing innovator, probably deserved better. His highlights for 1998 were the outside pole at the Las Vegas inaugural and fifth place at Rockingham in February.

Car No.: 28
Make & Model: Ford Taurus
Team Owner: Robert Yates
Wins: 0
Top 10: 5

28th

Kenny Irwin

Ford's answer to Jeff Gordon was Kenny Irwin, who like Gordon came up through USAC sprints and midgets. Irwin had shown great promise in the Craftsman Truck Series in 1997, and Ford installed him in Robert Yates' No. 28 in 1998, replacing Ernie Irvan. Irwin, 29, won Rookie of the Year and became the first rookie to win more than $1 million. Irwin, however, failed to live up to the "next Jeff Gordon" career plot, as if anyone could have. Irwin finished fifth at Atlanta in March, then won the pole there in November. In between came an extremely disappointing DNQ at Charlotte in May.

Car No.: 90
Make & Model: Ford Taurus
Team Owner: Junie Donlavey
Wins: 0
Top 10: 1

Dick Trickle

Fifty-year car owner Junie Donlavey had the best sponsorship of his life, from furniture retailer Heilig-Meyers, 1993 through 1998. Stubborn Donlavey stuck to his methods, as always, and went through a miscellany of drivers, with Bobby Hillin, Mike Wallace, and finally Dick Trickle wheeling the green-and-black No. 90 cars. Trickle, 57 at the end of the year, had run to the end of a remarkable career. Nevertheless, he helped Donlavey to the owner's only top-30 points finish of the decade and his first million-dollar season, as the rising tide floated all the boats. Trickle was 19th at New Hampshire in August (pictured here), last man on the lead lap.

29th

Kyle Petty

King Richard Petty turned over Petty Enterprises to son Kyle in 1998, and Kyle suddenly had to assume business responsibility for the historic organization. Kyle's pe2 team, formed in 1997, had to be folded into the general empire, and the new duties seemed to cost Kyle focus. He drifted to 30th in points and failed to record a top-five finish for the first time since 1983, his first full racing season, and did not lead a lap for the first time in his career. Kyle's 1998 season indicated NASCAR's increasing prosperity: he fell 15 positions in points from 1997 but increased his winnings by $300,000.

Car No.: 44
Make & Model: Pontiac Grand Prix
Team Owner: Richard Petty
Wins: 0
Top 10: 2

30th

Chapter 10

1999

Speed and Consistency

DALE JARRETT AND ROBERT YATES RACING FIND THE GROOVE

Dale Jarrett was only the second-happiest man in south Florida the day he clinched the 1999 Winston Cup at Homestead-Miami Speedway. While the media and friends swarmed around Jarrett and crew chief Todd Parrott, team owner Robert Yates quietly brushed away tears from behind his designer shades.

Understandable. Perfectly understandable.

It had taken Robert Yates Racing 11 eventful years to finally reach the top of the NASCAR hill. "A lot of people—some of them here, some of them not—had a part in this," Yates said that Sunday afternoon in Homestead. "It's been a long time coming. It was longer than I expected, longer than I wanted. That's one of the reasons we'll enjoy this as long as we can. This is for Davey and Ernie, too."

At the time, Jarrett was only the fourth man to drive full-time for Robert Yates Racing. The late Davey Allison won six poles and 15 races between its inception in 1989

Dale Jarrett

Easily the biggest victory of Dale Jarrett's championship season was his run to the roses in the Brickyard 400 at Indianapolis Motor Speedway. In addition to the $712,240 paycheck, his largest to date, Jarrett joined select company, with Jeff Gordon, Dale Earnhardt, and Ricky Rudd the only other drivers to win at the historic speedway. In addition, Jarrett became the second driver to win the Brickyard twice. Jarrett dominated, leading all but five of the last 120 laps, Bobby Labonte finishing more than three seconds behind. This was the last of Jarrett's four victories in 1999, the others at Richmond, Michigan, and summer Daytona.

Car No.: 88
Make & Model: Ford Taurus
Team Owner: Robert Yates
Wins: 4
Top 10: 29

and his death in a July 1993 aviation accident. Ernie Irvan won 10 poles and eight races between September of 1993 and his departure after 1998. Jarrett came aboard in 1995 while Irvan recovered from injuries suffered the previous year in Michigan. When Irvan returned full-time to the No. 28 Ford in 1996, Yates created the No. 88 Ford team for Jarrett.

Twice in the 1990s Yates was on the verge of winning the NASCAR championship. He and Allison needed only a decent finish in 1992's final race at Atlanta to win it all. Instead, Allison crashed out with—irony of ironies—Irvan and finished third to Alan Kulwicki and Bill Elliott. Eight months later, standing fifth in points at mid season, Allison was dead.

Two years later, Irvan was No. 2 in points when he crashed at Michigan and almost killed himself. He already had five poles and three victories, and was only 27 points behind Dale Earnhardt after 20 of 31 races. Irvan had led the most races, the most laps, and the most miles, and

After finishing second or third three years in a row, Dale Jarrett finally reached the top spot in 1999. It was also the first championship for Robert Yates Racing in its 11-year history.

seemed poised to give Robert Yates Racing a solid run for the Cup it had lost two years earlier. Given Earnhardt's performance down the stretch—nine top 10s in 12 starts—he might have won the title, anyway. But it gnawed at Yates that Irvan and his 1994 team never got a shot at seeing how they would have done.

That's why he didn't try to hide his tears at Homestead. It had been, as he said later that afternoon, a long, painful, and emotionally trying run to the top. So much work and worry, pain and prayers.

Jarrett's championship season was a thing of beauty. He didn't win a pole, but won four races: the spring race at Richmond, and the summer races at Michigan, Daytona Beach, and Indianapolis. He had six runner-up finishes, four thirds, five fourths, five fifths, and eight other finishes between sixth and 10th. There was only one DNF—in the season-opener at Daytona Beach—and he clinched the title in the next-to-last race of the 34-race season.

"That's always been what wins championships," Jarrett said of his No. 88 Quality Care Ford team's uncanny consistency. "You race as hard as you can, trying to gain as many positions as you can. That's where you gain points—whether it's two or 20 or 100—and how you win championships. There were days we weren't very good at the start, but the crew kept working on it. Several times this year we made something out of nothing."

Parrott marveled at his driver's grit and obsession with getting every point he could get. "If he couldn't win the race, he wanted to finish second," he said. "If he couldn't do that, he wanted to finish top five. If he didn't have a car capable of finishing top 10, we all tried to fight back to get it in the top 20. That's the way Dale drove all year. The reason we won the championship is because of his determination and desire."

Jarrett and Parrott started poorly: a wreck-related DNF 37th in February in Daytona Beach. They were second at Rockingham a week later, then 11th at Las Vegas, fifth at Atlanta, fourth at Darlington, and second in Texas. Their third place at Bristol in Round 7 moved them to second in the standings, 52 points behind Jeff Burton. They were eighth at Martinsville, second at Talladega, and fifth in the early-May race at Fontana.

The team's first victory—at Richmond's night race the third weekend in May—pushed Jarrett past Burton into the points lead. He stayed there the rest of the year on the strength of runs like this: fifth at Charlotte on Memorial Day weekend, then fifth at Dover, first at Michigan, third at Pocono, sixth at Sonoma, and first at Daytona Beach in July. He was fourth at Loudon, second at Pocono, first at Indianapolis, then fourth at Watkins Glen and Michigan before crashing to a 38th in the August night race at Bristol.

Jarrett went into the fall portion of the schedule leading Mark Martin by 213 points. And despite struggling down the stretch, he never was in serious jeopardy of losing his lead. He was 16th at Darlington over Labor Day weekend, then third at Richmond, 18th at Loudon, third at Dover, 10th at Martinsville, and seventh at Charlotte. He finished the year in typical Jarrett fashion: second at Talladega, fourth at Rockingham, sixth at Phoenix, a title-clinching fifth at Homestead, then second in the finale at Atlanta the third weekend in November.

The new champ finished 201 points ahead of Bobby Labonte, who was 118 ahead of Martin. Flamboyant rookie Tony Stewart was fourth and Burton fifth. The second five: three-time and defending champion Jeff Gordon, seven-time champion Earnhardt, former champion Rusty Wallace, Ward Burton, and Mike Skinner.

It took Labonte a while to get right in the Joe Gibbs–owned No. 18 Interstate Pontiac. His victories came in the summer at Dover, twice at Pocono, in Michigan, then the finale at Atlanta. Labonte closed with a rush: 10 consecutive top 10s, eight of them top fives. All told he had 18 other top fives and three other finishes between sixth and 10th, and only one DNF.

Martin's year was more steady than spectacular in the No. 6 Valvoline Ford owned by Jack Roush. He won at Rockingham in the spring and Dover in the fall, had 17 other top fives, and seven more finishes between sixth and 10th. He ended the decade as the only driver to rank top 10 in points every year, but didn't have a Winston Cup to show for it.

It was evident early that Stewart in the No. 20 Home Depot Pontiac was something special. He dominated the rookie class, winning Rookie of the Year by 121 points over Elliott Sadler. He won at Richmond in the spring and Phoenix and Homestead in the fall, had nine other top fives, and eight finishes between sixth and 10th. He was the first rookie in Cup history with three victories and the first in the modern era to finish top five in points. His $3.2 million in winnings doubled Kenny Irwin's 1998 rookie record.

Jeff Burton had a career breakout season in the No. 99 Exide Ford. He won at Las Vegas, Darlington, and Charlotte in the spring; Loudon in the summer; then Darlington and Rockingham in the fall. His spring victory at

At the age of 38, Ward Burton had the best season of his career in 1999, joining brother Jeff in the top 10 with a ninth-place finish.

Darlington featured the strangest finish in years. Burton was leading when he slammed the Turn 4 wall as rain began falling. He took the caution flag leading and found himself the surprise winner when rain stopped the race for good after 270 of 367 laps.

His $5.7 million included $1 million bonuses for winning the spring No Bull 5 race at Charlotte and the fall race at Darlington. But after leading the points early, inconsistency kept him from challenging for the title. He had three finishes in the teens, two in the 20s, and seven in the 30s, and steadily slipped backward as the season wound down.

Gordon led the tour with seven victories: in the spring at Daytona Beach, Atlanta, and Fontana; in the summer at Sonoma and Watkins Glen; then back-to-back at Martinsville and Charlotte in the fall. His lack of consistency—six finishes in the 30s and two in the 40s—kept

him from making a serious run at the championship.

After a poor 1998, Earnhardt showed flashes of his former brilliance. He won in the spring and fall at Talladega, and in the summer at Bristol. He had only four other top fives, but finished 14 others between sixth and 10th, easily more than anyone else. His last-lap, bump-and-run victory over Terry Labonte at Bristol was the year's most controversial finish. "I just wanted to rattle his cage, get him a little loose, and drive by," Earnhardt said at the time. "I didn't think I hit him that hard, but he lost it. I hate that it happened. I didn't mean it." Asked to respond, Labonte said, "Yeah, right." NASCAR refused to intervene, calling it a racing accident.

Wallace had a mediocre season: a victory at Bristol in the spring, but only six other top fives and nine finishes between sixth and 10th. His eighth place in points continued his streak of being top 10 for seven consecutive

The newest sensation on the Winston Cup circuit, 27-year-old Tony Stewart took three checkered flags with Joe Gibbs Racing in his rookie season to finish fourth overall.

Second-place finisher Bobby Labonte won five races in 1999 and ended the season with 10 consecutive top-10 finishes. After winning the final race at Atlanta, Labonte was still the runnerup in the championship, more than 200 points behind the leader, Dale Jarrett. In 2000, he would improve his position by one, claiming the title. He and Terry became the only brothers to ever win the Winston Cup championship.

years and 10 of the last 12. Ward Burton had 16 top 10s and Skinner had 14. The other three victories came from drivers outside the top 10: Terry Labonte in the spring in Texas, John Andretti in the spring at Martinsville, and Joe Nemechek (his breakthrough Cup victory) at Loudon in the fall.

Much of 1999's biggest news came off the track. In February, within days of the season-opening Daytona 500, NASCAR president Bill France Jr. introduced trusted right-hand man Mike Helton as the new senior vice president and chief operating officer of the Daytona Beach–based sanctioning body. While still technically the boss, the 65-year-old France—who would later begin extensive treatment for cancer—let it be known that from that day forward he'd spend more time chasing fish than watching racecars. "But I'm just a cell-phone call away," he said with a slight grin. Helton's reply: "Yes, sir, whatever you say."

The year's other major off-track story was recognition of stock car racing as a major television event. After years of underselling itself, NASCAR signed a six-year, $2.4 billion television contract with NBC and cable partner TBS, and with Fox and its FX and Fox Sports Net cable affiliates. The deal called for NBC and Fox to alternate coverage of the Daytona 500 through 2006. Fox or its affiliates will get the first half of each Winston Cup season, then NBC or TBS the second half.

The deal miffed some long time NASCAR-watchers. It especially angered drivers and owners old enough to remember when ESPN and CBS jumped in and televised racing when nobody else wanted it. "This just goes to show there's no loyalty in racing, that money does all the talking," said Kyle Petty. "CBS was doing the Daytona 500 when nobody else wanted it, and this is the thanks they get. And I'd hate to think of where NASCAR would be without ESPN. It's not right, but it shows how big we've become.

"Well let me tell you . . . bigger isn't always better. This is one of those times when it's not."

Ray Evernham Leaves Hendrick Motorsports for Dodge

Many NASCAR-watchers spent most of the 1990s thinking Jeff Gordon and Ray Evernham were among the best driver/crew chief combinations in modern Winston Cup history. The stats certainly supported that premise: 1993 Rookie of the Year, 30 poles, 47 victories, more than $31 million in only 225 starts, Winston Cup titles in 1995, 1997, and 1998, and top 10 finishes in 1994, 1996, and 1999.

Together, Gordon, Evernham, team owner Rick Hendrick, and the Rainbow Warriors won four Pepsi Southern 500s, three Coca-Cola World 600s, two Brickyard 400s, and two Daytona 500s. They won 23 more superspeedway races, eight races on short tracks, and five on road courses. Just for good measure, they won three $1 million bonuses in the Winston Million and No Bull 5 programs and three Winston all-star races. Almost every meaningful NASCAR record seemed theirs for the taking.

So imagine the uproar when rumors surfaced late in 1999 that Evernham might quit Hendrick Motorsports with eight races remaining. And imagine the uproar-squared when he virtually acknowledged he was quitting to lead Dodge's long-rumored return to Winston Cup in 2001.

"I hate to dodge the questions, but I can't tell you right now what I'm going to be doing," Evernham said late in September. "It's time I did something different. I don't mean to dodge all y'all's questions, but that's all I can say for the time being."

Much later—after Dodge executives confirmed "the worst-kept secret in racing" in an October press conference in New York City—Evernham said the challenge of reintroducing a new car to NASCAR was simply too tempting to turn down. As for his relationship with Gordon . . .

"He doesn't need me like when we came into Winston Cup together," he said. "Back then, I felt more like a father to him. I was older and had raced and worked with IROC [International Race of Champions] and on a Busch Series team. I was a coach and mentor at first, but Jeff grew to where he didn't need me as much. It's like when you're a parent and your children go off to college. Times change and relationships change, and that's what happened to us."

But Evernham's six-plus years of training and influence didn't leave with him. Witness: Gordon and interim crew chief Brian Whitesell won a 500-lapper at Martinsville and a 500-miler at Charlotte on consecutive weekends after Evernham had left to start building his Dodge program.

Car No.: 18
Make & Model:
  Pontiac Grand Prix
Team Owner:
  Joe Gibbs
Wins: 5
Top 10: 26

Bobby Labonte

With their Pontiacs fully refined by 1999, Bobby Labonte tore off to his best season, winning five times. Labonte again showed an uncanny talent to find the secret of a particular track, and this year the track tamed was Pocono, the peculiar triangular track in northeastern Pennsylvania. Labonte won both in June (shown here) and July on the way to five victories and a distant second in points. Bobby led only 28 of the 200 laps, including the last 15, but was able to hold off Jeff Gordon by a couple of car-lengths. Labonte also continued to win at Michigan and Atlanta.

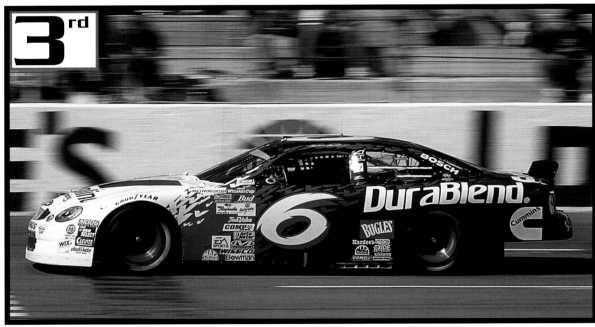

Car No.: 6
Make & Model: Ford Taurus
Team Owner: Jack Roush
Wins: 2
Top 10: 26

Mark Martin

Taken into perspective, Martin had a terrific decade in the 1990s, winning 30 races and never finishing lower than sixth in points. Yet, every time he was great, someone else was a little better, and Mark could count three heartbreaking second places in the championship battles. The 1999 season was no different, with Martin winning twice but falling 319 points behind runaway leader Dale Jarrett and 118 behind second-place Bobby Labonte. Martin won at Rockingham in February and Dover in September, but three finishes of 34th or worse killed his chances. Martin also tallied three second-places and five thirds. At Charlotte in October (seen here), Martin started fourth and finished fourth. Martin led to the second round of pit stops, with Bobby Labonte and winner Jeff Gordon taking control from there.

Car No.: 20
Make & Model:
  Pontiac Grand Prix
Team Owner:
  Joe Gibbs
Wins: 3
Top 10: 21

4th

Tony Stewart

Tony Stewart, at 27 just three months older than previous wonder Jeff Gordon, reset all the rookie records in 1999, winning three races and finishing fourth in points, with a rookie crew chief and what amounted to a new, Joe Gibbs-owned team. Stewart was especially impressive toward the end, winning back-to-back races at Phoenix and Homestead. The finish at the Homestead inaugural was controversial, with Stewart bumping by teammate and race-long leader Bobby Labonte for position off Tony's green-flag stop on Lap 248. He thus had the lead when the pit cycle was completed on Lap 257, Labonte finishing second.

5th

Car No.: 99
Make & Model: Ford Taurus
Team Owner: Jack Roush
Wins: 6
Top 10: 23

Jeff Burton

Jeff Burton emerged as a quiet challenger, more so than Jeff Gordon and Tony Stewart. By 1999, Burton had become a force, winning six races (second only to Gordon) and finishing fifth in points for the second year in a row. He also twice won Winston No Bull bonuses and more than doubled his 1998 season take, earning $5.7 million. One of those bonuses came from the rain-shortened Southern 500 at Darlington, where Burton led the most laps and was ahead when rain began to fall. Jeff did a rain dance, the race ended on Lap 270, and brother Ward had to sit and stew in second place.

Jeff Gordon

6th

Jeff Gordon, already a three-time champion at age 27, endured dramatic changes in 1999. Gordon continued to be the series' leading winner, with seven trophies. In late August, however, Gordon learned that Ray Evernham—the only crew chief he had had in NASCAR—would leave to direct Dodge's new program, announced that October. Gordon resisted Dodge's offers, staying with Chevrolet and Rick Hendrick and becoming part-owner of the No. 24 team. The big jewel was Gordon's second Daytona 500 victory (in just his seventh try). He ran down Rusty Wallace with 11 laps to go, using the lapped car of Ricky Rudd for a who-blinks-first move down the backstretch.

Car No.: 24
Make & Model: Chevrolet Monte Carlo
Team Owner: Rick Hendrick
Wins: 7
Top 10: 21

7th

Car No.: 3
Make & Model:
   Chevrolet Monte Carlo
Team Owner:
   Richard Childress
Wins: 3
Top 10: 21

Dale Earnhardt

Old master Dale Earnhardt bounced back in 1999 with three victories, his most since 1995, although he improved just one position in points over 1998, to seventh. For the fifth time, he finished second in the Daytona 500, then won twice on his own real estate at Talladega. In between, Earnhardt won at Bristol (shown here) with classic Earnhardt methods. He spun out leader Terry Labonte on the backstretch and beat Jimmy Spencer by a car-length, then pleaded not guilty while enduring the boos of 140,000 on a hot Saturday night. Earnhardt and Labonte had swapped the lead seven times over the final 122 laps.

8th

Car No.: 2
Make & Model: Ford Taurus
Team Owner: Roger Penske
Wins: 1
Top 10: 16

Rusty Wallace

Rusty Wallace won just one race for the third year in a row but fell from fourth to eighth in points, in part because of a slow start and two terrible finishes in the summer, at Pocono and New Hampshire. As always, Wallace excelled at Bristol's half-mile concrete fishbowl, out-running Mark Martin by .223 of a second—about two car-lengths. Wallace, however, had the car to beat. He started on the pole and led the first 197 laps. After a mid-race sort-out, Wallace returned to power, leading the last 149 rounds, with a caution on Lap 479 (of 500) closing the field for the finish run.

Car No.: 22
Make & Model: Pontiac Grand Prix
Team Owner: Bill Davis
Wins: 0
Top 10: 16

Ward Burton

Owner Bill Davis continued to build his racing apparatus in 1999, developing World of Outlaws star Dave Blaney as an eventual teammate for veteran Ward Burton and retaining talented Tommy Baldwin as Burton's crew chief, despite serious runs at Baldwin by other teams. Ward, older brother of Jeff, scored a career-best ninth in points, although he finished without a win. Burton won a pole at Michigan and pressed brother Jeff to the end at Darlington in September, being left with second place when rain came. Ward also finished second at Las Vegas and at Rockingham in the fall and finished no lower than 14th in the last nine races.

9th

Mike Skinner

Mike Skinner, in his first full season with crew chief Larry McReynolds, showed major gains, improving to 10th in points and winning two poles, at Pocono and Richmond. Skinner's go-or-blow nature was costly at several stops, however, including Texas in April (shown here), where Skinner crashed out on Lap 124, finishing 42nd. The Texas disaster came amid a terrible spring streak through which Skinner finished 21st or worse in five of seven races. Mike had started well, finishing no worse than sixth in the first four races. His best run of the year came at Charlotte in the fall, where he was third.

10th

Car No.: 31
Make & Model: Chevrolet Monte Carlo
Team Owner: Richard Childress
Wins: 0
Top 10: 14

11th

Jeremy Mayfield

Jeremy Mayfield seemed to be either very good or horrid through 1999 as change within the Penske and Kranefuss teams broke around him. The most striking change was the departure of crew chief Paul Andrews in May, with veteran Peter Sospenzo taking his place. Results, however, did not change so that anyone noticed. In 11 races with Andrews, Mayfield had shown fifth at Rockingham, second at Darlington, fifth at Texas, and seventh at California. With Sospenzo, he made top 10 at Charlotte, Dover, Pocono, Sonoma, Darlington, Charlotte, Rockingham, and Atlanta. Summer was terrible, with a 10-race stretch in which Jeremy finished better than 25nd only twice.

Car No.: 12
Make & Model: Ford Taurus
Team Owner: Roger Penske
Wins: 0
Top 10: 12

12th

Car No.: 5
Make & Model:
  Chevrolet Monte Carlo
Team Owner:
  Rick Hendrick
Wins: 1
Top 10: 7

Terry Labonte

Labonte kept alive his streak of winning at least once in each of his six years with Rick Hendrick, scoring at Texas in April. Overall, however, performance suffered, and Labonte finished out of the top 10 in points for the first time during his Hendrick years. Aside from the win, Terry had just five other top-10 finishes, and he had to use provisional starting spots an embarrassing nine times. Young crew chief Andy Graves left after the season to try his hand at Indy cars with Chip Ganassi, and Hendrick reinstalled Gary DeHart, who had guided Labonte to the championship in 1996, for the upcoming season.

13th

Car No.: 4
Make & Model: Chevrolet Monte Carlo
Team Owner: Larry McClure
Wins: 0
Top 10: 10

Bobby Hamilton

Capable regular Bobby Hamilton kept the fading Morgan-McClure team in the picture during 1999. Although he failed to win a race or a pole for the first time in four years, he propped up the organization with 10 top 10s, including a fourth place at Richmond in May. Shrewd Hamilton, meanwhile, had begun to build for his own future, staking out ground in the Craftsman Truck Series and maneuvering son Bobby Jr. into trucks and the Busch Series. Hamilton would spend one more year in the Kodak car, which would continue to drift backward in 2000.

Car No.: 1
Make & Model: Chevrolet Monte Carlo
Team Owner: Dale and Teresa Earnhardt
Wins: 0
Top 10: 5

Steve Park

Owner Dale Earnhardt showed patience with driver Steve Park, whose rookie season in 1999 had been ruined by injuries. A major acquisition was crew chief Paul Andrews, released in May by the Michael Kranefuss team and promptly snapped up by Earnhardt. Park began a gradual turnaround with a sixth at Michigan in June (his best of the year), then showed consistency down the stretch by finishing 15th or better in 10 of the final 11 races. Tough Bristol in April was an education, Park making the field with the last provisional (43rd) and struggling home 23rd, three laps down.

14th

15th

Ken Schrader

Ken Schrader, as usual, was steady, finishing his usual mid teens in points. Although he and the Andy Petree team reduced their DNFs to just one (in a wreck at Sears Point in June), overall results did not improve, with Schrader failing to record a top five for the first time since 1986. He did win the pole at Talladega in April. In September, Schrader reached agreement with Nelson Bowers' No. 36 team for 2000 (reportedly for substantially more money), ending a three-year tenure. At Atlanta in March (seen here), Schrader finished 26th, tumbling to 12th in points.

Car No.: 33
Make & Model: Chevrolet Monte Carlo
Team Owner: Andy Petree
Wins: 0
Top 10: 6

16th

Car No.: 40
Make & Model:
Chevrolet Monte Carlo
Team Owner:
Felix Sabates
Wins: 0
Top 10: 5

Sterling Marlin

Despite a crew chief change in midseason, with Scott Eggleston coming over from Joe Nemechek's companion team, veteran Sterling Marlin remained patient and brought stability to Felix Sabates' No. 40 team. Sterling, however, failed to find the winning form he had shown with Morgan-McClure, but it wasn't his fault. Marlin won the pole and finished fourth at Pocono in June, and he scored fourth place at Richmond in September. At Las Vegas in March, the team rallied somewhat from its disastrous start with a 15th-place run. The pole at Pocono, in record time, was the 10th of Marlin's career and first since 1995.

17th

Car No.: 43
Make & Model:
Pontiac Grand Prix
Team Owner: Richard Petty
Wins: 1
Top 10: 10

John Andretti

John Andretti, in his second season with the Petty team, produced a special highlight but endured several lows. In April at Martinsville, Richard Petty's best track, Andretti seized the lead from Jeff Burton with four laps to go and scored his, and Petty's, first victory since 1997 (shown here). On the other side, 10 DNFs, including early wrecks in three straight races in August and September, dropped Andretti and crew from 11th to 17th in points. Andretti, however, seemed to have found a home with the Pettys as the decade ended, with Kyle Petty increasingly taking over team operations.

18th

Wally Dallenbach Jr.

Wally Dallenbach, who somehow never seemed to last long anywhere, had his hopes up as he began his first full season with Rick Hendrick in 1999. Dallenbach had taken the ride mid season the year before, when starter Ricky Craven was dismissed shortly after returning from injuries. The 1999 campaign was Dallenbach's best in some ways, as he finished 18th in points and earned $1,741,178—more than double what he had made in any previous year. His best finish, however, was fifth at Pocono in July, and the always-puzzling No. 25 team settled into mediocrity afterward.

Car No.: 25
Make & Model: Chevrolet Monte Carlo
Team Owner: Rick Hendrick
Wins: 0
Top 10: 6

Car No.: 28
Make & Model: Ford Taurus
Team Owner: Robert Yates
Wins: 0
Top 10: 6

19th

Kenny Irwin

The "next Jeff Gordon" tag had faded after Kenny Irwin's disappointing performance in 1998. Results improved in 1999 but hung in the mid range, with Robert Yates's once-powerful No. 28 team seemingly having lost his way. Irwin showed flashes of his skill and commitment by roaring from 41st to third in the Daytona 500 and winning poles at Texas (April) and Darlington's Southern 500. Irwin, however, never rose above 18th in points after the false start and was out the door after the season. At Rockingham in February, Irwin quickly came down from his Daytona peak, finishing 23rd.

20th

Jimmy Spencer

Jimmy Spencer's long relationship with owner Travis Carter continued through 1999, although the effort was complicated by the arrival of aging teammate Darrell Waltrip. Waltrip, however, helped bring aboard sponsor Kmart, due to replace Winston as sponsor of Spencer's No. 23 in 2000. Sound complicated? It did to Spencer, who at times chafed under the extra weight of Waltrip's No. 66 group. Spencer made all the races in 2000 but slipped six positions in points. The high point was a strong second to Dale Earnhardt at Bristol in August. The next week at Darlington (seen here) Jimmy finished 15th.

Car No.: 23
Make & Model: Ford Taurus
Team Owner: Travis Carter
Wins: 0
Top 10: 4

21st

Car No.: 94
Make & Model: Ford Taurus
Team Owner: Bill Elliott
Wins: 0
Top 10: 2

Bill Elliott

Bill Elliott learned in late summer that long time sponsor McDonald's would leave after the 2000 season. Although he held out hope for the team he had formed in 1995, the McDonald's announcement was the beginning of the end, with Elliott enduring an uncomfortable 18 months with his lame-duck sponsor to the end of 2000. Spring and summer were best for Awesome Bill, with 10th at Talladega in April starting a streak of strong runs, including bright qualifying results at Dover, Michigan, Pocono, and Sears Point. Elliott faded after that, finishing no better than 20th in the final five races.

Kenny Wallace

Kenny Wallace had built a solid relationship with sponsor Square D through four years with Fil Martocci, and he carried the company to Andy Petree's team in 1999, as teammate to Ken Schrader. The Martocci team collapsed thereafter. Petree, fighting for a place in the sun among Winston Cup owners, was determined to expand his operation, and the Wallace/Square D situation played that way. The new team was all over the chart in 1999, with Kenny, youngest of the Wallace brothers, scoring second at New Hampshire in July but managing only four other top 10s. Always a good qualifier, Wallace started outside-front at Richmond in May.

22nd

Car No.: 55
Make & Model: Chevrolet Monte Carlo
Team Owner: Andy Petree
Wins: 0
Top 10: 5

23rd

Car No.: 97
Make & Model: Ford Taurus
Team Owner: Jack Roush
Wins: 0
Top 10: 5

Chad Little

Chad Little was quietly consistent in his second year with Jack Roush, who continued to draw the lifeblood of racing from sponsor John Deere. Overall results sagged a little, with Chad making just five top fives, including three from August on. His best start of the season was fourth at Daytona in July, next to teammate Mark Martin. Otherwise, Chad was pretty much invisible. He did well in the Daytona 500, finishing ninth, best among the Roush cars. He and the No. 97 team fell into the pattern the next week at Rockingham (shown here), however, with Little finishing 21st.

Car No.: 21
Make & Model: Ford Taurus
Team Owner: Wood Brothers
Wins: 0
Top 10: 1

24th

Elliott Sadler

The dark cloud settled in quickly over Elliott Sadler's Winston Cup career, rookie with the Wood Brothers team in 1999. Sadler, like the Woods, a border Virginian, had won five races in two Busch Series seasons and was considered a serious prospect. Wrecks in the first five races, however, hurt Sadler's morale, and it took him a year to regain his feet. In addition, Tony Stewart overshadowed Sadler with the greatest rookie season in history. Sadler had hoped for better at Martinsville, the Woods' home track (shown here), but he started 36th and finished 28th, three laps behind.

Kevin Lepage

Jack Roush needed a trained hand to replace Ted Musgrave at the end of 1998, so he hired Kevin Lepage, veteran Busch and Busch North competitor from Vermont who had gained a foothold in Winston Cup with struggling Joe Falk. Lepage had no better luck with the curious No. 16 than had Musgrave and Wally Dallenbach before him. He finished 13th in the Daytona 500 (shown here), his best until a fifth at Darlington in September. Lepage needed 11 provisional starting spots before tearing off an improbable pole at Atlanta in the season finale; he had taken a provisional the week before at Miami.

25th

Car No.: 16
Make & Model: Ford Taurus
Team Owner: Jack Roush
Wins: 0
Top 10: 2

26th

Car No.: 44
Make & Model:
  Pontiac Grand Prix
Team Owner:
  Kyle Petty
Wins: 0
Top 10: 9

Kyle Petty

Kyle Petty abandoned his disguise in 1999, officially folding his pe2 team into ancestral Petty Enterprises and taking over leadership from his father, Richard, who faded from all but ceremonial view. Life and business got no easier for Kyle, as his No. 44 team, broken up by the move from Charlotte to Greensboro, stumbled through April, failing to qualify at Las Vegas and Texas. Kyle grabbed the bottom rung in May and began to pull himself up, scoring top 10s in three of the final six races and improving five positions in points in that stretch. Even with the DNQs, Petty gained four spots over 1998.

27th

Car No.: 60
Make & Model:
  Chevrolet Monte Carlo
Team Owner: Jim Mattei
Wins: 0
Top 10: 2

Geoff Bodine

One-of-a-kind Geoff Bodine in 1998 played out the last string with the team he bought in 1993 and sold to Jim Mattei in 1998—at the end of the season, he was out. Bodine admirer Joe Bessey, who had worked through Busch North into Busch Grand National in the early 1990s, set sail for Winston Cup in late 1998 and hired Geoff to drive in 1999, with backing from a Philadelphia electricity wholesaler. Not all the news was bad, with Bodine qualifying top 10 five times from August on (including Dover, shown here) and finishing third at Martinsville in September. Bodine had turned 50 in April and was showing wear.

Johnny Benson

No one believed Johnny Benson lost his touch during his two years with Jack Roush; he was a good driver before and a good driver afterward. In 1999, he sagged to 28th in points in Roush's five-car stable, and by the end of the year he wanted out. Roush obliged him, leaving Benson without a solid ride for 2000. Roush basically had over-expanded, and the No. 26 team was more or less a paperweight for the General Mills sponsorship, which the next year migrated to the Pettys. Johnny struggled to the finish with just two top 10s and 12 provisional starts. He *did* start outside-front at Darlington in March.

28th

Car No.: 26
Make & Model: Ford Taurus
Team Owner: Jack Roush
Wins: 0
Top 10: 2

Car No.: 7
Make & Model: Chevrolet Monte Carlo
Team Owner: Wood Brothers
Wins: 0
Top 10: 3

Michael Waltrip

After three years with the Wood Brothers, Michael Waltrip pitched in with Jim Mattei's No. 7 in 1999, replacing Geoff Bodine. It was never clear whether the No. 7 team was investment or toy to owner Mattei, who sold out to Jim Smith the following season. Waltrip, as usual, was game with a less-than-adequate team, which went from what looked like strong sponsorship from Philips to NationsRent mid year. There were few highlights, one being fifth place in the Daytona 500 and a No. 5 start at the Brickyard. Overall, however, the campaign was discouraging.

29th

Joe Nemechek

Nemechek endured another year of quiet turmoil with Felix Sabates' Team Sabco. The highlight film showed his first career victory at New Hampshire in September and poles at summer Daytona, fall Martinsville, and fall Talladega. The prelude and postscript to Nemechek's win at New Hampshire were five finishes of 19th or worse leading up, and finishes of 30th or worse in three of the next four following. It is not surprising that Nemechek finished 30th in points. Joe's runs at Rockingham (shown here) were middling, with 24th place in February and 26th place in October. Both driver and owner had their eyes elsewhere for 2000.

30th

Car No.: 42
Make & Model: Chevrolet Monte Carlo
Team Owner: Felix Sabates
Wins: 1
Top 10: 3

Darrell Waltrip

With Kmart firmly behind him as driver and spokesman, Darrell Waltrip took up with Travis Carter's team as running mate to Jimmy Spencer. Waltrip's career was about over, and he finally admitted it in August, announcing that the 2000 season would be his last. At 52, he had hung on a few years too long. Waltrip's sad decline was apparent when he used his four champion provisionals in the first four races of the year, then failed to qualify at Dover in June. It became painful when he couldn't make speed in five of the last nine races of the season, including the finale at Atlanta.

Car No.: 66
Make & Model: Ford Taurus
Team Owner: Carl Haas & Travis Carter
Wins: 0
Top 10: 0

Ernie Irvan

The meteoric career of Ernie Irvan crashed to earth in 1999, with Irvan announcing his retirement in August. Repeated injuries finally convinced him to step away from the danger, ending one of the more remarkable comeback stories in NASCAR history. Nearly killed at Michigan in 1994, he returned to win twice in 1996 and once in 1997, but the clock ran down in 1999. The MB2 team finished the season with Dick Trickle (one race, at Michigan) and rising star Jerry Nadeau before settling on Ken Schrader for 2000. Irvan's best of the year was sixth at Las Vegas in March.

Car No.: 36
Make & Model: Pontiac Grand Prix
Team Owner: MB2
Wins: 0
Top 10: 5

Dale Earnhardt Jr.

The stars of the next decade began to emerge in 1999, and primary among them was Dale Earnhardt Jr., son of the seven-time champion. Junior made his debut in a Budweiser-dressed car at, of all places, Charlotte, nerve center of racing, previewing his full-season, Bud-backed rookie effort in 2000. Junior did not do bad, finishing 16th (shown here), three laps down. Young Earnhardt, 25, had earned the try, winning championships in both his seasons in the Busch Series. He ran four more races in Dad's cars in 1999—New Hampshire, Michigan, Richmond and Atlanta—with a best of 10th at Richmond

Car No.: 8
Make & Model: Chevrolet Monte Carlo
Team Owner: Dale Earnhardt
Wins: 0
Top 10: 1

Ricky Rudd

Ricky Rudd knew it was all over as owner by spring 1999, with sponsor Tide migrating to Cal Wells' new team. Still, his streak of consecutive winning seasons, dating to 1983, was important to him, and he pressed on like a soldier to the end, falling just short at Bristol, Talladega, and Phoenix down the stretch. In late summer, Rudd had agreed to begin in 2000 with Robert Yates, and by late fall 1999, he had wound down his business to a skeleton crew. He auctioned what he could at Thanksgiving, merged with Yates what he could, and quietly closed a six-year try at making it on his own.

Car No.: 10
Make & Model: Ford Taurus
Team Owner: Ricky Rudd
Wins: 0
Top 10: 5

Car No.: 17
Make & Model: Ford Taurus
Team Owner: Jack Roush
Wins: 0
Top 10: 1

Matt Kenseth

Matt Kenseth, modest young fellow from Wisconsin, earned respect from Mark Martin during two years in Busch, and Martin recommended him to owner Jack Roush. Roush graduated Kenseth and sponsor DeWalt tools for a five-race tryout in 1999, beginning at Michigan in August. Matt's other auditions were at Richmond, Dover, Charlotte, and Rockingham. Kenseth was especially impressive at Dover in September, where he had done well filling in for Bill Elliott the year before; he finished fourth, behind Martin, Tony Stewart, and Dale Jarrett. Kenseth quickly was cast as Dale Jr.'s top rival for 2000.

Appendix

1990 Season

Daytona 500
Daytona Beach, Fla.
February 18

1. Derrike Cope — Chevrolet
2. Terry Labonte — Oldsmobile
3. Bill Elliott — Ford
4. Ricky Rudd — Chevrolet
5. Dale Earnhardt — Chevrolet

Pontiac Excitement 400
Richmond, Va.
February 25

1. Mark Martin — Ford
2. Dale Earnhardt — Chevrolet
3. Ricky Rudd — Chevrolet
4. Bill Elliott — Ford
5. Dick Trickle — Pontiac

Goodwrench 500
Rockingham, N.C.
March 4

1. Kyle Petty — Pontiac
2. Geoff Bodine — Ford
3. Ken Schrader — Chevrolet
4. Sterling Marlin — Oldsmobile
5. Rusty Wallace — Pontiac

Motorcraft Quality Parts 500
Hampton, Ga.
March 18

1. Dale Earnhardt — Chevrolet
2. Morgan Shepherd — Ford
3. Ernie Irvan — Oldsmobile
4. Ken Schrader — Chevrolet
5. Mark Martin — Ford

TranSouth 500
Darlington, S.C.
April 1

1. Dale Earnhardt — Chevrolet
2. Mark Martin — Ford
3. Davey Allison — Ford
4. Geoff Bodine — Ford
5. Morgan Shepherd — Ford

Valleydale Meats 500
Bristol, Tenn.
April 8

1. Davey Allison — Ford
2. Mark Martin — Ford
3. Ricky Rudd — Chevrolet
4. Terry Labonte — Oldsmobile
5. Rick Wilson — Oldsmobile

First Union 400
North Wilkesboro, N.C.
April 22

1. Brett Bodine — Buick
2. Darrell Waltrip — Chevrolet
3. Dale Earnhardt — Chevrolet
4. Ricky Rudd — Chevrolet
5. Morgan Shepherd — Ford

Hanes Activewear 500
Martinsville, Va.
April 29

1. Geoff Bodine — Ford
2. Rusty Wallace — Pontiac
3. Morgan Shepherd — Ford
4. Darrell Waltrip — Chevrolet
5. Dale Earnhardt — Chevrolet

Winston 500
Talladega, Ala.
May 6

1. Dale Earnhardt — Chevrolet
2. Greg Sacks — Chevrolet
3. Mark Martin — Ford
4. Ernie Irvan — Oldsmobile
5. Michael Waltrip — Pontiac

Coca-Cola 600
Concord, N.C.
May 27

1. Rusty Wallace — Pontiac
2. Bill Elliott — Ford
3. Mark Martin — Ford
4. Michael Waltrip — Pontiac
5. Ernie Irvan — Oldsmobile

Budweiser 500
Dover, Del.
June 3

1. Derrike Cope — Chevrolet
2. Ken Schrader — Chevrolet
3. Dick Trickle — Pontiac
4. Mark Martin — Ford
5. Sterling Marlin — Oldsmobile

Banquet Frozen Foods 300
Sonoma, Calif.
June 10

1. Rusty Wallace — Pontiac
2. Mark Martin — Ford

Miller Genuine Draft 500
Pocono, Pa.
June 17

1. Harry Gant — Oldsmobile
2. Rusty Wallace — Pontiac
3. Geoff Bodine — Ford
4. Brett Bodine — Buick
5. Davey Allison — Ford

Miller Genuine Draft 400
Brooklyn, Mich.
June 24

1. Dale Earnhardt — Chevrolet
2. Ernie Irvan — Oldsmobile
3. Geoff Bodine — Ford
4. Mark Martin — Ford
5. Harry Gant — Oldsmobile

Pepsi 400
Daytona Beach, Fla.
July 7

1. Dale Earnhardt — Chevrolet
2. Alan Kulwicki — Ford
3. Ken Schrader — Chevrolet
4. Terry Labonte — Oldsmobile
5. Sterling Marlin — Oldsmobile

AC Spark Plug 500
Pocono, Pa.
July 22

1. Geoff Bodine — Ford
2. Bill Elliott — Ford
3. Rusty Wallace — Pontiac
4. Dale Earnhardt — Chevrolet
5. Davey Allison — Ford

DieHard 500
Talladega, Ala.
July 29

1. Dale Earnhardt — Chevrolet
2. Bill Elliott — Ford
3. Sterling Marlin — Oldsmobile
4. Alan Kulwicki — Ford
5. Ricky Rudd — Chevrolet

Budweiser at the Glen
Watkins Glen, N.Y.
August 12

1. Ricky Rudd — Chevrolet

2. Geoff Bodine — Ford
3. Brett Bodine — Buick
4. Michael Waltrip — Pontiac
5. Mark Martin — Ford

Champion Spark Plug 400
Brooklyn, Mich.
August 19

1. Mark Martin — Ford
2. Greg Sacks — Chevrolet
3. Rusty Wallace — Pontiac
4. Bill Elliott — Ford
5. Ricky Rudd — Chevrolet

Busch 500
Bristol, Tenn.
August 25

1. Ernie Irvan — Chevrolet
2. Rusty Wallace — Pontiac
3. Mark Martin — Ford
4. Terry Labonte — Oldsmobile
5. Sterling Marlin — Oldsmobile

Heinz Southern 500
Darlington, S.C.
September 2

1. Dale Earnhardt — Chevrolet
2. Ernie Irvan — Chevrolet
3. Alan Kulwicki — Ford
4. Bill Elliott — Ford
5. Harry Gant — Oldsmobile

Miller Genuine Draft 400
Richmond, Va.
September 9

1. Dale Earnhardt — Chevrolet
2. Mark Martin — Ford
3. Darrell Waltrip — Chevrolet
4. Bill Elliott — Ford
5. Rusty Wallace — Pontiac

Peak Antifreeze 500
Dover, Del.
September 16

1. Bill Elliott — Ford
2. Mark Martin — Ford
3. Dale Earnhardt — Chevrolet
4. Harry Gant — Oldsmobile
5. Michael Waltrip — Pontiac

Goody's 500
Martinsville, Va.
September 23

1. Geoff Bodine — Ford
2. Dale Earnhardt — Chevrolet
3. Mark Martin — Ford
4. Brett Bodine — Buick
5. Harry Gant — Oldsmobile

Tyson Holly Farms 400
North Wilkesboro, N.C.
September 30

1. Mark Martin — Ford
2. Dale Earnhardt — Chevrolet
3. Brett Bodine — Buick
4. Bill Elliott — Ford
5. Ken Schrader — Chevrolet

Mello Yello 500
Concord, N.C.
October 6

1. Davey Allison — Ford
2. Morgan Shepherd — Ford
3. Michael Waltrip — Pontiac
4. Kyle Petty — Pontiac
5. Alan Kulwicki — Ford

AC Delco 500
Rockingham, N.C.
October 21

1. Alan Kulwicki — Ford
2. Bill Elliott — Ford
3. Harry Gant — Oldsmobile
4. Geoff Bodine — Ford
5. Ken Schrader — Chevrolet

Checker 500
Phoenix, Ariz.
November 4

1. Dale Earnhardt — Chevrolet
2. Ken Schrader — Chevrolet
3. Morgan Shepherd — Ford
4. Darrell Waltrip — Chevrolet
5. Bill Elliott — Ford

Atlanta Journal 500
Hampton, Ga.
November 18

1. Morgan Shepherd — Ford
2. Geoff Bodine — Ford
3. Dale Earnhardt — Chevrolet
4. Dale Jarrett — Ford
5. Darrell Waltrip — Chevrolet

1991 Season

Daytona 500
Daytona Beach, Fla.
February 17

1. Ernie Irvan — Chevrolet
2. Sterling Marlin — Ford
3. Joe Ruttman — Oldsmobile
4. Rick Mast — Oldsmobile
5. Dale Earnhardt — Chevrolet

Pontiac Excitement 400
Richmond, Va.
February 24

1. Dale Earnhardt — Chevrolet
2. Ricky Rudd — Chevrolet
3. Harry Gant — Oldsmobile
4. Rusty Wallace — Pontiac
5. Alan Kulwicki — Ford

Goodwrench 500
Rockingham, N.C.
March 3

1. Kyle Petty — Pontiac
2. Ken Schrader — Chevrolet
3. Harry Gant — Oldsmobile
4. Ricky Rudd — Chevrolet
5. Bill Elliott — Ford

Motorcraft Quality Parts 500
Hampton, Ga.
March 18

1. Ken Schrader — Chevrolet
2. Bill Elliott — Ford
3. Dale Earnhardt — Chevrolet
4. Morgan Shepherd — Ford
5. Michael Waltrip — Pontiac

TranSouth 500
Darlington, S.C.
April 7

1. Ricky Rudd — Chevrolet
2. Davey Allison — Ford
3. Michael Waltrip — Pontiac
4. Mark Martin — Ford
5. Rusty Wallace — Pontiac

Valleydale Meats 500
Bristol, Tenn.
April 14

1. Rusty Wallace — Pontiac
2. Ernie Irvan — Chevrolet
3. Davey Allison — Ford
4. Mark Martin — Ford
5. Ricky Rudd — Chevrolet

First Union 400
North Wilkesboro, N.C.
April 21

1. Darrell Waltrip — Chevrolet
2. Dale Earnhardt — Chevrolet
3. Jimmy Spencer — Chevrolet
4. Morgan Shepherd — Ford
5. Ken Schrader — Chevrolet

Hanes 500
Martinsville, Va.
April 28

1. Dale Earnhardt — Chevrolet
2. Kyle Petty — Pontiac
3. Darrell Waltrip — Chevrolet
4. Brett Bodine — Buick
5. Harry Gant — Oldsmobile

Winston 500
Talladega, Ala.
May 6

1. Harry Gant — Oldsmobile
2. Darrell Waltrip — Chevrolet
3. Dale Earnhardt — Chevrolet
4. Sterling Marlin — Ford
5. Michael Waltrip — Pontiac

Coca-Cola 600
Concord, N.C.
May 26

1. Davey Allison — Ford
2. Ken Schrader — Chevrolet
3. Dale Earnhardt — Chevrolet
4. Harry Gant — Oldsmobile
5. Dale Jarrett — Ford

Budweiser 500
Dover, Del.
June 2

1. Ken Schrader — Chevrolet
2. Dale Earnhardt — Chevrolet
3. Harry Gant — Oldsmobile
4. Ernie Irvan — Chevrolet
5. Mark Martin — Ford

Banquet Frozen Foods 300
Sonoma, Calif.
June 9

1. Davey Allison — Ford
2. Ricky Rudd — Chevrolet
3. Rusty Wallace — Pontiac
4. Ernie Irvan — Chevrolet
5. Ken Schrader — Chevrolet

Champion Spark Plug 500
Pocono, Pa.
June 16

1. Darrell Waltrip — Chevrolet
2. Dale Earnhardt — Chevrolet
3. Mark Martin — Ford
4. Harry Gant — Oldsmobile
5. Geoff Bodine — Ford

Miller Genuine Draft 400
Brooklyn, Mich.
June 23

1. Davey Allison — Ford
2. Hut Stricklin — Buick
3. Mark Martin — Ford
4. Dale Earnhardt — Chevrolet
5. Ernie Irvan — Chevrolet

Pepsi 400
Daytona Beach, Fla.
July 6

1. Bill Elliott — Ford

2. Geoff Bodine — Ford
3. Davey Allison — Ford
4. Ken Schrader — Chevrolet
5. Ernie Irvan — Chevrolet

Miller Genuine Draft 500
Pocono, Pa.
July 21

1. Rusty Wallace — Pontiac
2. Mark Martin — Ford
3. Geoff Bodine — Ford
4. Hut Stricklin — Buick
5. Sterling Marlin — Ford

DieHard 500
Talladega, Ala.
July 28

1. Dale Earnhardt — Chevrolet
2. Bill Elliott — Ford
3. Mark Martin — Ford
4. Ricky Rudd — Chevrolet
5. Sterling Marlin — Ford

Budweiser at the Glen
Watkins Glen, N.Y.
August 11

1. Ernie Irvan — Chevrolet
2. Ricky Rudd — Chevrolet
3. Mark Martin — Ford
4. Rusty Wallace — Pontiac
5. Dale Jarrett — Ford

Champion Spark Plug 400
Brooklyn, Mich.
August 18

1. Dale Jarrett — Ford
2. Davey Allison — Ford
3. Rusty Wallace — Pontiac
4. Mark Martin — Ford
5. Bill Elliott — Ford

Bud 500
Bristol, Tenn.
August 24

1. Alan Kulwicki — Ford
2. Sterling Marlin — Ford
3. Ken Schrader — Chevrolet
4. Mark Martin — Ford
5. Ricky Rudd — Chevrolet

Heinz Southern 500
Darlington, S.C.
September 1

1. Harry Gant — Oldsmobile
2. Ernie Irvan — Chevrolet
3. Ken Schrader — Chevrolet
4. Derrike Cope — Chevrolet
5. Terry Labonte — Oldsmobile

Miller Genuine Draft 400
Richmond, Va.
September 7

1. Harry Gant — Oldsmobile
2. Davey Allison — Ford
3. Rusty Wallace — Pontiac
4. Ernie Irvan — Chevrolet
5. Ricky Rudd — Chevrolet

Peak Antifreeze 500
Dover, Del.
September 15

1. Harry Gant — Oldsmobile
2. Geoff Bodine — Ford
3. Morgan Shepherd — Ford
4. Hut Stricklin — Buick
5. Michael Waltrip — Pontiac

Goody's 500
Martinsville, Va.
September 22

1. Harry Gant — Oldsmobile
2. Brett Bodine — Buick
3. Dale Earnhardt — Chevrolet
4. Ernie Irvan — Chevrolet
5. Mark Martin — Ford

Tyson Holly Farms 400
North Wilkesboro, N.C.
September 29

1. Dale Earnhardt — Chevrolet
2. Harry Gant — Oldsmobile
3. Morgan Shepherd — Ford
4. Davey Allison — Ford
5. Mark Martin — Ford

Mello Yello 500
Concord, N.C.
October 6

1. Geoff Bodine — Ford
2. Davey Allison — Ford
3. Alan Kulwicki — Ford
4. Harry Gant — Oldsmobile
5. Sterling Marlin — Ford

AC Delco 500
Rockingham, N.C.
October 20

1. Davey Allison — Ford
2. Harry Gant — Oldsmobile
3. Mark Martin — Ford
4. Geoff Bodine — Ford
5. Ken Schrader — Chevrolet

Pyroil 500
Phoenix, Ariz.
November 3

1. Davey Allison — Ford

2. Darrell Waltrip — Chevrolet
3. Sterling Marlin — Ford
4. Alan Kulwicki — Ford
5. Rusty Wallace — Pontiac

Hardee's 500
Hampton, Ga.
November 17

1. Mark Martin — Ford
2. Ernie Irvan — Chevrolet
3. Bill Elliott — Ford
4. Harry Gant — Oldsmobile
5. Dale Earnhardt — Chevrolet

1992 Season

Daytona 500
Daytona Beach, Fla.
February 16

1. Davey Allison — Ford
2. Morgan Shepherd — Ford
3. Geoff Bodine — Ford
4. Alan Kulwicki — Ford
5. Dick Trickle — Oldsmobile

Goodwrench 500
Rockingham, N.C.
March 1

1. Bill Elliott — Ford
2. Davey Allison — Ford
3. Harry Gant — Oldsmobile
4. Michael Waltrip — Pontiac
5. Ken Schrader — Chevrolet

Pontiac Excitement 400
Richmond, Va.
March 8

1. Bill Elliott — Ford
2. Alan Kulwicki — Ford
3. Harry Gant — Oldsmobile
4. Davey Allison — Ford
5. Darrell Waltrip — Chevrolet

Motorcraft Quality Parts 500
Hampton, Ga.
March 15

1. Bill Elliott — Ford
2. Harry Gant — Oldsmobile
3. Dale Earnhardt — Chevrolet
4. Davey Allison — Ford
5. Dick Trickle — Ford

TranSouth 500
Darlington, S.C.
March 29

1. Bill Elliott — Ford
2. Harry Gant — Oldsmobile
3. Mark Martin — Ford
4. Davey Allison — Ford

5. Ricky Rudd — Chevrolet

Food City 500
Bristol, Tenn.
April 5

1. Alan Kulwicki — Ford
2. Dale Jarrett — Chevrolet
3. Ken Schrader — Chevrolet
4. Terry Labonte — Oldsmobile
5. Dick Trickle — Ford

First Union 400
North Wilkesboro, N.C.
April 12

1. Davey Allison — Ford
2. Rusty Wallace — Pontiac
3. Ricky Rudd — Chevrolet
4. Geoff Bodine — Ford
5. Harry Gant — Oldsmobile

Hanes 500
Martinsville, Va.
April 26

1. Mark Martin — Ford
2. Sterling Marlin — Ford
3. Darrell Waltrip — Chevrolet
4. Terry Labonte — Oldsmobile
5. Harry Gant — Oldsmobile

Winston 500
Talladega, Ala.
May 3

1. Davey Allison — Ford
2. Bill Elliott — Ford
3. Dale Earnhardt — Chevrolet
4. Sterling Marlin — Ford
5. Ernie Irvan — Chevrolet

Coca-Cola 600
Concord, N.C.
May 24

1. Dale Earnhardt — Chevrolet
2. Ernie Irvan — Chevrolet
3. Kyle Petty — Pontiac
4. Davey Allison — Ford
5. Harry Gant — Oldsmobile

Budweiser 500
Dover, Del.
May 31

1. Harry Gant — Oldsmobile
2. Dale Earnhardt — Chevrolet
3. Rusty Wallace — Pontiac
4. Ernie Irvan — Chevrolet
5. Darrell Waltrip — Chevrolet

Save Mart 300
Sonoma, Calif.
June 7

1. Ernie Irvan — Chevrolet
2. Terry Labonte — Oldsmobile
3. Mark Martin — Ford
4. Ricky Rudd — Chevrolet
5. Bill Elliott — Ford

Champion Spark Plug 500
Pocono, Pa.
June 14

1. Alan Kulwicki — Ford
2. Mark Martin — Ford
3. Bill Elliott — Ford
4. Ken Schrader — Chevrolet
5. Davey Allison — Ford

Miller Genuine Draft 400
Brooklyn, Mich.
June 21

1. Davey Allison — Ford
2. Darrell Waltrip — Chevrolet
3. Alan Kulwicki — Ford
4. Kyle Petty — Pontiac
5. Ricky Rudd — Chevrolet

Pepsi 400
Daytona Beach, Fla.
July 4

1. Ernie Irvan — Chevrolet
2. Sterling Marlin — Ford
3. Dale Jarrett — Chevrolet
4. Geoff Bodine — Ford
5. Bill Elliott — Ford

Miller Genuine Draft 500
Pocono, Pa.
July 19

1. Darrell Waltrip — Chevrolet
2. Harry Gant — Oldsmobile
3. Alan Kulwicki — Ford
4. Ricky Rudd — Chevrolet
5. Ted Musgrave — Ford

DieHard 500
Talladega, Ala.
July 26

1. Ernie Irvan — Chevrolet
2. Sterling Marlin — Ford
3. Davey Allison — Ford
4. Ricky Rudd — Chevrolet
5. Bill Elliott — Ford

Budweiser at the Glen
Watkins Glen, N.Y.
August 9

1. Kyle Petty — Pontiac
2. Morgan Shepherd — Ford
3. Ernie Irvan — Chevrolet
4. Mark Martin — Ford
5. Wally Dallenbach Jr. — Ford

Champion Spark Plug 400
Brooklyn, Mich.
August 16

1. Harry Gant — Oldsmobile
2. Darrell Waltrip — Chevrolet
3. Bill Elliott — Ford
4. Ernie Irvan — Chevrolet
5. Davey Allison — Ford

Bud 500
Bristol, Tenn.
August 29

1. Darrell Waltrip — Chevrolet
2. Dale Earnhardt — Chevrolet
3. Ken Schrader — Chevrolet
4. Kyle Petty — Pontiac
5. Alan Kulwicki — Ford

Mountain Dew Southern 500
Darlington, S.C.
September 6

1. Darrell Waltrip — Chevrolet
2. Mark Martin — Ford
3. Bill Elliott — Ford
4. Brett Bodine — Ford
5. Davey Allison — Ford

Miller Genuine Draft 400
Richmond, Va.
September 12

1. Rusty Wallace — Pontiac
2. Mark Martin — Ford
3. Darrell Waltrip — Chevrolet
4. Dale Earnhardt — Chevrolet
5. Geoff Bodine — Ford

Peak Antifreeze 500
Dover, Del.
September 20

1. Ricky Rudd — Chevrolet
2. Bill Elliott — Ford
3. Kyle Petty — Pontiac
4. Davey Allison — Ford
5. Morgan Shepherd — Ford

Goody's 500
Martinsville, Va.
September 27

1. Geoff Bodine — Ford
2. Rusty Wallace — Pontiac
3. Brett Bodine — Ford
4. Kyle Petty — Pontiac
5. Alan Kulwicki — Ford

Tyson Holly Farms 400
North Wilkesboro, N.C.
October 5

1. Geoff Bodine — Ford

2. Mark Martin — Ford
3. Kyle Petty — Pontiac
4. Rusty Wallace — Pontiac
5. Sterling Marlin — Ford

Mello Yello 500
Concord, N.C.
October 12

1. Mark Martin — Ford
2. Alan Kulwicki — Ford
3. Kyle Petty — Pontiac
4. Jimmy Spencer — Ford
5. Ricky Rudd — Chevrolet

AC Delco 500
Rockingham, N.C.
October 25

1. Kyle Petty — Pontiac
2. Ernie Irvan — Chevrolet
3. Ricky Rudd — Chevrolet
4. Bill Elliott — Ford
5. Sterling Marlin — Ford

Pyroil 500
Phoenix, Ariz.
November 1

1. Davey Allison — Ford
2. Mark Martin — Ford
3. Darrell Waltrip — Chevrolet
4. Alan Kulwicki — Ford
5. Jimmy Spencer — Ford

Hooters 500
Hampton, Ga.
November 15

1. Bill Elliott — Ford
2. Alan Kulwicki — Ford
3. Geoff Bodine — Ford
4. Jimmy Spencer — Ford
5. Terry Labonte — Chevrolet

1993 Season

Daytona 500
Daytona Beach, Fla.
February 14

1. Dale Jarrett — Chevrolet
2. Dale Earnhardt — Chevrolet
3. Geoff Bodine — Ford
4. Hut Stricklin — Ford
5. Jeff Gordon — Chevrolet

Goodwrench 500
Rockingham, N.C.
February 28

1. Rusty Wallace — Pontiac
2. Dale Earnhardt — Chevrolet
3. Ernie Irvan — Chevrolet
4. Alan Kulwicki — Ford

5. Mark Martin — Ford

Pontiac Excitement 400
Richmond, Va.
March 7

1. Davey Allison — Ford
2. Rusty Wallace — Pontiac
3. Alan Kulwicki — Ford
4. Dale Jarrett — Chevrolet
5. Kyle Petty — Pontiac

Motorcraft 500
Hampton, Ga.
March 20

1. Morgan Shepherd — Ford
2. Ernie Irvan — Chevrolet
3. Rusty Wallace — Pontiac
4. Jeff Gordon — Chevrolet
5. Ricky Rudd — Chevrolet

TranSouth 500
Darlington, S.C.
March 28

1. Dale Earnhardt — Chevrolet
2. Mark Martin — Ford
3. Dale Jarrett — Chevrolet
4. Ken Schrader — Chevrolet
5. Rusty Wallace — Pontiac

Food City 500
Bristol, Tenn.
April 4

1. Rusty Wallace — Pontiac
2. Dale Earnhardt — Chevrolet
3. Kyle Petty — Pontiac
4. Jimmy Spencer — Ford
5. Davey Allison — Ford

First Union 400
North Wilkesboro, N.C.
April 18

1. Rusty Wallace — Pontiac
2. Kyle Petty — Pontiac
3. Ken Schrader — Chevrolet
4. Davey Allison — Ford
5. Darrell Waltrip — Chevrolet

Hanes 500
Martinsville, Va.
April 25

1. Rusty Wallace — Pontiac
2. Davey Allison — Ford
3. Dale Jarrett — Chevrolet
4. Darrell Waltrip — Chevrolet
5. Kyle Petty — Pontiac

Winston 500
Talladega, Ala.
May 2

1. Ernie Irvan — Chevrolet
2. Jimmy Spencer — Ford
3. Dale Jarrett — Chevrolet
4. Dale Earnhardt — Chevrolet
5. Joe Ruttman — Ford

Save Mart Supermarkets 300
Sonoma, Calif.
May 16

1. Geoff Bodine — Ford
2. Ernie Irvan — Chevrolet
3. Ricky Rudd — Chevrolet
4. Ken Schrader — Chevrolet
5. Kyle Petty — Pontiac

Coca-Cola 600
Concord, N.C.
May 30

1. Dale Earnhardt — Chevrolet
2. Jeff Gordon — Chevrolet
3. Dale Jarrett — Chevrolet
4. Ken Schrader — Chevrolet
5. Ernie Irvan — Chevrolet

Budweiser 500
Dover, Del.
June 6

1. Dale Earnhardt — Chevrolet
2. Dale Jarrett — Chevrolet
3. Davey Allison — Ford
4. Mark Martin — Ford
5. Ken Schrader — Chevrolet

Champion Spark Plug 500
Pocono, Pa.
June 13

1. Kyle Petty — Pontiac
2. Ken Schrader — Chevrolet
3. Harry Gant — Chevrolet
4. Jimmy Spencer — Ford
5. Ted Musgrave — Ford

Miller Genuine Draft 400
Brooklyn, Mich.
June 20

1. Ricky Rudd — Chevrolet
2. Jeff Gordon — Chevrolet
3. Ernie Irvan — Chevrolet
4. Dale Jarrett — Chevrolet
5. Rusty Wallace — Pontiac

Pepsi 400
Daytona Beach, Fla.
July 3

1. Dale Earnhardt — Chevrolet
2. Sterling Marlin — Ford
3. Ken Schrader — Chevrolet
4. Ricky Rudd — Chevrolet
5. Jeff Gordon — Chevrolet

Slick 50 300
Loudon, N.H.
July 11

1. Rusty Wallace — Pontiac
2. Mark Martin — Ford
3. Davey Allison — Ford
4. Dale Jarrett — Chevrolet
5. Ricky Rudd — Chevrolet

Miller Genuine Draft 500
Pocono, Pa.
July 18

1. Dale Earnhardt — Chevrolet
2. Rusty Wallace — Pontiac
3. Bill Elliott — Ford
4. Morgan Shepherd — Ford
5. Brett Bodine — Ford

DieHard 500
Talladega, Ala.
July 25

1. Dale Earnhardt — Chevrolet
2. Ernie Irvan — Chevrolet
3. Mark Martin — Ford
4. Kyle Petty — Pontiac
5. Dale Jarrett — Chevrolet

Budweiser at the Glen
Watkins Glen, N.Y.
August 8

1. Mark Martin — Ford
2. Wally Dallenbach Jr. — Ford
3. Jimmy Spencer — Ford
4. Bill Elliott — Ford
5. Ken Schrader — Chevrolet

Champion Spark Plug 400
Brooklyn, Mich.
August 15

1. Mark Martin — Ford
2. Morgan Shepherd — Ford
3. Jeff Gordon — Chevrolet
4. Dale Jarrett — Chevrolet
5. Ted Musgrave — Ford

Bud 500
Bristol, Tenn.
August 28

1. Mark Martin — Ford
2. Rusty Wallace — Pontiac
3. Dale Earnhardt — Chevrolet
4. Harry Gant — Chevrolet
5. Rick Mast — Ford

Mountain Dew Southern 500
Darlington, S.C.
September 5

1. Mark Martin — Ford

2. Brett Bodine — Ford
3. Rusty Wallace — Pontiac
4. Dale Earnhardt — Chevrolet
5. Ernie Irvan — Ford

Miller Genuine Draft 400
Richmond, Va.
September 11

1. Rusty Wallace — Pontiac
2. Bill Elliott — Ford
3. Dale Earnhardt — Chevrolet
4. Ricky Rudd — Chevrolet
5. Brett Bodine — Ford

Splitfire Spark Plug 500
Dover, Del.
September 19

1. Rusty Wallace — Pontiac
2. Ken Schrader — Chevrolet
3. Darrell Waltrip — Chevrolet
4. Dale Jarrett — Chevrolet
5. Harry Gant — Chevrolet

Goody's 500
Martinsville, Va.
September 26

1. Ernie Irvan — Ford
2. Rusty Wallace — Pontiac
3. Jimmy Spencer — Ford
4. Ricky Rudd — Chevrolet
5. Dale Jarrett — Chevrolet

Tyson/Holly Farms 400
North Wilkesboro, N.C.
October 3

1. Rusty Wallace — Pontiac
2. Dale Earnhardt — Chevrolet
3. Ernie Irvan — Ford
4. Kyle Petty — Pontiac
5. Ricky Rudd — Chevrolet

Mello Yello 500
October 10
Concord, N.C.

1. Ernie Irvan — Ford
2. Mark Martin — Ford
3. Dale Earnhardt — Chevrolet
4. Rusty Wallace — Pontiac
5. Jeff Gordon — Chevrolet

AC Delco 500
Rockingham, N.C.
October 24

1. Rusty Wallace — Pontiac
2. Dale Earnhardt — Chevrolet
3. Bill Elliott — Ford
4. Harry Gant — Chevrolet
5. Mark Martin — Ford

Slick 50 500
Phoenix, Ariz.
October 31

1. Mark Martin   Ford
2. Ernie Irvan   Ford
3. Kyle Petty   Pontiac
4. Dale Earnhardt   Chevrolet
5. Bill Elliott   Ford

Hooters 500
Hampton, Ga.
November 24

1. Rusty Wallace   Pontiac
2. Ricky Rudd   Chevrolet
3. Darrell Waltrip   Chevrolet
4. Bill Elliott   Ford
5. Dick Trickle   Chevrolet

1994 Season

Daytona 500
Daytona Beach, Fla.
February 20

1. Sterling Marlin   Chevrolet
2. Ernie Irvan   Ford
3. Terry Labonte   Chevrolet
4. Jeff Gordon   Chevrolet
5. Morgan Shepherd   Ford

Goodwrench 500
Rockingham, N.C.
February 27

1. Rusty Wallace   Ford
2. Sterling Marlin   Chevrolet
3. Rick Mast   Ford
4. Mark Martin   Ford
5. Ernie Irvan   Ford

Pontiac Excitement 400
Richmond, Va.
March 6

1. Ernie Irvan   Ford
2. Rusty Wallace   Ford
3. Jeff Gordon   Chevrolet
4. Dale Earnhardt   Chevrolet
5. Kyle Petty   Pontiac

Purolator 500
Hampton, Ga.
March 13

1. Ernie Irvan   Ford
2. Morgan Shepherd   Ford
3. Darrell Waltrip   Chevrolet
4. Jeff Burton   Ford
5. Mark Martin   Ford

TranSouth Financial 400
Darlington, S.C.
March 27

1. Dale Earnhardt   Chevrolet
2. Mark Martin   Ford
3. Bill Elliott   Ford
4. Dale Jarrett   Chevrolet
5. Lake Speed   Ford

Food City 500
Bristol, Tenn.
April 10

1. Dale Earnhardt   Chevrolet
2. Ken Schrader   Chevrolet
3. Lake Speed   Ford
4. Geoff Bodine   Ford
5. Michael Waltrip   Pontiac

First Union 400
North Wilkesboro, N.C.
April 17

1. Terry Labonte   Chevrolet
2. Rusty Wallace   Ford
3. Ernie Irvan   Ford
4. Kyle Petty   Pontiac
5. Dale Earnhardt   Chevrolet

Hanes 500
Martinsville, Va.
April 24

1. Rusty Wallace   Ford
2. Ernie Irvan   Ford
3. Mark Martin   Ford
4. Darrell Waltrip   Chevrolet
5. Morgan Shepherd   Ford

Winston Select 500
Talladega, Ala.
May 1

1. Dale Earnhardt   Chevrolet
2. Ernie Irvan   Ford
3. Michael Waltrip   Pontiac
4. Jimmy Spencer   Ford
5. Ken Schrader   Chevrolet

Save Mart Supermarkets 300
Sonoma, Calif.
May 15

1. Ernie Irvan   Ford
2. Geoff Bodine   Ford
3. Dale Earnhardt   Chevrolet
4. Wally Dallenbach Jr. Pontiac
5. Rusty Wallace   Ford

Coca-Cola 600
Concord, N.C.
May 19

1. Jeff Gordon   Chevrolet
2. Rusty Wallace   Ford
3. Geoff Bodine   Ford
4. Dale Jarrett   Chevrolet

5. Ernie Irvan   Ford

Budweiser 500
Dover, Del.
June 5

1. Rusty Wallace   Ford
2. Ernie Irvan   Ford
3. Ken Schrader   Chevrolet
4 Mark Martin   Ford
5. Jeff Gordon   Chevrolet

UAW-GM Teamwork 500
Pocono, Pa.
June 12

1. Rusty Wallace   Ford
2. Dale Earnhardt   Chevrolet
3. Ken Schrader   Chevrolet
4. Morgan Shepherd   Ford
5. Mark Martin   Ford

Miller Genuine Draft 400
Brooklyn, Mich.
June 19

1. Rusty Wallace   Ford
2. Dale Earnhardt   Chevrolet
3. Mark Martin   Ford
4. Ricky Rudd   Ford
5. Morgan Shepherd   Ford

Pepsi 400
Daytona Beach, Fla.
July 2

1. Jimmy Spencer   Ford
2. Ernie Irvan   Ford
3. Dale Earnhardt   Chevrolet
4. Mark Martin   Ford
5. Ken Schrader   Chevrolet

Slick 50 300
Loudon, N.H.
July 10

1. Ricky Rudd   Ford
2. Dale Earnhardt   Chevrolet
3. Rusty Wallace   Ford
4. Mark Martin   Ford
5. Todd Bodine   Ford

Miller Genuine Draft 500
Pocono, Pa.
July 17

1. Geoff Bodine   Ford
2. Ward Burton   Chevrolet
3. Joe Nemechek   Chevrolet
4. Jeff Burton   Ford
5. Morgan Shepherd   Ford

DieHard 500
Talladega, Ala.
July 24

1. Jimmy Spencer — Ford
2. Bill Elliott — Ford
3. Ernie Irvan — Ford
4. Ken Schrader — Chevrolet
5. Sterling Marlin — Chevrolet

Brickyard 400
Indianapolis, Ind.
August 6

1. Jeff Gordon — Chevrolet
2. Brett Bodine — Ford
3. Bill Elliott — Ford
4. Rusty Wallace — Ford
5. Dale Earnhardt — Chevrolet

The Bud at the Glen
Watkins Glen, N.Y.
August 14

1. Mark Martin — Ford
2. Ernie Irvan — Ford
3. Dale Earnhardt — Chevrolet
4. Ken Schrader — Chevrolet
5. Ricky Rudd — Ford

GM Goodwrench Dealer 400
Brooklyn, Mich.
August 21

1. Geoff Bodine — Ford
2. Mark Martin — Ford
3. Rick Mast — Ford
4. Rusty Wallace — Ford
5. Bobby Labonte — Pontiac

Goody's 500
Bristol, Tenn.
August 27

1. Rusty Wallace — Ford
2. Mark Martin — Ford
3. Dale Earnhardt — Chevrolet
4. Darrell Waltrip — Chevrolet
5. Bill Elliott — Ford

Mountain Dew Southern 500
Darlington, S.C.
September 4

1. Bill Elliott — Ford
2. Dale Earnhardt — Chevrolet
3. Morgan Shepherd — Ford
4. Ricky Rudd — Ford
5. Sterling Marlin — Chevrolet

Miller Genuine Draft 400
Richmond, Va.
September 10

1. Terry Labonte — Chevrolet
2. Jeff Gordon — Chevrolet
3. Dale Earnhardt — Chevrolet
4. Rusty Wallace — Ford
5. Ricky Rudd — Ford

Splitfire Spark Plug 500
Dover, Del.
September 18

1. Rusty Wallace — Ford
2. Dale Earnhardt — Chevrolet
3. Darrell Waltrip — Chevrolet
4. Ken Schrader — Chevrolet
5. Geoff Bodine — Ford

Goody's 500
Martinsville, Va.
September 25

1. Rusty Wallace — Ford
2. Dale Earnhardt — Chevrolet
3. Bill Elliott — Ford
4. Kenny Wallace — Ford
5. Dale Jarrett — Chevrolet

Tyson/Holly Farms 400
North Wilkesboro, N.C.
October 2

1. Geoff Bodine — Ford
2. Terry Labonte — Chevrolet
3. Rick Mast — Ford
4. Rusty Wallace — Ford
5. Mark Martin — Ford

Mello Yello 500
Concord, N.C.
October 9

1. Dale Jarrett — Chevrolet
2. Morgan Shepherd — Ford
3. Dale Earnhardt — Chevrolet
4. Ken Schrader — Chevrolet
5. Lake Speed — Ford

AC Delco 500
Rockingham, N.C.
October 23

1. Dale Earnhardt — Chevrolet
2. Rick Mast — Ford
3. Morgan Shepherd — Ford
4. Ricky Rudd — Ford
5. Terry Labonte — Chevrolet

Slick 50 500
Phoenix, Ariz.
October 30

1. Terry Labonte — Chevrolet
2. Mark Martin — Ford
3. Sterling Marlin — Chevrolet
4. Jeff Gordon — Chevrolet
5. Ted Musgrave — Ford

Hooters 500
Hampton, Ga.
November 13

1. Mark Martin — Ford

2. Dale Earnhardt — Chevrolet
3. Todd Bodine — Ford
4. Lake Speed — Ford
5. Mike Wallace — Ford

1995 Season

Daytona 500
Daytona Beach, Fla.
February 19

1. Sterling Marlin — Chevrolet
2. Dale Earnhardt — Chevrolet
3. Mark Martin — Ford
4. Ted Musgrave — Ford
5. Dale Jarrett — Ford

Goodwrench 500
Rockingham, N.C.
February 26

1. Jeff Gordon — Chevrolet
2. Bobby Labonte — Chevrolet
3. Dale Earnhardt — Chevrolet
4. Ricky Rudd — Ford
5. Dale Jarrett — Ford

Pontiac Excitement 400
Richmond, Va.
March 5

1. Terry Labonte — Chevrolet
2. Dale Earnhardt — Chevrolet
3. Rusty Wallace — Ford
4. Ken Schrader — Chevrolet
5. Sterling Marlin — Chevrolet

Purolator 500
Hampton, Ga.
March 12

1. Jeff Gordon — Chevrolet
2. Bobby Labonte — Chevrolet
3. Terry Labonte — Chevrolet
4. Dale Earnhardt — Chevrolet
5. Dale Jarrett — Ford

TranSouth Financial 400
Darlington, S.C.
March 26

1. Sterling Marlin — Chevrolet
2. Dale Earnhardt — Chevrolet
3. Ted Musgrave — Ford
4. Todd Bodine — Ford
5. Derrike Cope — Ford

Food City 500
Bristol, Tenn.
April 2

1. Jeff Gordon — Chevrolet
2. Rusty Wallace — Ford
3. Darrell Waltrip — Chevrolet
4. Bobby Hamilton — Pontiac

5. Ricky Rudd   Ford

First Union 400
North Wilkesboro, N.C.
April 9

1. Dale Earnhardt   Chevrolet
2. Jeff Gordon   Chevrolet
3. Mark Martin   Ford
4. Rusty Wallace   Ford
5. Steve Grissom   Chevrolet

Hanes 500
Martinsville, Va.
April 23

1. Rusty Wallace   Ford
2. Ted Musgrave   Ford
3. Jeff Gordon   Chevrolet
4. Darrell Waltrip   Chevrolet
5. Mark Martin   Ford

Winston Select 500
Talladega, Ala.
April 30

1. Mark Martin   Ford
2. Jeff Gordon   Chevrolet
3. Morgan Shepherd   Ford
4. Darrell Waltrip   Chevrolet
5. Bobby Labonte   Chevrolet

Save Mart Supermarkets 300
Sonoma, Calif.
May 7

1. Dale Earnhardt   Chevrolet
2. Mark Martin   Ford
3. Jeff Gordon   Chevrolet
4. Ricky Rudd   Ford
5. Terry Labonte   Chevrolet

Coca-Cola 600
Concord, N.C.
May 28

1. Bobby Labonte   Chevrolet
2. Terry Labonte   Chevrolet
3. Michael Waltrip   Pontiac
4. Sterling Marlin   Chevrolet
5. Ricky Rudd   Ford

Miller Genuine Draft 500
Dover, Del.
June 4

1. Kyle Petty   Pontiac
2. Bobby Labonte   Chevrolet
3. Ted Musgrave   Ford
4. Hut Stricklin   Ford
5. Dale Earnhardt   Chevrolet

UAW-GM Teamwork 500
Pocono, Pa.
June 11

1. Terry Labonte   Chevrolet
2. Ted Musgrave   Ford
3. Ken Schrader   Chevrolet
4. Sterling Marlin   Chevrolet
5. Hut Stricklin   Ford

Miller Genuine Draft 400
Brooklyn, Mich.
June 18

1. Bobby Labonte   Chevrolet
2. Jeff Gordon   Chevrolet
3. Rusty Wallace   Ford
4. John Andretti   Ford
5. Morgan Shepherd   Ford

Pepsi 400
Daytona Beach, Fla.
July 1

1. Jeff Gordon   Chevrolet
2. Sterling Marlin   Chevrolet
3 Dale Earnhardt   Chevrolet
4. Mark Martin   Ford
5. Ted Musgrave   Ford

Slick 50 300
Loudon, N.H.
July 9

1. Jeff Gordon   Chevrolet
2. Morgan Shepherd   Ford
3. Mark Martin   Ford
4. Terry Labonte   Chevrolet
5. Ricky Rudd   Ford

Miller Genuine Draft 500
Pocono, Pa.
July 16

1. Dale Jarrett   Ford
2. Jeff Gordon   Chevrolet
3. Ricky Rudd   Ford
4. Ted Musgrave   Ford
5. Bill Elliott   Ford

DieHard 500
Talladega, Ala.
July 23

1. Sterling Marlin   Chevrolet
2. Dale Jarrett   Ford
3. Dale Earnhardt   Chevrolet
4. Morgan Shepherd   Ford
5. Bill Elliott   Ford

Brickyard 400
Indianapolis, Ind.
August 5

1. Dale Earnhardt   Chevrolet
2. Rusty Wallace   Ford
3. Dale Jarrett   Ford
4. Bill Elliott   Ford
5. Mark Martin   Ford

The Bud at the Glen
Watkins Glen, N.Y.
August 13

1. Mark Martin   Ford
2. Wally Dallenbach Jr.   Pontiac
3. Jeff Gordon   Chevrolet
4. Ricky Rudd   Ford
5. Terry Labonte   Chevrolet

GM Goodwrench Dealer 400
Brooklyn, Mich.
August 20

1. Bobby Labonte   Chevrolet
2. Terry Labonte   Chevrolet
3. Jeff Gordon   Chevrolet
4. Sterling Marlin   Chevrolet
5. Rusty Wallace   Ford

Goody's 500
Bristol, Tenn.
August 26

1. Terry Labonte   Chevrolet
2 Dale Earnhardt   Chevrolet
3. Dale Jarrett   Ford
4. Darrell Waltrip   Chevrolet
5. Mark Martin   Ford

Mountain Dew Southern 500
Darlington, S.C.
September 3

1. Jeff Gordon   Chevrolet
2. Dale Earnhardt   Chevrolet
3. Rusty Wallace   Ford
4. Ward Burton   Pontiac
5. Michael Waltrip   Pontiac

Miller Genuine Draft 400
Richmond, Va.
September 9

1. Rusty Wallace   Ford
2. Terry Labonte   Chevrolet
3. Dale Earnhardt   Chevrolet
4. Dale Jarrett   Ford
5. Bobby Hamilton   Pontiac

MBNA 500
Dover, Del.
September 17

1. Jeff Gordon   Chevrolet
2. Bobby Hamilton   Pontiac
3. Rusty Wallace   Ford
4. Joe Nemechek   Chevrolet
5. Dale Earnhardt   Chevrolet

Goody's 500
Martinsville, Va.
September 24

1. Dale Earnhardt   Chevrolet

2. Terry Labonte   Chevrolet
3. Rusty Wallace   Ford
4. Bobby Hamilton   Pontiac
5. Geoff Bodine   Ford

Tyson/Holly Farms 400
North Wilkesboro, N.C.
October 1

1. Mark Martin   Ford
2. Rusty Wallace   Ford
3. Jeff Gordon   Chevrolet
4. Terry Labonte   Chevrolet
5. Ricky Rudd   Ford

UAW-GM Quality 500
Concord, N.C.
October 8

1. Mark Martin   Ford
2. Dale Earnhardt   Chevrolet
3. Terry Labonte   Chevrolet
4. Ricky Rudd   Ford
5. Dale Jarrett   Ford

AC Delco 400
Rockingham, N.C.
October 22

1. Ward Burton   Pontiac
2. Rusty Wallace   Ford
3. Mark Martin   Ford
4. Terry Labonte   Chevrolet
5. Jeff Burton   Ford

Dura Lube 500
Phoenix, Ariz.
October 29

1. Ricky Rudd   Ford
2. Derrike Cope   Ford
3. Dale Earnhardt   Chevrolet
4. Rusty Wallace   Ford
5. Jeff Gordon   Chevrolet

NAPA 500
Hampton, Ga.
November 12

1. Dale Earnhardt   Chevrolet
2. Sterling Marlin   Chevrolet
3. Rusty Wallace   Ford
4. Bill Elliott   Ford
5. Ward Burton   Pontiac

1996 Season

Daytona 500
Daytona Beach, Fla.
February 18

1. Dale Jarrett   Ford
2. Dale Earnhardt   Chevrolet
3. Ken Schrader   Chevrolet
4. Mark Martin   Ford

5. Jeff Burton   Ford

Goodwrench 400
Rockingham, N.C.
February 25

1. Dale Earnhardt   Chevrolet
2. Dale Jarrett   Ford
3. Ricky Craven   Chevrolet
4. Ricky Rudd   Ford
5. Steve Grissom   Chevrolet

Pontiac Excitement 400
Richmond, Va.
March 3

1. Jeff Gordon   Chevrolet
2. Dale Jarrett   Ford
3. Ted Musgrave   Ford
4. Jeff Burton   Ford
5. Mark Martin   Ford

Purolator 500
Hampton, Ga.
March 10

1. Dale Earnhardt   Chevrolet
2. Terry Labonte   Chevrolet
3. Jeff Gordon   Chevrolet
4. Ernie Irvan   Ford
5. Jeremy Mayfield   Ford

TranSouth Financial 400
Darlington, S.C.
March 24

1. Jeff Gordon   Chevrolet
2. Bobby Labonte   Chevrolet
3. Ricky Craven   Chevrolet
4. Rusty Wallace   Ford
5. Terry Labonte   Chevrolet

Food City 500
Bristol, Tenn.
March 31

1. Jeff Gordon   Chevrolet
2. Terry Labonte   Chevrolet
3. Mark Martin   Ford
4. Dale Earnhardt   Chevrolet
5. Rusty Wallace   Ford

First Union 400
North Wilkesboro, N.C.
April 14

1. Terry Labonte   Chevrolet
2. Jeff Gordon   Chevrolet
3. Dale Earnhardt   Chevrolet
4. Robert Pressley   Chevrolet
5. Sterling Marlin   Chevrolet

Goody's Headache Powder 500
Martinsville, Va.
April 21

1. Rusty Wallace   Ford
2. Ernie Irvan   Ford
3. Jeff Gordon   Chevrolet
4. Jeremy Mayfield   Ford
5. Dale Earnhardt   Chevrolet

Winston Select 500
Talladega, Ala.
April 28

1. Sterling Marlin   Chevrolet
2. Dale Jarrett   Ford
3. Dale Earnhardt   Chevrolet
4. Terry Labonte   Chevrolet
5. Michael Waltrip   Ford

Save Mart Supermarkets 300
Sonoma, Calif.
May 5

1. Rusty Wallace   Ford
2. Mark Martin   Ford
3. Wally Dallenbach Jr.   Ford
4. Dale Earnhardt   Chevrolet
5. Terry Labonte   Chevrolet

Coca-Cola 600
Concord, N.C.
May 25

1. Dale Jarrett   Ford
2. Dale Earnhardt   Chevrolet
3. Terry Labonte   Chevrolet
4. Jeff Gordon   Chevrolet
5. Ken Schrader   Chevrolet

Miller Genuine Draft 500
Dover, Del.
June 2

1. Jeff Gordon   Chevrolet
2. Terry Labonte   Chevrolet
3. Dale Earnhardt   Chevrolet
4. Ernie Irvan   Ford
5. Bobby Labonte   Chevrolet

UAW-GM Teamwork 500
Pocono, Pa.
June 16

1. Jeff Gordon   Chevrolet
2. Ricky Rudd   Ford
3. Geoff Bodine   Ford
4. Mark Martin   Ford
5. Bobby Hamilton   Pontiac

Miller Genuine Draft 400
Brooklyn, Mich.
June 23

1. Rusty Wallace   Ford
2. Terry Labonte   Chevrolet
3. Sterling Marlin   Chevrolet
4. Jimmy Spencer   Ford
5. Ernie Irvan   Ford

Pepsi 400
Daytona Beach, Fla.
July 6

1. Sterling Marlin — Chevrolet
2. Terry Labonte — Chevrolet
3. Jeff Gordon — Chevrolet
4. Dale Earnhardt — Chevrolet
5. Ernie Irvan — Ford

Jiffy Lube 300
Loudon, N.H.
July 14

1. Ernie Irvan — Ford
2. Dale Jarrett — Ford
3. Ricky Rudd — Ford
4. Jeff Burton — Ford
5. Robert Pressley — Chevrolet

Miller Genuine Draft 500
Pocono, Pa.
July 21

1. Rusty Wallace — Ford
2. Ricky Rudd — Ford
3. Dale Jarrett — Ford
4. Ernie Irvan — Ford
5. Johnny Benson — Pontiac

DieHard 500
Talladega, Ala.
July 28

1. Jeff Gordon — Chevrolet
2. Dale Jarrett — Ford
3. Mark Martin — Ford
4. Ernie Irvan — Ford
5. Jimmy Spencer — Ford

Brickyard 400
Indianapolis, Ind.
August 3

1. Dale Jarrett — Ford
2. Ernie Irvan — Ford
3. Terry Labonte — Chevrolet
4. Mark Martin — Ford
5. Morgan Shepherd — Ford

The Bud at the Glen
Watkins Glen, N.Y.
August 11

1. Geoff Bodine — Ford
2. Terry Labonte — Chevrolet
3. Mark Martin — Ford
4. Jeff Gordon — Chevrolet
5. Bobby Labonte — Chevrolet

GM Goodwrench Dealer 400
Brooklyn, Mich.
August 18

1. Dale Jarrett — Ford

2. Mark Martin — Ford
3. Terry Labonte — Chevrolet
4. Ernie Irvan — Ford
5. Jeff Gordon — Chevrolet

Goody's Headache Powder 500
Bristol, Tenn.
August 24

1. Rusty Wallace — Ford
2. Jeff Gordon — Chevrolet
3. Mark Martin — Ford
4. Dale Jarrett — Ford
5. Terry Labonte — Chevrolet

Mountain Dew Southern 500
Darlington, S.C.
September 1

1. Jeff Gordon — Chevrolet
2. Hut Stricklin — Ford
3. Mark Martin — Ford
4. Ken Schrader — Chevrolet
5. John Andretti — Ford

Miller 400
Richmond, Va.
September 7

1. Ernie Irvan — Ford
2. Jeff Gordon — Chevrolet
3. Jeff Burton — Ford
4. Dale Jarrett — Ford
5. Terry Labonte — Chevrolet

MBNA 500
Dover, Del.
September 15

1. Jeff Gordon — Chevrolet
2. Rusty Wallace — Ford
3. Dale Jarrett — Ford
4. Bobby Labonte — Chevrolet
5. Mark Martin — Ford

Hanes 500
Martinsville, Va.
September 22

1. Jeff Gordon — Chevrolet
2. Terry Labonte — Chevrolet
3. Bobby Hamilton — Pontiac
4. Rick Mast — Pontiac
5. John Andretti — Ford

Tyson/Holly Farms 400
North Wilkesboro, N.C.
September 29

1. Jeff Gordon — Chevrolet
2. Dale Earnhardt — Chevrolet
3. Dale Jarrett — Ford
4. Jeff Burton — Ford
5. Terry Labonte — Chevrolet

UAW-GM Quality 500
Concord, N.C.
October 6

1. Terry Labonte — Chevrolet
2. Mark Martin — Ford
3. Dale Jarrett — Ford
4. Sterling Marlin — Chevrolet
5. Ricky Craven — Chevrolet

AC Delco 400
Rockingham, N.C.
October 20

1. Ricky Rudd — Ford
2. Dale Jarrett — Ford
3. Terry Labonte — Chevrolet
4. Ernie Irvan — Ford
5. Jeff Burton — Ford

Dura Lube 500
Phoenix, Ariz.
October 27

1. Bobby Hamilton — Pontiac
2. Mark Martin — Ford
3. Terry Labonte — Chevrolet
4. Ted Musgrave — Ford
5. Jeff Gordon — Chevrolet

NAPA 500
Hampton, Ga.
November 10

1. Bobby Labonte — Chevrolet
2. Dale Jarrett — Ford
3. Jeff Gordon — Chevrolet
4. Dale Earnhardt — Chevrolet
5. Terry Labonte — Chevrolet

1997 Season

Daytona 500
Daytona Beach, Fla.
February 16

1. Jeff Gordon — Chevrolet
2. Terry Labonte — Chevrolet
3. Ricky Craven — Chevrolet
4. Bill Elliott — Ford
5. Sterling Marlin — Chevrolet

GM Goodwrench 400
Rockingham, N.C.
February 23

1. Jeff Gordon — Chevrolet
2. Dale Jarrett — Ford
3. Jeff Burton — Ford
4. Ricky Rudd — Ford
5. Ricky Craven — Chevrolet

Pontiac Excitement 400
Richmond, Va.
March 2

1. Rusty Wallace — Ford
2. Geoffrey Bodine — Ford
3. Dale Jarrett — Ford
4. Jeff Gordon — Chevrolet
5. Bobby Hamilton — Pontiac

Primestar 500
Hampton, Ga.
March 9

1. Dale Jarrett — Ford
2. Ernie Irvan — Ford
3. Morgan Shepherd — Pontiac
4. Bobby Labonte — Pontiac
5. Jeff Burton — Ford

TranSouth Financial 400
Darlington, S.C.
March 23

1. Dale Jarrett — Ford
2. Ted Musgrave — Ford
3. Jeff Gordon — Chevrolet
4. Jeff Burton — Ford
5. Bobby Labonte — Pontiac

Interstate Batteries 500
Fort Worth, Tex.
April 6

1. Jeff Burton — Ford
2. Dale Jarrett — Ford
3. Bobby Labonte — Pontiac
4. Terry Labonte — Chevrolet
5. Ricky Rudd — Ford

Food City 500
Bristol, Tenn.
April 13

1. Jeff Gordon — Chevrolet
2. Rusty Wallace — Ford
3. Terry Labonte — Chevrolet
4. Dale Jarrett — Ford
5. Mark Martin — Ford

Goody's 500
Martinsville, Va.
April 20

1. Jeff Gordon — Chevrolet
2. Bobby Hamilton — Pontiac
3. Mark Martin — Ford
4. Terry Labonte — Chevrolet
5. Rusty Wallace — Ford

Save Mart Supermarkets 300
Sonoma, Calif.
May 4

1. Mark Martin — Ford
2. Jeff Gordon — Chevrolet
3. Terry Labonte — Chevrolet
4. Dale Jarrett — Ford
5. Darrell Waltrip — Chevrolet

Winston 500
Talladega, Ala.
May 10

1. Mark Martin — Ford
2. Dale Earnhardt — Chevrolet
3. Bobby Labonte — Pontiac
4. John Andretti — Ford
5. Jeff Gordon — Chevrolet

Coca-Cola 600
Concord, N.C.
May 25

1. Jeff Gordon — Chevrolet
2. Rusty Wallace — Ford
3. Mark Martin — Ford
4. Bill Elliott — Ford
5. Jeff Burton — Ford

Miller 500
Dover, Del.
June 1

1. Ricky Rudd — Ford
2. Mark Martin — Ford
3. Jeff Burton — Ford
4. Jeremy Mayfield — Ford
5. Kyle Petty — Pontiac

Pocono 500
Pocono, Pa.
June 8

1. Jeff Gordon — Chevrolet
2. Jeff Burton — Ford
3. Dale Jarrett — Ford
4. Mark Martin — Ford
5. Jeremy Mayfield — Ford

Miller 400
Brooklyn, Mich.
June 15

1. Ernie Irvan — Ford
2. Bill Elliott — Ford
3. Mark Martin — Ford
4. Ted Musgrave — Ford
5. Jeff Gordon — Chevrolet

California 500 presented by NAPA
Fontana, Calif.
June 22

1. Jeff Gordon — Chevrolet
2. Terry Labonte — Chevrolet
3. Ricky Rudd — Ford
4. Ted Musgrave — Ford
5. Jimmy Spencer — Ford

Pepsi 400
Daytona Beach, Fla.
July 5

1. John Andretti — Ford

2. Terry Labonte — Chevrolet
3. Sterling Marlin — Chevrolet
4. Dale Earnhardt — Chevrolet
5. Dale Jarrett — Ford

Jiffy Lube 300
Loudon, N.H.
July 13

1. Jeff Burton — Ford
2. Dale Earnhardt — Chevrolet
3. Rusty Wallace — Ford
4. Steve Grissom — Chevrolet
5. Mark Martin — Ford

Pennsylvania 500
Pocono, Pa.
July 20

1. Dale Jarrett — Ford
2. Jeff Gordon — Chevrolet
3. Jeff Burton — Ford
4. Ted Musgrave — Ford
5. Mark Martin — Ford

Brickyard 400
Indianapolis, Ind.
August 2

1. Ricky Rudd — Ford
2. Bobby Labonte — Pontiac
3. Dale Jarrett — Ford
4. Jeff Gordon — Chevrolet
5. Jeremy Mayfield — Ford

The Bud at the Glen
Watkins Glen, N.Y.
August 10

1. Jeff Gordon — Chevrolet
2. Geoff Bodine — Ford
3. Rusty Wallace — Ford
4. Robby Gordon — Chevrolet
5. Mark Martin — Ford

DeVilbiss 400
Brooklyn, Mich.
August 17

1. Mark Martin — Ford
2. Jeff Gordon — Chevrolet
3. Ted Musgrave — Ford
4. Ernie Irvan — Ford
5. Dale Jarrett — Ford

Goody's 500
Bristol, Tenn.
August 23

1. Dale Jarrett — Ford
2. Mark Martin — Ford
3. Dick Trickle — Ford
4. Jeff Burton — Ford
5. Steve Grissom — Chevrolet

Mountain Dew Southern 500
Darlington, S.C.
August 31

1. Jeff Gordon — Chevrolet
2. Jeff Burton — Ford
3. Dale Jarrett — Ford
4. Bill Elliott — Ford
5. Ricky Rudd — Ford

Exide NASCAR Select Batteries 400
Richmond, Va.
September 6

1. Dale Jarrett — Ford
2. Jeff Burton — Ford
3. Jeff Gordon — Chevrolet
4. Geoff Bodine — Ford
5. Rusty Wallace — Ford

CMT 300
Loudon, N.H.
September 14

1. Jeff Gordon — Chevrolet
2. Ernie Irvan — Ford
3. Bobby Hamilton — Pontiac
4. Steve Grissom — Chevrolet
5. Ricky Craven — Chevrolet

MBNA 400
Dover, Del.
September 21

1. Mark Martin — Ford
2. Dale Earnhardt — Chevrolet
3. Kyle Petty — Pontiac
4. Bobby Labonte — Pontiac
5. Dale Jarrett — Ford

Hanes 500
Martinsville, Va.
September 29

1. Jeff Burton — Ford
2. Dale Earnhardt — Chevrolet
3. Bobby Hamilton — Pontiac
4. Jeff Gordon — Chevrolet
5. Bill Elliott — Ford

UAW-GM Teamwork 500
Concord, N.C.
October 5

1. Dale Jarrett — Ford
2. Bobby Labonte — Pontiac
3. Dale Earnhardt — Chevrolet
4 Mark Martin — Ford
5. Jeff Gordon — Chevrolet

DieHard 500
Talladega, Ala.
October 12

1. Terry Labonte — Chevrolet

2. Bobby Labonte — Pontiac
3. John Andretti — Ford
4. Ken Schrader — Chevrolet
5. Ernie Irvan — Ford

AC Delco 400
Rockingham, N.C.
October 27

1. Bobby Hamilton — Pontiac
2. Dale Jarrett — Ford
3. Ricky Craven — Chevrolet
4. Jeff Gordon — Chevrolet
5. Dick Trickle — Ford

Dura Lube 500
Phoenix, Ariz.
November 2

1. Dale Jarrett — Ford
2. Rusty Wallace — Ford
3. Bobby Hamilton — Pontiac
4. Ken Schrader — Chevrolet
5. Dale Earnhardt — Chevrolet

NAPA 500
Hampton, Ga.
November 16

1. Bobby Labonte — Pontiac
2. Dale Jarrett — Ford
3. Mark Martin — Ford
4. Jeff Green — Chevrolet
5. Derrike Cope — Pontiac

1998 Season

Daytona 500
Daytona Beach, Fla.
February 15

1. Dale Earnhardt — Chevrolet
2. Bobby Labonte — Pontiac
3. Jeremy Mayfield — Ford
4. Ken Schrader — Chevrolet
5. Rusty Wallace — Ford

Goodwrench 400
Rockingham, N.C.
February 22

1. Jeff Gordon — Chevrolet
2. Rusty Wallace — Ford
3. Mark Martin — Ford
4. Jimmy Spencer — Ford
5. Geoff Bodine — Ford

Las Vegas 400
Las Vegas, Nev.
March 1

1. Mark Martin — Ford
2. Jeff Burton — Ford
3. Rusty Wallace — Ford
4. Johnny Benson — Ford

5. Jeremy Mayfield — Ford

PrimeStar 500
Hampton, Ga.
March 9

1. Bobby Labonte — Pontiac
2. Dale Jarrett — Ford
3. Jeremy Mayfield — Ford
4. Rusty Wallace — Ford
5. Kenny Irwin — Ford

TranSouth Financial 400
Darlington, S.C.
March 22

1. Dale Jarrett — Ford
2. Jeff Gordon — Chevrolet
3. Rusty Wallace — Ford
4. Jeremy Mayfield — Ford
5. Jeff Burton — Ford

Food City 500
Bristol, Tenn.
March 29

1. Jeff Gordon — Chevrolet
2. Terry Labonte — Chevrolet
3. Dale Jarrett — Ford
4. Jeff Burton — Ford
5. Johnny Benson — Ford

Texas 500
Fort Worth, Tex.
April 5

1. Mark Martin — Ford
2. Chad Little — Ford
3. Robert Pressley — Ford
4. Joe Nemechek — Chevrolet
5. Johnny Benson — Ford

Goody's 500
Martinsville, Va.
April 20

1. Bobby Hamilton — Chevrolet
2. Ted Musgrave — Ford
3. Dale Jarrett — Ford
4. Dale Earnhardt — Chevrolet
5. Randy LaJoie — Chevrolet

DieHard 500
Talladega, Ala.
April 26

1. Bobby Labonte — Pontiac
2. Jimmy Spencer — Ford
3. Dale Jarrett — Ford
4. Terry Labonte — Chevrolet
5. Jeff Gordon — Chevrolet

California 500
Fontana, Calif.
May 3

1. Mark Martin — Ford
2. Jeremy Mayfield — Ford
3. Terry Labonte — Chevrolet
4. Jeff Gordon — Chevrolet
5. Darrell Waltrip — Chevrolet

Coca-Cola 600
Concord, N.C.
May 24

1. Jeff Gordon — Chevrolet
2. Rusty Wallace — Ford
3. Bobby Labonte — Pontiac
4. Mark Martin — Ford
5. Dale Jarrett — Ford

MBNA Platinum 400
Dover, Del.
May 31

1. Dale Jarrett — Ford
2. Jeff Burton — Ford
3. Jeff Gordon — Chevrolet
4. Bobby Labonte — Pontiac
5. Jeremy Mayfield — Ford

Pontiac 400
Richmond, Va.
June 6

1. Terry Labonte — Chevrolet
2. Dale Jarrett — Ford
3. Rusty Wallace — Ford
4. Ken Schrader — Chevrolet
5. Mark Martin — Ford

Miller Lite 400
Brooklyn, Mich.
June 14

1. Mark Martin — Ford
2. Dale Jarrett — Ford
3. Jeff Gordon — Chevrolet
4. Jeff Burton — Ford
5. Jeremy Mayfield — Ford

Pocono 500
Pocono, Pa.
June 21

1. Jeremy Mayfield — Ford
2. Jeff Gordon — Chevrolet
3. Dale Jarrett — Ford
4. Jeff Burton — Ford
5. Mark Martin — Ford

Save Mart/Kragen 350
Sonoma, Calif.
June 28

1. Jeff Gordon — Chevrolet
2. Bobby Hamilton — Chevrolet
3. John Andretti — Pontiac
4. Bobby Labonte — Pontiac
5. Rusty Wallace — Ford

Jiffy Lube 300
Loudon, N.H.
July 12

1. Jeff Burton — Ford
2. Mark Martin — Ford
3. Jeff Gordon — Chevrolet
4. Rusty Wallace — Ford
5. Mike Skinner — Chevrolet

Pennsylvania 500
Pocono, Pa.
July 26

1. Jeff Gordon — Chevrolet
2. Mark Martin — Ford
3. Jeff Burton — Ford
4. Bobby Labonte — Pontiac
5. Dale Jarrett — Ford

Brickyard 400
Indianapolis, Ind.
August 1

1. Jeff Gordon — Chevrolet
2. Mark Martin — Ford
3. Bobby Labonte — Pontiac
4. Mike Skinner — Chevrolet
5. Dale Earnhardt — Chevrolet

The Bud at the Glen
Watkins Glen, N.Y.
August 9

1. Jeff Gordon — Chevrolet
2. Mark Martin — Ford
3. Mike Skinner — Chevrolet
4. Rusty Wallace — Ford
5. Dale Jarrett — Ford

Pepsi/DeVilbiss 400
Brooklyn, Mich.
August 16

1. Jeff Gordon — Chevrolet
2. Bobby Labonte — Pontiac
3. Dale Jarrett — Ford
4. Mark Martin — Ford
5. Jeff Burton — Ford

Goody's 500
Bristol, Tenn.
August 22

1. Mark Martin — Ford
2. Jeff Burton — Ford
3. Rusty Wallace — Ford
4. Dale Jarrett — Ford
5. Jeff Gordon — Chevrolet

Farm Aid/CMT 300
Loudon, N.H.
August 29

1. Jeff Gordon — Chevrolet

2. Mark Martin — Ford
3. John Andretti — Pontiac
4. Dale Jarrett — Ford
5. Jeff Burton

Pepsi Southern 500
Darlington, S.C.
September 6

1. Jeff Gordon — Chevrolet
2. Jeff Burton — Ford
3. Dale Jarrett — Ford
4. Dale Earnhardt — Chevrolet
5. Jeremy Mayfield — Ford

Exide NASCAR Select Batteries 400
Richmond, Va.
September 12

1. Jeff Burton — Ford
2. Jeff Gordon — Chevrolet
3. Mark Martin — Ford
4. Ken Schrader — Chevrolet
5. John Andretti — Pontiac

MBNA Gold 400
Dover, Del.
September 20

1. Mark Martin — Ford
2. Jeff Gordon — Chevrolet
3. Jeremy Mayfield — Ford
4. Bobby Labonte — Pontiac
5. Rusty Wallace — Ford

NAPA AutoCare 500
Martinsville, Va.
September 27

1. Ricky Rudd — Ford
2. Jeff Gordon — Chevrolet
3. Mark Martin — Ford
4. Rich Bickle — Ford
5. Jeff Burton — Ford

UAW-GM 500
Concord, NC
October 4

1. Mark Martin — Ford
2. Ward Burton — Pontiac
3. Jeff Burton — Ford
4. Bobby Hamilton — Chevrolet
5. Jeff Gordon — Chevrolet

Winston 500
Talladega, Ala.
October 11

1. Dale Jarrett — Ford
2. Jeff Gordon — Chevrolet
3. Terry Labonte — Chevrolet
4. Jimmy Spencer — Ford
5. Jeremy Mayfield — Ford

Pepsi 400
Daytona Beach, Fla.
October 17

1. Jeff Gordon — Chevrolet
2. Bobby Labonte — Pontiac
3. Mike Skinner — Chevrolet
4. Jeremy Mayfield — Ford
5. Rusty Wallace — Ford

Dura Lube/Kmart 500
Phoenix, Ariz.
October 25

1. Rusty Wallace — Ford
2. Mark Martin — Ford
3. Dale Earnhardt — Chevrolet
4. Jeff Burton — Ford
5. Ted Musgrave — Ford

AC Delco 400
Rockingham, N.C.
November 1

1. Jeff Gordon — Chevrolet
2. Dale Jarrett — Ford
3. Rusty Wallace — Ford
4. Mark Martin — Ford
5. Jeff Burton — Ford

NAPA 500
Hampton, Ga.
November 8

1. Jeff Gordon — Chevrolet
2. Dale Jarrett — Ford
3. Mark Martin — Ford
4. Jeff Burton — Ford
5. Todd Bodine — Chevrolet

1999 Season

Daytona 500
Daytona Beach, Fla.
February 14

1. Jeff Gordon — Chevrolet
2. Dale Earnhardt — Chevrolet
3. Kenny Irwin — Ford
4. Mike Skinner — Chevrolet
5. Michael Waltrip — Chevrolet

Dura Lube/Kmart 400
Rockingham, N.C.
February 21

1. Mark Martin — Ford
2. Dale Jarrett — Ford
3. Bobby Labonte — Pontiac
4. Jeff Burton — Ford
5. Jeremy Mayfield — Ford

Las Vegas 400
Las Vegas, Nev.
March 7

1. Jeff Burton — Ford
2. Ward Burton — Pontiac
3. Jeff Gordon — Chevrolet
4. Mike Skinner — Chevrolet
5. Bobby Labonte — Pontiac

Cracker Barrel 500
Hampton, Ga.
March 14

1. Jeff Gordon — Chevrolet
2. Bobby Labonte — Pontiac
3. Mark Martin — Ford
4. Jeff Burton — Ford
5. Dale Jarrett — Ford

TranSouth Financial 400
Darlington, S.C.
March 21

1. Jeff Burton — Ford
2. Jeremy Mayfield — Ford
3. Jeff Gordon — Chevrolet
4. Dale Jarrett — Ford
5. Mark Martin — Ford

PrimeStar 500
Fort Worth, Tex.
March 26

1. Terry Labonte — Chevrolet
2. Dale Jarrett — Ford
3. Bobby Labonte — Pontiac
4. Rusty Wallace — Ford
5. Jeremy Mayfield — Ford

Food City 500
Bristol, Tenn.
April 11

1. Rusty Wallace — Ford
2. Mark Martin — Ford
3. Dale Jarrett — Ford
4. John Andretti — Pontiac
5. Jeff Burton — Ford

Goody's Body Pain 500
Martinsville, Va.
April 18

1. John Andretti — Pontiac
2. Jeff Burton — Ford
3. Jeff Gordon — Chevrolet
4. Mike Skinner — Chevrolet
5. Mark Martin — Ford

DieHard 500
Talladega, Ala.
April 25

1. Dale Earnhardt — Chevrolet
2. Dale Jarrett — Ford
3. Mark Martin — Ford
4. Bobby Labonte — Pontiac
5. Tony Stewart — Pontiac

California 500
Fontana, Calif.
May 2

1. Jeff Gordon — Chevrolet
2. Jeff Burton — Ford
3. Bobby Labonte — Pontiac
4. Tony Stewart — Pontiac
5. Dale Jarrett — Ford

Pontiac Excitement 400
Richmond, Va.
May 15

1. Dale Jarrett — Ford
2. Mark Martin — Ford
3. Bobby Labonte — Pontiac
4. Bobby Hamilton — Chevrolet
5. Rusty Wallace — Ford

Coca-Cola 600
Concord, N.C.
May 30

1. Jeff Burton — Ford
2. Bobby Labonte — Pontiac
3. Mark Martin — Ford
4. Tony Stewart — Pontiac
5. Dale Jarrett — Ford

MBNA Platinum 400
Dover, Del.
June 6

1. Bobby Labonte — Pontiac
2. Jeff Gordon — Chevrolet
3. Mark Martin — Ford
4. Tony Stewart — Pontiac
5. Dale Jarrett — Ford

Kmart 400
Brooklyn, Mich.
June 13

1. Dale Jarrett — Ford
2. Jeff Gordon — Chevrolet
3. Jeff Burton — Ford
4. Ward Burton — Pontiac
5. Bobby Labonte — Pontiac

Pocono 500
Pocono, Pa.
June 20

1. Bobby Labonte — Pontiac
2. Jeff Gordon — Chevrolet
3. Dale Jarrett — Ford
4. Sterling Marlin — Chevrolet
5. Mark Martin — Ford

Save Mart/Kragen 350
Sonoma, Calif.
June 27

1. Jeff Gordon — Chevrolet

2. Mark Martin — Ford
3. John Andretti — Pontiac
4. Rusty Wallace — Ford
5. Jimmy Spencer — Ford

Pepsi 400
Daytona Beach, Fla.
July 3

1. Dale Jarrett — Ford
2. Dale Earnhardt — Chevrolet
3. Jeff Burton — Ford
4. Mike Skinner — Chevrolet
5. Bobby Labonte — Pontiac

Jiffy Lube 300
Loudon, N.H.
July 11

1. Jeff Burton — Ford
2. Kenny Wallace — Chevrolet
3. Jeff Gordon — Chevrolet
4. Dale Jarrett — Ford
5. Bill Elliott — Ford

Pennsylvania 500
Pocono, Pa.
July 25

1. Bobby Labonte — Pontiac
2. Dale Jarrett — Ford
3. Mark Martin — Ford
4. Tony Stewart — Pontiac
5. Wally Dallenbach Jr. — Chevrolet

Brickyard 400
Indianapolis, Ind.
August 7

1. Dale Jarrett — Ford
2. Bobby Labonte — Pontiac
3. Jeff Gordon — Chevrolet
4. Mark Martin — Ford
5. Jeff Burton — Ford

Frontier at the Glen
Watkins Glen, N.Y.
August 15

1. Jeff Gordon — Chevrolet
2. Ron Fellows — Chevrolet
3. Rusty Wallace — Ford
4. Dale Jarrett — Ford
5. Jerry Nadeau — Ford

Pepsi 400 presented by Meijer
Brooklyn, Mich.
August 22

1. Bobby Labonte — Pontiac
2. Jeff Gordon — Chevrolet
3. Tony Stewart — Pontiac
4. Dale Jarrett — Ford
5. Dale Earnhardt — Chevrolet

Goody's Headache Powder 500
Bristol, Tenn.
August 28

1. Dale Earnhardt — Chevrolet
2. Jimmy Spencer — Ford
3. Ricky Rudd — Ford
4. Jeff Gordon — Chevrolet
5. Tony Stewart — Pontiac

Pepsi Southern 500
Darlington, S.C.
September 5

1. Jeff Burton — Ford
2. Ward Burton — Pontiac
3. Jeremy Mayfield — Ford
4. Mark Martin — Ford
5. Kevin Lepage — Ford

Exide NASCAR Select Batteries 400
Richmond, Va.
September 11

1. Tony Stewart — Pontiac
2. Bobby Labonte — Pontiac
3. Dale Jarrett — Ford
4. Sterling Marlin — Chevrolet
5. Kenny Irwin — Ford

Dura Lube/Kmart 300
Loudon, N.H.
September 19

1. Joe Nemechek — Chevrolet
2. Tony Stewart — Pontiac
3. Bobby Labonte — Pontiac
4. Jeff Burton — Ford
5. Jeff Gordon — Chevrolet

MBNA Gold 400
Dover, Del.
September 26

1. Mark Martin — Ford
2. Tony Stewart — Pontiac
3. Dale Jarrett — Ford
4. Matt Kenseth — Ford
5. Bobby Labonte — Pontiac

NAPA AutoCare 500
Martinsville, Va.
October 3

1. Jeff Gordon — Chevrolet
2. Dale Earnhardt — Chevrolet
3. Geoffrey Bodine — Chevrolet
4. Rusty Wallace — Ford
5. Kenny Wallace — Ford

UAW-GM Quality 500
Concord, N.C.
October 11

1. Jeff Gordon — Chevrolet

2. Bobby Labonte — Pontiac
3. Mike Skinner — Chevrolet
4. Mark Martin — Ford
5. Ward Burton — Pontiac

Winston 500
Talladega, Ala.
October 17

1. Dale Earnhardt — Chevrolet
2. Dale Jarrett — Ford
3. Ricky Rudd — Ford
4. Ward Burton — Pontiac
5. Kenny Wallace — Chevrolet

Pop Secret Microwave Popcorn 400
Rockingham, N.C.
October 24

1. Jeff Burton — Ford
2. Ward Burton — Pontiac
3. Bobby Labonte — Pontiac
4. Dale Jarrett — Ford
5. Rusty Wallace — Ford

Checker Auto Parts/Dura Lube 500
Phoenix, Ariz.
November 7

1. Tony Stewart — Pontiac
2. Mark Martin — Ford
3. Bobby Labonte — Pontiac
4. Jeff Burton — Ford
5. Ricky Rudd — Ford

Pennzoil 400 presented by Kmart
Homestead, Fla.
November 14

1. Tony Stewart — Pontiac
2. Bobby Labonte — Pontiac
3. Jeff Burton — Ford
4. Mark Martin — Ford
5. Dale Jarrett — Ford

NAPA 500
Hampton, Ga.
November 21

1. Bobby Labonte — Pontiac
2. Dale Jarrett — Ford
3. Jeremy Mayfield — Ford
4. Mark Martin — Ford
5. Jeff Burton — Ford

Index